Saltwater Aquariums

3rd Edition

by Gregory Skomal, PhD

for dummies®
A Wiley Brand

Saltwater Aquariums For Dummies®, 3rd Edition

Published by: **John Wiley & Sons, Inc.**, 111 River Street, Hoboken, NJ 07030-5774, www.wiley.com

Copyright © 2020 by John Wiley & Sons, Inc., Hoboken, New Jersey

Published simultaneously in Canada

For general information on our other products and services, please contact our Customer Care Department within the U.S. at 877-762-2974, outside the U.S. at 317-572-3993, or fax 317-572-4002. For technical support, please visit www.wiley.com/techsupport.

Wiley publishes in a variety of print and electronic formats and by print-on-demand. Some material included with standard print versions of this book may not be included in e-books or in print-on-demand. If this book refers to media such as a CD or DVD that is not included in the version you purchased, you may download this material at http://booksupport.wiley.com. For more information about Wiley products, visit www.wiley.com.

Library of Congress Control Number: 2019952061

ISBN: 978-1-119-61268-1; ISBN 978-1-119-61275-9 (ebk); ISBN 978-1-119-61276-6 (ebk)

Manufactured in the United States of America

C10014699_101519

Contents at a Glance

Table of Contents

Introduction

Congratulations, my friend! You've just taken the first step into the world of saltwater aquariums, and I welcome you. Stop looking for complicated books with laborious equations on filtration and water chemistry. Don't grab a book just because it has a lot of pretty photos of elegant saltwater fish! The complete hassle-free guide to setting up a saltwater aquarium is *Saltwater Aquariums For Dummies,* 3rd Edition, and, fortunately for you, it's in your hands right now.

Saltwater Aquariums For Dummies, 3rd Edition is a fun reference book that walks you through the entire aquarium process from selecting the proper equipment to choosing the right fish. I even help you choose the right pet store because, believe me, they aren't all alike. I know, you've been told that saltwater aquariums are complicated, need constant attention, and cost a lot. But times have changed since the introduction of the goldfish bowl, and new technologies are making the saltwater aquarium hobby a fast-growing pastime that, with a little diligence, can be mastered by everyone with the average-size pocketbook.

That being said, relax and read on. I keep it simple, and I don't skimp on the facts. If all goes as planned, your aquarium will be set up in no time, and you and your family will be smiling for a long time to come.

About This Book

There's something about fish that I find fascinating, and the thought of keeping them in my home is exciting. I am truly a fish fanatic. I find fish fun, too, so I guess I'm really a fish "funatic" and hope you are as well. You and I aren't alone; people have been keeping fish in captivity for centuries. Among the first fish kept in captivity were the common goldfish dating back to 265 A.D. in China. Care and husbandry of fishes have come a long way over the centuries.

The world of fish is both enthralling and complex. In this newest edition of this book, my goal is to boil down the complexity and give you everything you need to know to set up and maintain a successful saltwater aquarium. Doing so requires a general knowledge of fish, their anatomy, and biology. You also need a thorough understanding of their proper care and husbandry. Saltwater aquariums have come a long way since my last edition. More saltwater fishes and invertebrates are being raised in captivity, which is much better for the environment. And new technologies are making this hobby much easier and, therefore, more enjoyable. I cover all these advancements in this new edition.

In this book, I offer you a look at the watery world of saltwater fishes and invertebrates, and I show you what makes these animals so unique. I also examine the aquarium and the importance of meeting the biological needs of fish. In the process, I describe the critical differences between freshwater and saltwater aquariums. I walk you through the basics of aquarium setup and proper maintenance. I cover proper nutrition and feeding as well as fish health issues. And I even cover some advanced marine aquarium techniques. And, although I'm repeating myself, I present all this info with a painless and simple approach.

Foolish Assumptions

When writing this book, I make the following assumptions about you:

>> I assume you know little to nothing about aquariums, filtration, fish, or invertebrates.

>> I assume you have no formal schooling in biology.

>> I assume you have a genuine interest in these subjects to the point that you want to keep saltwater creatures in captivity.

>> I assume this interest is so great that you're willing to do what it takes to keep your saltwater pets happy and healthy.

That's it! If you've previously had a freshwater aquarium or you know a little more than I expect, then feel free to skip over sections of this book or merely breeze through them to make sure you have a firm handle on the subject.

Icons Used in This Book

As is typical of *For Dummies* books, a number of small pictures called *icons* appear in the margins of this book that highlight various aspects of the text. Here's what they mean:

If I use this icon, it means that I want you to make a special effort to remember the point that I'm making. This information needs to be emphasized and reemphasized so that it sinks in. Most of this is common sense. For example, the correct temperature for a tropical aquarium is important to remember, but I won't ask you to commit the chemical composition of seawater to memory.

When you see this icon, it means that the paragraph next to it is something I suggest you do to help you accomplish the task at hand or information that will keep your aquarium and its inhabitants healthy.

As you'd expect, this icon is indicative of a potential problem or dangerous situation associated with the topic being discussed. Pay particular attention to these icons because they may involve your fish, but they're more likely to affect you and those around you.

In most cases, this icon highlights information that is technical by nature and not critical to the task at hand. If you simply aren't interested in the topic, pass over it.

Where to Go from Here

Well, now that you and I have had an opportunity to meet, it's time to move on to the real important stuff: saltwater aquariums. Where you go from here largely depends on your personal level of expertise. If you have never owned an aquarium, then simply turn the page, and start at square one.

If, however, you already have some saltwater pets in mind and want to start by building your aquarium, go to Part 2. Perhaps you want to review the table of contents or index and see what topics tickle your fancy. You can also refer to the Cheat Sheet at www.dummies.com for more helpful advice that you can refer to whenever you need to. Go for it. Enjoy!

1

Getting Started with Saltwater Aquarium Basics

Discover all the great reasons to have a saltwater aquarium, what you need to get started in your new hobby, and what it takes to keep your new pets happy and healthy for years to come.

Explore fish anatomy, biology, and physiology, find out about how fishes are classified, and familiarize yourself with all the families most commonly kept in the saltwater aquarium.

Choose the best fish species for your new saltwater aquarium by understanding where they come from, their daily habits, their dietary preferences, and their disposition.

Survey the fascinating and diverse world of marine invertebrates and discover about their biology, the way they live, and the most common aquarium species.

Find out how to select healthy fish and invertebrates for your saltwater aquarium, the best way to get them to their new home, why isolating new pets in a quarantine tank is important, and ultimately how you can add them to your aquarium.

Chapter **1**

Taking Your First Salty Steps

You can find a variety of reasons to purchase, set up, and maintain a healthy aquarium in your home. Perhaps your child wants a saltwater aquarium, and you're wrestling with the decision. In this chapter, I help you make that decision with a broad overview of what saltwater aquarium keeping entails.

Perhaps the best way to describe the experience of having an aquarium is to tell you why I started keeping an aquarium when I was young. Prompted by the early television shows of underwater explorer Jacques Cousteau, I was in awe of the ocean and its inhabitants, particularly tropical coral reefs and all the beautiful creatures that inhabit them. During those same years, I was fortunate to travel to the coral reefs of the Caribbean and swim among those very creatures. Swimming about the reef with a mask and a snorkel, I explored all the nooks, watched the fish, and admired the beauty for hours and hours. Soon I learned to scuba dive and take underwater photos, but that wasn't enough, especially when I had to return to cold Connecticut waters. I had to have these animals in my home all the time. So I set up an aquarium and was able to experience much of what I enjoyed while swimming with the fish. Later, inspired by these childhood experiences, I became a marine biologist.

Knowing about Wet Pets and Where to Buy Them

Most of the ornamental fishes sold in pet stores are freshwater fish, many of which are spawned and raised in captivity. Although they represent only a fraction of the number of fishes sold, saltwater species have been traditionally harvested from the wild. More and more saltwater species are bred in captivity every year, and many countries are starting to ban the collection of fish and invertebrates in their waters. As a result, you should make every effort to choose captive-bred animals for your aquarium. Nonetheless, you will still encounter fish or invertebrates for your saltwater aquarium that have been captured and taken from their native habitat.

Here I discuss the basics about buying your saltwater pets and locating a reliable fish dealer to help you get started.

Focusing on saltwater critters

The most popular of these saltwater fish come primarily from coral reefs. Of course, natural reef systems can be hurt if great care isn't taken to protect them and harvest fish wisely. If managed properly, the coral reefs around the world can be harvested without harm because they are extremely productive. Take care, however, not to purchase fish that may have been harvested in areas that don't adhere to the sound conservation of natural reefs. If you can, try to purchase *captive-bred* fish.

TIP

To make sure that your fish are harvested without harm to the environment, check with the Marine Aquarium Council (www.marineaquariumcouncil.org).

Saltwater aquarium pets typically include both fish and invertebrates. In Chapter 2, I go into great detail about fish and not only tell you about their scales, fins, and gills, but I also give you an overview of the fish families that you're most likely to encounter in the pet store. Knowing all about fish families is one thing, but which fishes are right for you? Well, Chapter 3 helps you choose those fish species that are best for the beginner and tells you about fish that school, fish that are active at night, and even those species best avoided.

Invertebrates, however, are different from fish. They belong to many kinds of groups, such as insects, clams, corals, and worms. The basic feature that unites invertebrates is the fact that they lack a backbone. In Chapter 4, you find out all about invertebrate groups, how they are classified, who's who, and which ones would make nice additions to your aquarium. After reading Chapter 4, you will know that invertebrates for the aquarium include shrimp, coral, and anemones, to name a few.

WHAT'S IN A NAME?

As you know, humans have a tendency to name living things, which is called *taxonomy,* and it can be a problem because humans speak many different languages. So, for example, what you call a *shark* in English is called a *tiburón* in Spanish. To get around the confusion associated with language differences, a scientific naming scheme was set up many years ago. The language that was chosen for scientific naming is Latin. But don't worry, you don't need to learn the entire language!

At the ultimate level, all fish and other living creatures are classified into species. So, when I say that there are more than 20,000 kinds of marine fishes, I mean that there are that many species. A bluefish is one species, and a grouper is another. When a species is scientifically classified, it's given a scientific name that is composed of two parts: the *genus* and the species. For example, the scientific name of the threadfin butterflyfish is *Chaetodon auriga,* and that of the spotfin butterflyfish is *Chaetodon ocellatus.* The first (capitalized) name refers to the genus to which both species belong. A genus is a scientific grouping of similar species. If you look at these two fish, you can see that they're extremely similar. The second name refers only to that species and no other.

This classification scheme continues as you group similar *genera* (plural for genus) into *families.* Then you group similar families into *orders,* similar orders into *classes,* and similar classes into *phyla* (singular is phylum). All the different phyla make up the kingdom *Animalia,* for the animals. There are also subdivisions of these categories, like *suborder* and *infraclass.* It gets pretty complicated.

So, at the risk of boring you to tears, I'll give you an example: The Great White Shark has the genus and species name of *Carcharodon carcharias.* It belongs to the family Lamnidae, the order Lamniformes, the superorder Selachimorpha, the subclass Elasmobranchii, the class Chondrichthyes, the superclass Gnathostomata, the subphylum Vertebrata, and the phylum Chordata. Whew!

For the purposes of this book, I stick with the most common names and the genus, species, and family, so don't worry about all this classification stuff right now.

Finding a really fishy dealer

Establishing a rapport with the right dealer is important to the entire aquarium process, from the initial purchase to treating diseases to troubleshooting. This book gets you started and helps you keep a healthy aquarium, but no book can anticipate all the new developments in the aquarium trade that your dealer will have immediate access to.

I explain working with a dealer and getting your new pets home in Chapter 5. Although this is a pretty straightforward process, you discover that minimizing the stress of travel is as important as the way you place the fish into your tank.

Understanding Your Responsibilities

Fish and invertebrates kept in an aquarium live in an artificial environment and are faced with several challenges for survival. Unfortunately, most of these challenges can't be met by the fish and must be provided by you, the *aquarist.* When you take it upon yourself to set up an aquarium, you're accepting the responsibility of meeting all the needs of its inhabitants. Without you, your aquarium and all its occupants are doomed.

REMEMBER

Your responsibilities include ensuring high water quality, proper feeding, correct water temperature, a balanced fish community of the proper density, appropriate habitat and shelter, and sufficient lighting — to name a few.

Your fish are no longer in the wild; they're your pets, and they need you. The fish are totally dependent on you to meet their everyday needs. If they get sick or diseased, you must treat them.

Table 1-1 lists the biological needs of your fish and invertebrates. I include the kinds of equipment that provide for these needs in order to introduce you to some common aquarium components, and I highlight the corresponding chapter in this book.

TABLE 1-1   ## What Exactly Do My Fish Need?

Biological Need	Equipment	Chapter
Water	Aquarium tank	6
Clean water	Filters, protein skimmer	7
Oxygen	Aerators, power heads	7
Correct water temperature	Aquarium heater	8
Adequate lighting	Aquarium light	8
Housing and protection	Aquarium ornamentation	9
Food	Aquarium foods	16
Disease treatment	Aquarium treatments	18

Getting Started with Your First Saltwater Aquarium

By taking the time to properly plan your aquarium now, you can save a lot of time and money down the road. After all, you want to set it up once and set it up right.

What equipment do I need?

In order to meet the needs of your fish that are highlighted in Table 1-1, you should buy much of your equipment right from the start. After all, you can't bring home any fish from your dealer unless you have something to put them into.

Part 2 of the book tells you about the equipment essential to a successful marine aquarium:

>> Chapter 6 describes aquarium tanks and tells you where and on what to set up the new aquarium.

>> Chapter 7 helps you understand filtration and describes the many kinds of filters. By reading this chapter, you'll also know what kind of filter to buy. Of course, Chapter 7 also explains that adding oxygen to the water is very important. Hence, you find out about powerheads and other equipment for doing so.

>> Chapter 8 offers valuable information about heating and lighting your aquarium. Because most species of fish and invertebrates come from tropical waters, heating your aquarium is very important; this chapter tells you how to do so. Tropical regions are also known for bright sunshine, and lighting your aquarium is equally important. Many kinds of lights are available, and the one you choose much depends on whether you plan to house invertebrates; Chapter 8 helps you make the right choice.

>> Chapter 9 brings together all the odds and ends necessary to round out your aquarium. These items include aquarium gravel, rocks and coral, and, of course, salt. Other equipment, such as cleaning tools, nets, and water quality test kits are needed to maintain a healthy aquarium. These items are also discussed in Chapter 9 because you may as well buy them now.

What about brackish water aquariums?

Although most folks reading this book are interested in aquariums that are strictly saltwater, some are interested in aquariums that are not quite fresh and not quite salt. Chapter 10 is a special chapter dedicated to *brackish* water aquariums. This kind of aquarium is for those who would like to keep critters and plants that live in areas where freshwater and saltwater meet. These aquariums have less salt in them than the average marine aquarium. Chapter 10 explains brackish water systems and their inhabitants and tells you what you need to set one up.

How do I set up the aquarium?

Chapter 11 puts all the pieces of the saltwater aquarium puzzle together and tells you how to set up the system from start to finish. However, unlike the typical freshwater aquarium, the marine system needs to mature as your filtration starts to work. Therefore, you really can't add fish until your aquarium has had a chance to establish itself over a couple of weeks. How will you know? That depends on water chemistry.

Understanding Water Chemistry and Algae

Before you can add fish to your new saltwater aquarium, you need to establish and maintain excellent, well-balanced water quality through filtration. This means that you need to understand a little bit about water chemistry. But don't panic. It may sound complex, but it's actually pretty simple.

In Part 3, you discover these important new concepts:

>> Chapter 12 tells you about the importance of nitrogen in your aquarium and shows you the simple way to monitor nitrogen levels.

>> Chapter 13 offers you greater detail about some of the other water components that you already know about, like salt, oxygen, and pH. Monitoring these aspects of water quality is simple and important for maintaining a healthy system.

>> Chapter 14 gives you more than you ever wanted to know about algae, the marine plant-like inhabitant of your aquarium. Algae, in general, are good for your system, but can be a nuisance if the wrong kinds explode in your tank.

Knowing all this water chemistry is important only if you put it to good use. Chapter 15 outlines the important daily, weekly, and monthly steps that you need to take to keep your aquarium clean and, therefore, your new pets happy. These simple activities, which may take only a minute or two, provide the preventive upkeep so that you can avoid future problems.

Keeping Your Fish and Invertebrates Healthy

With good choices for your first aquarium pets (Part 1), the right equipment (Part 2), and well-balanced water chemistry (Part 3), you're well prepared to keep your fish and invertebrates alive and happy. Adding them to the new system is pretty straightforward (Chapter 5), but keeping them healthy involves good food, the prevention of stress, and the right treatments for disease (Part 4).

What do I feed my fish and invertebrates?

Chapter 16 explains that some fish eat other fish and invertebrates, some eat strictly algae and plants, and some eat both. You need to meet the dietary needs of your new pets, and that chapter also tells how, when, and how much to feed your fish and invertebrates.

What if my wet pets get sick?

REMEMBER

The best way to treat disease in your saltwater aquarium is to prevent it.

Fish and invertebrates that are stressed by poor water quality, other tank inhabitants, or poor feeding may ultimately get sick. Chapter 17 explains the concept of stress and how to prevent it and, thereby, avoid disease altogether.

If, however, one of your aquarium inhabitants does get sick, Chapter 18 tells you how to diagnose the disease and treat it. Of course, you won't be able to tell if your fish are sick unless you pay attention to them. Therefore, Chapter 19 offers some great information about how to observe and enjoy your aquarium inhabitants. This chapter tells you how to watch your pets, keep an aquarium log, and even take pictures.

Avoiding the Wrong Aquarium Pets

As collection and captive breeding techniques improve, you will find more and more species of fish and invertebrates offered at your pet store. However, not all these critters are compatible, well suited for the beginner, or prove easy to keep in captivity.

Chapters 20 and 21 provide two simple lists of ten kinds of fish and invertebrates to avoid for a variety of reasons. This doesn't mean that you can't eventually keep some of these critters in your tank, but, in some cases, you may simply need a little more experience before doing so.

Recognizing Why Aquariums Are So Great

Not everybody has had the opportunity to explore the coral reefs of the Caribbean, but most have seen the beauty of these areas on television and the internet. Yet why watch them on a screen when you can see the creatures live in your home and at a fraction of the cost of traveling to the tropics? The following lists some reasons why I love aquariums.

Fish watching

I can watch fish for hours, but, admittedly, I'm a bit strange. Still, the more you watch your aquarium, the better off your aquarium will be. You'll get to know all the subtleties of your fish; you'll name them; you'll know about their individual personalities (oh, they have them); you'll watch as they interact; and, most importantly, you'll know immediately if something isn't quite right. Each animal in your aquarium is your pet, and, like any pet, by watching it daily, you'll know when it acts normally and when something is wrong. You can diagnose problems as they arise and not after it's too late.

Relaxation

Fish and invertebrates are entertaining creatures, and just sitting and watching them can be very relaxing. As far as I'm concerned, relaxation is one of the very best reasons to have an aquarium. Studies show that spending time in front of the aquarium reduces stress. Also, if you have insomnia, try fish watching — count fins, not sheep.

A fishy family affair

It may sound a bit corny, but fishkeeping is fun for the whole family. By bringing the kids into the process, you help them learn the responsibility involved in taking care of pets. Every child will want to feed the fish, and you can show them how to do it properly. Daily, weekly, and monthly maintenance duties become easier if they're shared by all. Also, if everybody has a vested interest in the aquarium, the aquarium will be better off. In fact, family pets often get more attention than those owned by a single person.

REMEMBER

Your child may want an aquarium and promise to take care of it. Please realize, however, that with any pet, he or she has to commit to *maintaining* the aquarium. The responsibilities are similar to those associated with keeping a dog or cat. The child may not always have the high level of interest he or she expresses early on — just look at my kids. You have to be prepared to not only emphasize the importance of aquarium maintenance to your child but also be willing to pick up the slack for him or her.

Fishy friends

You aren't the only one who will enjoy your aquarium. How many times have you been to a friend's house who has an aquarium, and you couldn't help but check it out? So, too, will your friends when they visit. Think of your aquarium as a pet and a piece of furniture combined. Don't hide it away in a back room. People appreciate a house that's nicely decorated, and people generally like pets. Your aquarium will offer both amenities at once, and you'll be the talk of the town.

It's a natural thing

Perhaps you too are an aspiring marine biologist. I can think of no better way of getting started than by owning an aquarium. Many studies on fish biology have been conducted on animals kept in aquaria. In fact, a lot what scientists know about marine life comes from studies on captive fish. Fish and invertebrates are living animals that eat, grow, exhibit unique behaviors, and act and react to their environment and to other animals. As an amateur biologist, you can discover a lot about fish in your own home. The whole family will understand the importance of and gain a respect for nature by having a piece of it in your home.

TECHNICAL
STUFF

The study of fish is known as *ichthyology*. Scientists who study the biology of fish are known as *ichthyologists*. That means that by owning an aquarium with fish in it, you become an amateur ichthyologist.

The ideal pet

Have you ever had to quiet a dog, clean up an unsightly pet mess, go find the cat, or hope that the mailman doesn't get bitten? If you answer yes to any of these, you know what owning a typical pet is like. Fish, on the other hand, never give you these problems. They don't bark or bite or scratch. If you're tired of dealing with the typical pet, try the tropical pet instead.

REMEMBER

Keeping an aquarium requires a commitment. If you can't commit to your tropical fish, either drop the idea or wait until you can make that commitment. You wouldn't get a dog if you didn't have time to feed it, so don't get an aquarium if you can't take care of it.

MY PASSION FOR FISH AND SALTWATER AQUARIUMS

I am a very avid fish enthusiast, but my passion doesn't only apply to fish. In general, all creatures of the ocean, including the ocean itself, are my playground and office. That's right, I not only study the ocean in my spare time, I do so when I go to work every day.

I have been fascinated by the ocean and its inhabitants since the days when Jacques Cousteau was entertaining us with beautiful images of Earth's inner space, the underwater world. I watched every episode as a kid, and this inspired me to set up an aquarium when I was less than a decade old. Oh, like most, I started with a small freshwater system, which turned into a large freshwater system, which turned into a large saltwater system, which turned into multiple saltwater systems, and so on. And believe it or not, most of what I know about aquariums was self-taught through a lot of trial and error with my buddies. As my aquariums became more elaborate, I learned slowly and often at the expense of my mother's pocketbook. Aquariums in those days were expensive and cumbersome to set up. Filtration was primitive, and few people made the bold move to saltwater.

My passion for the ocean motivated me to become a marine biologist, and I'm very fortunate to say that I am actually living my dream of traveling around the world studying fish both in the wild and in the aquarium.

Chapter **2**

Some Things Fishy

W hat is it that made you want to set up an aquarium? The fancy equipment? The opportunity to find out about water chemistry? The nitrogen cycle? I doubt it. I bet it has a lot to do with your fascination with the beauty of the critters that live in the sea. I share that fascination with you — in this chapter, I share some important information about fish.

Figuring Out What a Fish Is

The group of aquatic animals that people refer to as fishes has been around for more than 400 million years and is the most numerous and diverse of the major vertebrate groups. (*Vertebrates* are different from *invertebrates* in that they have a *vertebral column*, or backbone.)

REMEMBER

I use the words *fish* and *fishes*, but you probably thought the plural of *fish* was *fish*. Actually, when you're referring to more than one kind of fish, known as a *species*, the plural of *fish* is *fishes*, as in "there are many kinds of fishes in the ocean." However, when you're talking about more than one fish of the same kind, then the plural is *fish*, like "these damsels are beautiful fish."

Fishes have permeated all the waters of the world, adapting an incredible variety of forms, lifestyles, and behaviors. From the seasonal freshwater streams, desert springs, and salty bays to the coral reefs, open oceans, and deep abyss, these incredible animals have found suitable homes. More than 34,000 species of fishes currently inhabit the earth and many more are being discovered every year.

Because saltwater covers more than 70 percent of the earth's surface, and freshwater less than 1 percent, you may expect to find many more marine (saltwater) species than freshwater species of fishes. Surprisingly, though, only 58 percent of the world's fish species live exclusively in saltwater. By far, most (46 percent) of these live in the narrow band of water less than 700 feet deep along coastlines. As you move into the warm tropical waters of coral reefs, the number of species dramatically increases. It's these fishes that are usually the most sought after for aquariums because of their incredible beauty.

Understanding the Basics of Fish Anatomy

Because there are about 20,000 kinds (species) of marine fish, the typical fish is difficult to describe. However, for the most part, all fishes have some common characteristics. Water is 800 times denser than air, so fish have developed a variety of ways to move, breath, and feed in a dense medium. These involve the body shape, fins, scales, and swim bladder (see Figure 2-1).

Body shape

You can discover a great deal about a species of fish by looking at its body shape. Fishes that are streamlined or bullet-shaped are well-adapted to open water. A couple of examples of these fishes include tunas and sharks. Flat or deep-bodied fish live on or close to the bottom. Just look at a flounder and you'll see what I mean.

Fins

Almost all species of fish have fins in one form or another. The fins are critically important appendages that allow the fish to propel, stabilize, maneuver, and stop. In many cases, fins are used to protect the fish, as well. Lionfish, for example, have fins with long, protective, poisonous spines.

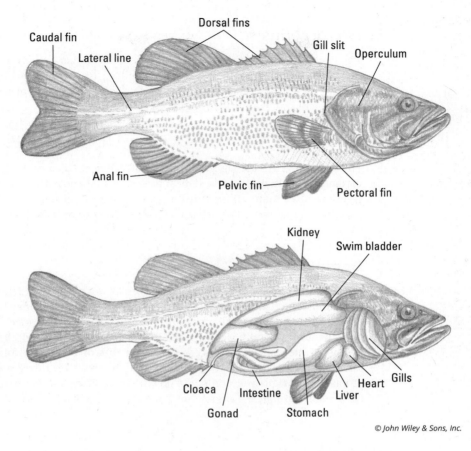

Caudal fin

Dorsal fins

Lateral line

Gill slit

Operculum

Anal fin

Pelvic fin

Pectoral fin

Kidney

Swim bladder

Cloaca

Intestine

Liver

Heart

Gills

Gonad

Stomach

FIGURE 2-1:
Knowing the anatomy of a fish comes in mighty handy as you advance in the aquarium hobby.

Depending on the type of fish and where it lives, the fins take on many shapes and functions. Bottom, sedentary, and slower-moving fishes possess rounded fins, whereas faster, open-water fishes generally have longer, pointed fins.

In general, the supporting structures of fish fins are hard spines and soft rays. Anyone who has handled a fish knows that the spines can be sharp. These bony structures provide protection against predators, which can include humans, of course.

Fins come in ones or twos, so they're either paired or unpaired. Paired fins include the pectorals and pelvics, whereas unpaired fins are the dorsal fin(s), caudal fin, and anal fin.

Pectoral fins

The pectoral fins are the most forward fins, and if fish had arms, these would be them. These fins act to help the fish stabilize, turn, maneuver, hover, and swim backwards. The pectoral fins are generally found just behind or below the gills on each side of the fish, under the midline of the body.

Pelvic fins

The pelvic fins are the leg fins, so to speak. They are also paired and are the most variable in position. In some fishes, the pelvics lie under the fish toward the rear. In others, like many tropical fishes, the pelvics are closer to the head under the pectorals. In general, the pelvic fins act as brakes while helping to stabilize and turn the fish.

Dorsal fin

This unpaired fin is found protruding from the top of the fish. The dorsal fin helps to stabilize the fish and keep it moving straight. Dorsal fins may be long or short, elaborate or simple, singular or multiple. The spines of the dorsal fin can be sharp, and this makes handling some fish difficult. I've been "spined" by a few fish, and it's not a pleasant experience. The dorsal fins of most fish fold down to help streamline the fish while it's moving through the water. However, the dorsal fins of sharks are rigid and don't fold down, which gives sharks their classic look as they move through the water. Some species of fish, such as goldfish, don't have a dorsal fin.

Anal fin

The anal fin is another unpaired fin that helps stabilize the fish when it swims. This fin is located on the underside of the fish behind the anal vent and before the tail fin.

Caudal fin

The caudal or tail fin is an unpaired fin that's largely responsible for propelling the fish forward. This fin can also assist in turning and braking. The shape of the tail can tell you a lot about the lifestyle of a fish. Faster fishes, like tuna and sharks, have deeply forked tails, whereas many slower, deep-bodied, bottom fishes have square or rounded tails. The tail of the eel is pointed, and this fish moves along the bottom like a snake moves through the grass.

Scales

The bodies of most fish are covered with scales. The scales are composed of a hard, bony substance and serve to protect the fish, reducing the chance of injuries and infection. Covering the scales is a very thin layer of *epidermal* (skin) tissue that contains mucous cells. These cells produce that slimy texture you feel when you pick up a fish. This mucous coating not only protects the fish against injury and infection, but also helps the fish to swim more easily in the water, reducing the friction between the body and the dense medium.

The scales of a fish are actually translucent and lack color. The vibrant colors of tropical fishes come from specialized pigment cells, called *chromatophores*, in the deeper dermal layer of the skin. Fish that are clear, such as the freshwater glass-fish, lack these pigments. The color of a fish depends on the types of chromatophores present.

There are generally three types in fish:

» *Melanophores* give fish the darker colors of black, brown, and blue.

» *Xanthophores* produce the colors of red, yellow, and orange.

» *Iridophores* reflect light, producing a silvery shine that's common to many fishes.

The bodies of sharks and rays are covered with specialized scales called *denticles.* These actually look like tiny teeth that are pointed toward the tail of the shark. The denticles have the texture of sandpaper and give the shark that rough feeling, but only when you rub the shark toward its head. Not that a lot of people have the opportunity to pet a shark!

Swim bladder

Living in the dense medium of water presents a few problems for fish, and one of these is buoyancy. Maintaining a certain level in the water column without having to expend a lot of energy is important if you live on and about a coral reef. Therefore, most species of fish have a special organ called the *swim bladder.* This gas-filled sac in the abdominal cavity acts as a life vest that keeps the fish at the correct level in the water column.

Fishes have many types of swim bladders, ranging from the simple single-chambered sac of the trout to the three-chambered bladder of the codfish. There are two types of mechanisms to fill the swim bladder with air:

>> Some fish have direct connections between the esophagus and the bladder and simply swallow air to fill it.

>> Others must rely on gas exchange from specialized blood vessels in the circulatory system to fill the bladder.

In addition to its role in buoyancy control, the swim bladder also helps to amplify sound for better hearing in certain species of fish.

Not all species of marine fish have swim bladders. For example, the sharks and their close relatives, the rays, have large, fatty livers instead of swim bladders to help maintain buoyancy. Their skeleton is composed of cartilage, which also reduces their density in water. Many of the tunas also lack swim bladders; their streamlined bodies and forward speed help them to maintain buoyancy.

Feeding

Just as the body form of a fish can tell you a lot about its swimming habits, the mouth can tell you something about its feeding habits. Bottom-feeders have downward pointing mouths, whereas surface feeders have mouths that are upward-pointing. However, for most tropical reef fishes, the mouth is at the end of the snout.

The size of the mouth is usually related to the size of the fish's preferred food. For example, large predatory fish, like sharks and barracuda, have large mouths armed with teeth for biting and consuming other fish. On the other hand, fishes that normally feed on small invertebrates, such as butterflyfish, have smaller mouths. Some tropical marine fishes have specialized mouths for unique feeding strategies. The sharp "beak" of the parrotfish aids this fish when feeding on the coral reef. The basking shark, which feeds on tiny plankton, has a mouth that opens very wide and specialized "rakers" on the gills that sift the water.

Most marine fish have a relatively straightforward digestive system that varies little from species to species. In general, food passes from the mouth, down the esophagus, to the stomach, through the intestine, and out the anal vent. However, several species of fish lack true stomachs and have elongated, supercoiled intestines. Sharks and rays are different in that they possess a specialized large intestine called the *spiral valve.*

Respiration

One of the most basic needs of fish is oxygen. Like land animals, fish are living creatures that require oxygen to live. However, unlike other animals, fish must obtain oxygen from the water in which they live. Hence, they have specialized organs, called *gills*, which allow them to extract oxygen from the water. The gills of a fish are similar to human lungs only to the extent that they provide oxygen to and remove carbon dioxide from the blood. This oxygen is then transported by the blood to the tissues, where it is utilized to produce energy in a series of chemical reactions called *respiration*.

Although a few kinds of fish can breathe air from the water's surface, fish would certainly die without gills. In addition, water contains much less oxygen than air, and fish must breath 10 to 30 times more water to get the same amount of oxygen that a land animal would get from air.

Most fish have four gills on each side of the head, which are protected by a singular gill cover or *operculum*. Sharks and their relatives possess five to seven gills, each with its own *gillslit*.

When a fish breathes, water is drawn into the mouth and passed over the gills and out the operculum or gillslits. As water passes over the membranes and filaments of the gills, oxygen is removed, and carbon dioxide is excreted. To accomplish this, the gills have a high number of blood vessels that deliver the oxygen to the rest of the fish via the circulatory system. Oxygen and carbon dioxide aren't the only substances exchanged by the gills. The gills also excrete large amounts of ammonia, and as Chapter 12 discusses, ammonia is something that *you* need to get rid of as well (from the aquarium, that is).

Other organs

Fish typically possess general circulatory, digestive, respiratory, and nervous system features common to most vertebrates. If you're interested in finding out more, examine the suggested reading list in Appendix A for more detailed descriptions of the unique anatomy of fishes.

Senses

With few exceptions, fish have no less than five senses that they use to feed, avoid predators, communicate, and reproduce.

Sight

The eyes of most fishes are similar to those of humans, except that they lack eyelids, and their irises work much slower. Some species of sharks, however, have special eyelid-type structures, called *nictitating membranes,* which protect the eyes. Fish eye lenses are spherical, which helps to focus light on the retina underwater. The location of the lens in fish eyes makes most fish nearsighted. Fish are generally thought to be able to detect color, and some can even see ultraviolet light, although this varies from species to species.

WARNING

Rapid changes in light intensity tend to shock or startle fish, so be sure you provide gradual changes in light to allow your pets to accommodate and avoid temporary blindness.

Sound

Water is a much more efficient conductor of sound than air. Therefore, sound carries much farther and faster in water. Most fish don't have noticeable external ears, but they do have two inner ears. The auditory component of the inner ear consists of the *sacculus* and the *lagena,* which house the sensory components of hearing, the *otoliths.* Sound vibrations pass through the water and through the fish's body, and then reverberate off the otoliths within the inner ear. In some cases, the swim bladder articulates with the ear to amplify the sound.

Hearing is an important sense for the fish. Although sharks and rays don't possess otoliths, their inner ear structure allows for the directional detection of low-frequency sounds.

Smell

Every fish has external nostrils, called *nares,* which draw water into and out of the olfactory organs located above its mouth and below its eyes. Water flows through the nares and into the olfactory pits where odors are perceived and communicated to the brain via a large nerve.

The olfactory system of fish isn't attached to the respiratory system as it is in humans but remains isolated from the mouth and gills. Smell is particularly important in prey and mate detection in fishes.

Taste

This sense in fishes is especially helpful in the identification of both food and noxious substances. Although taste buds are only found in human mouths, those of fish occur in the mouth and also on the external surfaces of the skin, lips, and fins. Catfishes have special *barbels* with taste buds that help the fish to detect food items in the murky waters in which they live.

Touch

Fish have a specialized sensory system called the *lateral line,* which allows them to detect water movements. Sensory receptors lying along the surface of the fish's body in low pits or grooves detect water displacement and, therefore, give the fish the sensation of touch. The lateral line is easily visible along the sides of most fish. This unique system helps the fish detect other fishes, sense water movement and currents, and avoid obstacles.

In addition to the lateral line system, sharks and rays possess sophisticated sensory organs called the *ampullae of Lorenzini,* which allow them to detect weak electrical fields. Imagine being able to find your prey by sensing the electricity that it generates. This would allow you to hunt at night or to detect a critter that is hiding in the sand.

Recognizing the Differences between Fresh and Salted

Just what are the differences between saltwater and freshwater fish? Why can't you just move a saltwater fish into freshwater and vice versa? Put simply, it's because they would die, and in this section I explain why.

In general, the freshwater species of fish are hardier than their marine counterparts, having evolved to withstand the rapid and dramatic changes in water conditions that occur inland. Most marine species have lived in constant and stable environmental conditions. Therefore, they don't have the ability to deal with sudden changes, such as those that may occur in the home aquarium. This, of course, makes saltwater fish more difficult to maintain in captivity.

As the name implies, saltwater contains much higher concentrations of dissolved salt (sodium chloride) than freshwater does. Although salt is the major constituent, there are many other dissolved elements as well, and they all occur in higher concentrations than found in freshwater. The amount of these dissolved salts in water is referred to as its *salinity* or *specific gravity.* In Chapter 13, I discuss the chemistry of saltwater in great detail, so I won't bore you with it here.

Maintaining proper salt balance in your body is critical for your survival, and it's also true for all living things including fish. To better understand how salinity impacts the survival of fish, you need explore the process of osmosis and osmoregulation, which the following sections do.

Osmosis

Because fish live in water, they're surrounded by the chemistry of the water they live in. Also, keep in mind that a fish has water and dissolved salts in its body as well. So a fish surrounded by freshwater has more salts in its body than outside its body, and a fish surrounded by saltwater has fewer salts in its body than outside.

Both of these situations can create real problems for the fish because the process called *osmosis* causes water to flow through cell membranes from areas of low salts (salinity) to areas of high salts. This means that fish in freshwater are constantly subjected to an influx of water because their cells are more saline than their environment. On the other hand, marine fish are always threatened by the loss of water from their cells because their environment is more saline.

Osmoregulation

Although anatomically the two groups of fishes are similar in appearance, they have evolved to very different ways of living in these chemically different environments. As a means of maintaining their internal salinity, freshwater fish drink little water and produce large quantities of dilute urine. On the other hand, most marine fish drink large quantities of water and eliminate salts in small amounts of highly concentrated urine and feces, as well as at the gills. So the kidneys of these groups are very different.

Sharks and their close relatives, the rays, are exceptions to this pattern in marine fish. These species concentrate urea in their tissues and blood to offset the loss of water.

This aspect of water balance is called *osmoregulation*. It's important to understand the basic principles of osmoregulation because it has large implications for fish held in captivity. Freshwater fish can't be kept in saltwater and vice versa because their bodies simply can't adapt to the change. As for saltwater fish:

>> Marine fish must burn a lot of energy to prevent the loss of water and excrete salt, so they require good nutrition and good health.

>> Because marine fish drink large amounts of water, the quality of water must be excellent.

>> Abrupt changes in salinity disturb the internal chemistry of marine fishes.

Therefore, marine fishkeeping can be a little more difficult than the maintenance of a freshwater system. But with a little extra effort, it can also be more rewarding.

Identifying Common Tropical Marine Fish Families

In this section, I touch upon the various families of fish that commonly inhabit coral reefs and whose members may be available for your tropical marine aquarium. The diversity of these fishes is daunting. They're found throughout the world along the band of warm water at the earth's lower latitudes. By no means is this a complete list of tropical marine fish families, however, because there are literally thousands of species and hundreds of families. (I strongly recommend that you consult with the references listed in Appendix A for more comprehensive information about fish species.) In this section, I include some illustrations of common members of these families. You can also see beautiful color photos of specific fish species in the color section of this book.

Angelfishes

The angelfishes are often confused with the butterflyfishes, having ornate colors and deep, flattened bodies. The angels, however, belong to the family Pomacanthidae and can be readily distinguished from the butterflies by the presence of a spine on the gill cover. Angelfishes are popular aquarium fish originating from coral reefs throughout the world. Some grow quite large, exceeding 24 inches, but others rarely exceed a few inches. Angels come in a variety of colors and patterns, sometimes changing as the fish matures from juvenile to adult. In general, angelfish can be offered a variety of foods, but some large adults can be somewhat finicky, preferring sponges and corals, which means they can't be kept in the reef tank. The pygmy or dwarf angels like the one shown in Figure 2-2 are well suited for a home aquarium, whereas other species of angelfish grow larger, are prone to being territorial, and do better in larger public and private displays.

© John Wiley & Sons, Inc.

FIGURE 2-2:
Touched by
an angelfish.

Blennies

These long, slender, very active fishes belong to the family Blenniidae, which includes about 401 species. They generally live near, on, or in the bottom and have comb-like teeth for cropping algae. Blennies prefer nooks and crannies for hiding. One blenny, the false cleanerfish, is known to mimic the cleaner wrasse, but when the host fish approaches, this blennie bites off a piece of fin instead of cleaning the fish. It's best to avoid this critter. Blennies generally eat a variety of foods, from algae to flake foods, and prefer hiding places such as caves and crevices. Most are less than 4 inches long and make peaceful additions to a fish-only or reef aquarium (a peaceful mix invertebrates and fish). There are also multiple kinds of tank-raised blennies now available for the home aquarium.

Boxfishes and trunkfishes

Fish of the family Ostraciidae, which contains 25 species, possess box-shaped bodies covered with bony plates, and they have no pelvic fins. These fish release poisons into the water when threatened and are, therefore, poorly suited for the average aquarium. Boxfishes are generally bottom-feeders that can be territorial and intolerant of their own kind.

Butterflyfishes

With 131 species, these popular aquarium fish belong to the family Chaetodontidae. They have oval, flattened bodies, terminal mouths, and stunning color patterns like those on the threadfin butterflyfish shown in Figure 2-3. The butterflies are well adapted to life on the coral reef, feeding on the reef itself while seeking algae, sponges, and corals. Although among the most beautiful, these aren't the hardiest of marine tropicals because they're sensitive to changes in water quality. Feeding in captivity can be difficult, and some species can be territorial. They aren't recommended for the inexperienced fish hobbyist and shouldn't be kept in the reef tank because they consume invertebrates.

FIGURE 2-3: The threadfin butterflyfish and its cousins are pretty and peaceful.

© John Wiley & Sons, Inc.

Cardinalfishes

This group of fish of the family Apogonidae includes about 350 species of slow-moving peaceful fishes. Large eyes, two separate erect dorsal fins, and a large head are characteristic of these fish. A common cardinalfish is the flamefish shown in Figure 2-4. Although nocturnal, cardinals can be acclimated to daytime feeding and activity. When kept with other tranquil species in a community tank, these fish are well suited for both fish-only and the reef tanks.

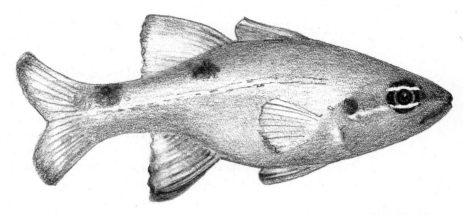

© John Wiley & Sons, Inc.

FIGURE 2-4:
The flamefish is a great addition to any reef tank.

Catfishes

Although there are about 34 families of catfishes, only two have species that live in saltwater. The most common marine aquarium catfishes belong to the family Plotosidae, which contains 42 species. These fish prefer to live in schools, so they're best kept in groups. Some species do, however, have highly venomous spines, so take care when handling them because the reaction to this venom can range from mild inflammation to, in rare cases, death.

Clownfishes and damselfishes

These fishes are popular in the aquarium trade for all levels of experience. Although comprising one family, the Pomacentridae, this group contains almost 400 species and is usually divided into the clownfishes and the damselfishes. The clownfishes are also called anemonefishes because in the wild, these small ornate fish are able to live unharmed among the stinging tentacles of anemones, which are soft invertebrates related to corals (see Chapter 4).

The clowns and anemones live in harmony and both receive protection from the relationship. This relationship can be mimicked in the aquarium as well, but clownfishes don't need anemones to survive in the aquarium. Clownfishes, like the one shown in Figure 2-5, are one of the few groups of marine species reared in captivity, and they do well in both reef and fish-only tanks.

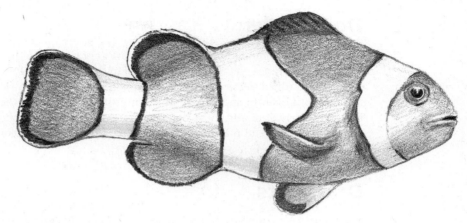

FIGURE 2-5:
Send in the
clownfish.

© John Wiley & Sons, Inc.

Damselfishes are considered by many to be the hardiest of the marine aquarium species and are, therefore, usually the first to be introduced into the new aquarium. These fish, however, can be territorial and aggressive, and if introduced too early to a new tank, less tolerant of new tank mates. Nonetheless, some of the damsels, like the sergeant major shown in Figure 2-6 or the blue green chromis, can be exciting additions to your tank, particularly when introduced in *shoals* (schools). Many species of damselfish will harm invertebrates, so they don't belong in the reef tank.

FIGURE 2-6:
The sergeant
major will
command your
attention.

© John Wiley & Sons, Inc.

Dottybacks

These fish of the family Pseudochromidae are very similar to the fairy basslets in size and appearance, yet they're distributed in the Indo-West Pacific, whereas the latter are confined to the Caribbean. This family contains the large genus *Pseudochromis,* comprised of about 70 species. Unfortunately, some of the dottybacks can be highly territorial and must be kept alone. Use care when choosing the right species for a peaceful marine aquarium. They adapt well to a reef tank with a lot of hiding places.

Dragonets

The family Callionymidae has 196 species of small, shallow-water fishes that live in the Indo-Pacific. Some species are drab colored and live over sand, but others can be very colorful. Sometimes called mandarinfish, these fishes eat tiny invertebrates and, therefore, thrive only in an established reef tank.

Fairy basslets

There are only 17 species of basslets of the family Grammatidae. These somewhat shy fish from the Caribbean prefer a lot of shelter, which they'll defend from other tank inhabitants. Although a beautiful addition to any tank, the basslet's finicky habits are best suited for the fish-only or reef tank of the experienced hobbyist.

Filefishes

Like their close relatives the triggerfishes, filefishes of the family Monacanthidae have a modified dorsal spine that locks into place. Unlike the triggers, these fish are more peaceful, less active, and generally smaller, making them better suited to a tropical community tank. However, you may have difficulty getting these fish to feed in captivity because they normally feed on coral and algae.

Gobies

Somewhat similar in body shape to the blennies, the gobies belong to the family Gobiidae (Figure 2-7). Gobies have modified pelvic fins that are united to form a sucking disk, which they use to attach to structures. This family is the largest of the marine fishes, with more than 250 genera and 1,800 species. Some are able to live out of water for extended periods, returning to water to wet their gills. Others live on sand or in close association with invertebrates, such as sea urchins, sponges, hard and soft corals, and shrimps. Like the blennies, gobies prefer hiding places and shelters. Some reef-dwelling gobies, like the neon goby, act as cleaner fish, removing parasites from other reef fishes at specified cleaning stations on the reef. Most gobies are brightly colored, peaceful, and relatively small in size, eating a wide variety of foods. They do well in fish-only tanks and are excellent additions to a reef tank. Like the blennies, there are now a number of tank-bred species available.

FIGURE 2-7: Gobies are the largest marine fish family.

Groupers and sea basses

Similar to the grunts and snappers, this group of fishes of the family Serranidae includes fast-growing, large, predatory fishes. Most, therefore, require larger fish-only aquaria if they're to be kept for any length of time. Nonetheless, with more than 500 species belonging to this family, a few smaller species are suitable for the peaceful aquarium of the beginner. Many of the groupers are nocturnal, spending most of their daytime hiding or lying on the bottom.

Grunts

These fast-growing, hardy fish are so named for the grunting noises they make when their swim bladders amplify the sound generated by the grinding of their teeth. Belonging to the family Haemulidae, which contains 134 species, the grunts accept a wide variety of foods but require a lot of space. It's best to keep only small juveniles in small schools. This family also contains the sweetlips fishes, which come from the Indo-Pacific. Sweetlips can be highly active like grunts, but they're excellent aquarium inhabitants as juveniles. They're generally brightly colored as juveniles, like the yellow sweetlips in Figure 2-8, but become drab as they get older. These fish have a quiet disposition, preferring a peaceful fish-only tank without aggressive tank mates.

FIGURE 2-8: The yellow sweetlips is a real sweetie.

Hawkfishes

So named for their habit of perching themselves on a rock waiting to ambush prey, the 33 species of hawkfishes belong to the family Cirrhitidae. With the exception of four to five smaller species that are suitable for the home aquarium, most hawkfishes are highly predatory and get too large in the peaceful marine aquarium.

Lionfishes and scorpionfishes

No aquarium book is complete without mention of these unusual fishes of the family Scorpaenidae. This family comprises more than 200 species of fish with stocky spiny heads and spiny fins armed with venom glands, like the lionfish. They're generally predators that hover or lie in wait for their prey, suddenly lunging at and engulfing it. Their often-camouflaged coloration aids them in doing so. For obvious reasons, these fish must be handled with great care. In captivity, they are generally peaceful but will readily consume smaller tank mates. For now, I suggest avoiding them.

Moray eels

These well known, unique fishes belong to the family Muraenidae, which contain more than 200 species. The morays lack pectoral and pelvic fins but possess small gill openings and long, fang-like teeth. Morays are generally nocturnal fish, feeding on other fish and invertebrates at night, spending most of their daytime hours in holes and crevices. In the wild, these fish will easily attain lengths in excess of 5 feet, but this size is not common in the average aquarium. Although moray eels readily accept a variety of foods, they are carnivorous and will consume smaller fish in the aquarium. These fish belong in a fish-only aquarium, but I don't recommend them for the beginner.

Parrotfishes

Belonging to the same suborder as the wrasses, the parrotfishes are grouped in the family Scaridae, which includes about 100 species. These fishes are best known for their fused teeth that form a bird-like beak; hence the name. The beak is used for biting off pieces of dead coral to get at the algae living within it. For this reason, parrotfishes aren't well suited for a reef aquarium. In general, they get relatively large, which makes them a poor choice for the average fish-only aquarium as well.

Porcupinefishes

These oddities of the marine aquarium belong to the family Diodontidae. These fish, whose scales possess spines, have the ability to inflate their bodies with water to ward off danger. Although relatively easy to keep in captivity, they generally attain too large a size for the average aquarist.

Puffers

Although the puffers look very much like porcupinefish without spines, they are included in a different family called the Tetraodontidae, which contains about 200 species. They're smaller than the porcupines and have fused, beak-like jaws. These fish will also inflate with water as a defense mechanism to avoid being eaten. Their flesh is poisonous when consumed. These fish are vigorous feeders in the aquarium, and some species can be aggressive. Smaller puffers, though, like the spotted sharpnose shown in Figure 2-9, are well suited for the beginner's aquarium.

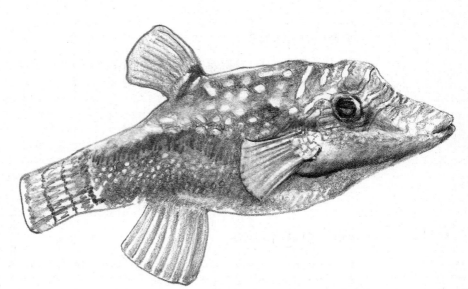

© John Wiley & Sons, Inc.

FIGURE 2-9:
The spotted sharpnose pufferfish is one of the smaller puffers.

Rabbitfishes

The family Siganidae originates from the Indo-Pacific and contains one genus with about two dozen species. Their flattened, oval bodies and small mouths are similar to those of surgeonfishes. Like rabbits, they prefer to browse on vegetative matter in the wild; in the aquarium, they'll consume algae and can be lured into taking vegetable foods as well. Although rabbitfish are hardy, these fish possess venom glands in their dorsal and anal spines, so use care when handling them. Many rabbitfish grow fast, so adequate swimming space is required in either a fish-only or reef tank.

Seahorses and pipefishes

These exotic fishes of the family Syngnathidae with more than 300 species are no strangers to the aquarium trade. The pipefishes lack the prehensile (wrapping and folding) tail, vertical swimming position, and angled head that are characteristic of the seahorses. Unfortunately, their feeding and water-quality requirements make them difficult for a beginner to maintain in an aquarium for any length of time. They don't compete well with other species for food. They're peaceful and do best in a quiet aquarium by themselves. The group is characterized by unusual reproductive behavior where the female deposits eggs into an abdominal pouch on the male. They're then fertilized and incubated by the male in this pouch.

Sharks

Scientists have identified at least 34 families and more than 500 species of sharks in the world, most of which have never been kept in aquaria. Sharks and their relatives, the rays, are different from the rest of the fish in this chapter. Their skeletons are composed of cartilage, they have teeth-like scales, and they have five to seven gillslits. Therefore, they belong to a completely different class of fish known as Chondrichthyes. Sharks in general grow too large for the home aquarium, can be, shall I say, very aggressive, and are sensitive to water quality. For these reasons alone, I don't recommend sharks for the average saltwater aquarium.

Snappers

These fishes of the family Lutjanidae with more than 100 species are another group of fast-growing, highly active fishes that aren't suitable as adults for the average marine aquarium. Several species in this family are commercially exploited for food throughout the world. They're predatory by nature, require a lot of space, and will quickly dominate an aquarium.

Squirrelfishes

These red fishes of the family Holocentridae, which contains 86 species, are normally nocturnal creatures in the wild, using their large eyes to feed at night. The family also includes the big eyes and soldierfish. In the aquarium, they can be conditioned to feed during the day. Their long bodies have two dorsal fins: a longer fin of spines and a shorter, soft-rayed fin close to the tail. Squirrelfish need a lot of space to accommodate their highly active nature and may be disruptive to a peaceful tank. In addition, they may consume smaller fish as they get larger. They prefer to live in schools and do well in a fish-only tank.

Surgeonfishes and tangs

These common aquarium fish belong to the family Acanthuridae comprising more than 80 species. They're characterized by high-profile, flattened, oval bodies. Their name is derived from the presence of two scalpel-like spines at the base of the caudal fin (tail). These are used in defense or during territorial disputes, so it's best to keep them alone. These schooling fish are *algal grazers* (feeding on algae) in the wild as well as in captivity, but they can be trained to take other kinds of food as well. In the wild, they reach sizes in excess of 15 inches, but they rarely reach half this size in captivity, depending on the species. Surgeonfish and tangs, like the one shown in Figure 2-10, can be kept in both fish-only and reef aquariums.

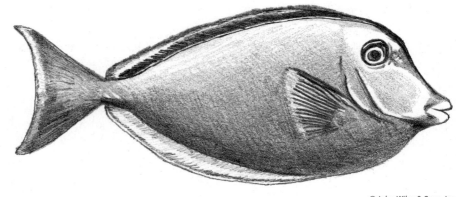

FIGURE 2-10:
Tangs, like this one, will graze on algae.

Triggerfishes

So named for their first dorsal fin that locks into place, triggerfishes, like the one in Figure 2-11, belong to the family Balistidae, which includes more than 40 species. Sound production in this group is common, produced by grinding the teeth or vibrating the swim bladder. The legendary Hawaiian name for the triggers is *humahuma nukunuku apua'a,* which means "the fish that sews with a needle and grunts like a pig." I'll stick to triggerfish! They can also rotate their eyes independently. The triggerfishes can be quite aggressive, having sharp teeth that are ideal for feeding on invertebrates in the wild. They readily accept any food in captivity, but their aggressive nature makes them unsuitable for the reef tank. These fish move primarily by using their dorsal and anal fins, saving the tail for emergencies. A bluejaw is a cheaper alternative to a cross-hatch, which tends to be a very expensive fish

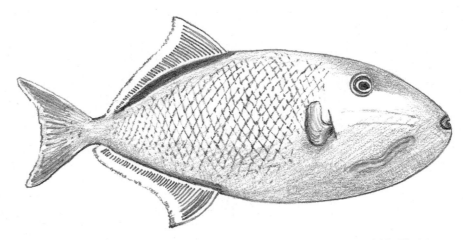

FIGURE 2-11:
The triggerfish isn't suitable for reef tanks.

Wormfishes

At one time included with the blennies and gobies, the family Microdesmidae contains almost 90 species of fishes that inhabit mostly tropical seas. Also called firefishes, the wormfishes have an eel-like body with an extended first dorsal ray. In the wild, these fish hover in groups close to the reef, feeding on small planktonic animals. They rapidly retreat to nooks in the reef when startled. These fishes can be kept in small groups, but they require plenty of hiding spaces.

Wrasses

The family Labridae has more than 500 species all over the world, not only in tropical waters. This group can be quite diverse with its members having a variety of body shapes, behaviors, and sizes. Many wrasse species are capable of changing sex as needed for reproductive purposes. Some are substrate burrowers that require sand, whereas others, like the canary wrasse, rest in crevices at night. Some members perform cleaning services similar to those provided by a few species of gobies. The more active species of wrasses can be disruptive to a peaceful tank, aggressive toward smaller fishes, or too large for the average aquarium. Most wrasses have special jaw plates, called *pharyngeal jaws,* which allow them to grind crabs, clams, snails, and sea urchins. Hence, keep them out of the reef tank.

Chapter **3**

Choosing the Best Fish for You

I n Chapter 2, I discuss the anatomy of fish and the general types (families) that are available to you. Now it's time to narrow your choices. To do so, you need a little more information about your options.

By far, the majority of marine fishes sold by pet dealers come from warm, tropical coral reefs. Brilliant colors, unique body shapes, and animated behavior make these fish preferred saltwater tank inhabitants. The coral reef ecosystem is a diverse community of algae, invertebrates, and vertebrate animals that function as a whole — it's the foundation upon which the community is built. For many species of fish, the coral reef is their home, providing food, protection, and companionship.

A number of fishes are well suited for the community marine aquarium. The important thing to do is to balance the types of fishes in your tank. Species of fish have varying lifestyles and different behaviors. Therefore, some fish live through-out water column of the tank, some in the middle, and some on the bottom. There are fishes that are compatible with invertebrates, and there are those that gobble them up. Some fishes are active in the daytime, some thrive at night. In your aquarium, you want to re-create the natural coral reef community by having fish at all activity levels, thereby minimizing competition, utilizing the entire aquar-ium, and creating a well-balanced community.

Considering Night and Day Fish

Fish, like most organisms, respond to changing light levels. This means that their activity patterns are tuned to day and night. Most of these activity patterns involve feeding or reproduction.

TECHNICAL STUFF

Fishes that are more active and feed during the day are called *diurnal,* and those that feed at night are called *nocturnal.* Because most of the fishes available for your aquarium are caught in the wild, they'll exhibit similar patterns in your home.

REMEMBER

Although some species may adapt to a diurnal lifestyle, you want to make sure that you don't stock your tank with fishes that are all nocturnal. I put together a list of nocturnal and diurnal species in Table 3-1, which you can use as a general guide when you purchase your fish.

TABLE 3-1

Activity Levels for Common Aquarium Fishes

Activity Level	Common Name	Family
Diurnal	Surgeonfishes	Acanthuridae
	Butterflyfishes	Chaetodontidae
	Gobies	Gobiidae
	Wrasses	Labridae
	Angelfishes	Pomacanthidae
	Damselfishes	Pomacentridae
	Parrotfishes	Scaridae
	Rabbitfishes	Siganidae
Nocturnal	Cardinalfishes	Apogonidae
	Porcupinefishes	Diodontidae
	Grunts	Haemulidae
	Squirrelfishes	Holocentridae
	Snappers	Lutjanidae
	Catfishes	Plotosidae
Both	Groupers	Serranidae
	Moray eels	Muraenidae
	Scorpionfishes	Scorpaenidae

Adding Schools to Your Aquarium

Many species of fish form natural groups called *schools*. Fishes swim in schools not to get smarter but to increase feeding success and to avoid predators. As many as half of all fish species form schools at some point in their lives. Some species, such as herrings, school for their entire lives, and others, like puffers, school only as juveniles.

TECHNICAL STUFF

Many authors use the terms *shoals* and *schools* interchangeably, but this isn't correct. Technically, shoals are groups of fish that are unorganized, and schools are groups of fish that are synchronized and polarized.

Schooling fish are an attractive addition to the aquarium. They add action to the tank because they rarely stop moving. They also increase the visibility and activity levels of their tank mates.

TIP

Of course, if you add schooling fish to your aquarium, don't try to mimic the numbers that occur in the wild. Your tank is simply too small, no matter how big it is. Keep the size of your school small, no more than five or six fish, taking into account the capacity of your aquarium. Also, it's not a good idea to buy one schooling fish and keep it alone. Try to imagine what that would feel like.

Understanding How Fish Interact with Each Other

Fish, like all animals, interact with each other in a variety of ways. This interaction can occur with individuals of the same species as well as between species.

TECHNICAL STUFF

Aggressive interactions are referred to as *agonistic*. Agonistic behavior between fish can be due to defense of a territory, a predatory attack, competition for food, or protection of mates, eggs, or young. Agonistic behavior usually results in a pecking order forming, in which some fish are subordinate to others. This is particularly true for coral reef fishes.

Of course, fish in the wild have a higher probability of avoiding each other. But when you bring fish into your home, they're forced to deal with each other in the confined space of your aquarium. Does this mean that they're always going to get along? No way! Take care to choose fish that are compatible, considering the following elements when selecting your new pets.

Size

One aspect of choosing fish that beginners will sometimes overlook is the maximum size of a particular species. A fish grows continuously throughout its life, and some species grow faster than others. You don't want a fish that will grow to 12 inches in less than a year. This situation will not only disrupt your aquarium capacity, but the larger fish will also undoubtedly dominate the tank. Some species are compatible with other species when they're smaller juveniles, but become solitary and aggressive as adults. These fish don't belong in the peaceful reef tank (an invertebrate aquarium with a few peaceful fishes) or fish-only tank.

TIP

Keep in mind that in the wild, bigger fish usually eat smaller fish and invertebrates. This will also happen in your aquarium, and it's just one more reason to keep large fishes out of the average aquarium. To be safe and avoid the event of one fish becoming the dinner of another, keep fishes of similar size in the fish-only and reef aquarium.

Attitude

Have you ever met somebody who always seems to have a bad attitude? Well, I have, and I've met a few fish like that, too. Some species simply have a surly disposition. Whether it's because they're territorial, defensive, or just plain hungry, these fish are not for the reef tank and don't fit into most peaceful fish-only aquariums.

REMEMBER

The best advice I can give you is to avoid aggressive fishes. Use the guides in both Chapter 2 and in this chapter to determine whether the species that you want is a problem child. Also, just because this book, another book, or a dealer tells you that a species isn't normally aggressive doesn't mean that your fish will be docile. Many species that are considered peaceful have been known to have a few bad seeds. Take the time to discuss your options with your dealer and keep a watchful eye on any new tank addition. If one of his fish is aggressive, the dealer should tell you (at least you hope he will), or you will undoubtedly find out one way or another. This is a good reason to establish a good rapport with a dealer.

Diet

In addition to size and attitude, always consider the diet of your tank inhabitants. In the "Finding Good Choices to Stock Your Aquarium" section in this chapter, I offer some recommended fishes with their food preferences. (Chapter 16 also includes some helpful feeding information.) Fish definitely have a variety of food preferences. Be wary of predatory fish, called *carnivores*, because they eat other fish and invertebrates.

REMEMBER

You really don't want to add large predators to your reef tank or fish-only tank: It's a bad mix (at least for the prey). In addition, don't choose fish that are going to be difficult to feed. For example, it's hard to feed fish with specialized diets, like those that eat only corals. Use the guide to fishes in this chapter and always consult with your dealer.

Creating a Peaceful Habitat

Without a doubt, fish have preferred habitats. The term *habitat* really just refers to the type of environment that a fish inhabits. For example, flounders prefer to live in a sandy-bottom habitat, and you're not likely to see one swimming at the surface. The best saltwater aquarium is well balanced with fishes that inhabit all levels of the tank. A couple of bottom-dwellers, a couple of topwater fellas, and a few midwater critters presents the most natural and pleasing appearance. It keeps any one part of the tank from getting overcrowded and helps to avoid agonistic interactions.

TIP

Know where your fishes come from. This way you'll not only impress your friends but also keep a region-specific natural aquarium with fishes from only one region of the world, if you so choose.

Tropical marine fishes come from four major regions of the world. In the "Finding Good Choices to Stock Your Aquarium" section, I tell you where specific fish come from and refer to the following regions for the fish that I recommend:

>> **Indo-West Pacific:** From South Africa and the Red Sea east through Indonesia and Australia to Hawaii and the South Pacific Islands to Easter Island. About 3,000 species live in this region, the most of any region.

>> **Eastern Pacific:** This region extends from the western coast of North America south along the tropical shores of Central America to the tropical and temperate shores of western South America. This region is separated from the Indo-West Pacific region by a huge expanse of ocean, and it contains about 1,300 species.

>> **Western Atlantic:** This region includes the temperate shores of eastern North America, the Gulf of Mexico, the Caribbean Sea, and the tropical and temperate shores of eastern South America. It contains about 2,000 species.

>> **Eastern Atlantic:** Tropical species of fish are limited to the Gulf of Guinea, a small area along the western coast of Africa. This region contains only about 500 species of tropical shore fishes.

Finding Good Choices to Stock Your Aquarium

When your tank is fully established, the water chemistry is balanced (see Chapters 12 and 13), and you're ready to stock your aquarium, I thoroughly recommend that you have a game plan in mind. Don't blindly go to your pet dealer and look for fish for your tank because that can result in fish incompatibility.

TIP

Preselect the kind of fish you want to start with, keeping in mind my suggestions in this section. (Also consult with some of the fish encyclopedias listed in Appendix A.) In other words, establish a good list of potential fish that you want to introduce into your aquarium. Remember to choose a variety of species that will live throughout the water column, from the top to the bottom.

This section gives you a list of tropical marine species that are relatively easy to care for. They're well suited for the beginner's peaceful tank where pH ranges from 8.1 to 8.3 and temperature is maintained between 75 and 79 degrees F. I list both the common and scientific names and try to include common representatives of each of the families that I review in Chapter 2. Bear in mind that common names vary from place to place, book to book, and store to store, but scientific names don't. In the following sections, I list the most common of the common names, if that makes any sense.

Also included is information on the level of the tank that the fish is most likely to inhabit, where it comes from, and its feeding preference. The size that I have listed for each fish is that usually attained in the home aquarium, which may be less than in the wild. In addition, for some species I include close relatives that are similar and equally suited for the aquarium.

REMEMBER

Bear in mind that every aquarium book has specific recommendations for fish that vary among authors. Aquarium hobbyists keep literally thousands of fish species, and no one author has a perfect list. The following sections include the species that I prefer, but others may be equally suitable.

Surgeonfishes and tangs (Acanthuridae)

The common names surgeonfish and tang both refer to members of this family, but these fishes have more in common than doctors and breakfast drinks. The family is typically called the surgeonfishes, but *acanthurids* are also called tangs, doctorfish, and unicornfish.

Lipstick tang, naso tang, or orange-spine unicornfish (Naso lituratus)

This species is another peaceful tang that's an attractive addition to a larger aquarium. The common name refers to the well-defined facial markings and red around the mouth of this fish. Remember that tangs and surgeons have two scalpels on each side of the tail, so be careful when handling these fish. Although the lipstick tang and other tangs are listed as herbivorous, they can be acclimated to other protein foods and flake foods. These tangs will grow quite large and require a lot of tank space.

>> **Distribution:** Indo-West Pacific

>> **Size:** 18 inches

>> **Food:** Herbivorous

>> **Tank level:** All levels

>> **Minimum tank size:** 130 gallons

Tomini tang (Ctenochaetus tominiensis)

The Tomini tang or Tomini surgeonfish is also a very colorful species with yellow, blue, and white highlights. This tang will be aggressive to other tangs but is peaceful with other fishes. The Tomini is moderately easy to care for and eats a variety of foods, but it should be offered a vegetarian diet.

>> **Distribution:** Western Central Pacific

>> **Size:** 6 inches

>> **Food:** Herbivorous

>> **Tank level:** All levels

>> **Minimum tank size:** 75 gallons

Yellow tang (Zebrasoma flavescens)

The yellow tang is one of the most colorful, common, and recognizable species in the aquarium industry. It's ideal for the beginner. The yellow tang eats a variety of foods, preferring a vegetarian diet. It's safe with all fishes, but it's best kept as a single specimen.

>> **Distribution:** Central and South Pacific

>> **Size:** 7 inches

>> **Food:** Herbivorous

>> **Tank level:** All levels

>> **Minimum tank size:** 75 gallons

Cardinalfishes (Apogonidae)

If you're looking for a calm, cool, and collected species of fish that blends with other mellow species and many invertebrates, keep your eyes open for a cardinalfish. This critter is the Ghandi of fish.

Flamefish or flame cardinalfish (Apogon maculatus)

The flamefish is one of the tranquil cardinalfishes that's well suited for the aquarium of the beginner. This fish has striking red coloration, prefers a peaceful aquarium, and takes all kinds of aquarium foods provided they will fit into its mouth. Because cardinalfishes are nocturnal by nature, they may be a bit shy at first. Feed these fish in the evening.

>> **Distribution:** Western Atlantic

>> **Size:** 3 inches

>> **Food:** Omnivorous

>> **Tank level:** Middle and lower levels

>> **Minimum tank size:** 15 gallons

Pajama cardinalfish (Sphaeramia nematoptera)

This species of cardinalfish is wearing those pajamas that my father refuses to throw out. It has three distinct color patterns on its body, each completely different. Like other cardinalfishes, the pajama has large eyes for nocturnal feeding and can be kept in groups. Be careful not to introduce boisterous fishes with cardinalfish because doing so will disrupt their quiet lifestyle. Cardinalfishes are ideal for the invertebrate reef tank. These fish are also available as captive bred and they readily breed in healthy saltwater tanks.

>> **Distribution:** Indo-West Pacific

>> **Size:** 3 inches

>> **Food:** Omnivorous

>> **Tank level:** Middle and lower levels

>> **Minimum tank size:** 20 gallons

Triggerfishes (Balistidae)

Although many species of triggerfishes are available to the aquarist, most aren't suitable for reef tanks. This is simply because many triggerfishes love invertebrates . . . for breakfast, lunch, and dinner.

The **Niger trigger fish** *(Odonus niger),* also called the redtooth trigger is a common relatively peaceful member of this family. This species is compatible in a fish-only aquarium. They may be shy initially but become more social with time.

>> **Distribution:** Indo-Pacific

>> **Size:** 19 inches

>> **Food:** Omnivorous

>> **Tank level:** All levels

>> **Minimum tank size:** 55 gallons

Blennies (Blenniidae)

The lovely little blennies are the all-around nice guys of the peaceful aquarium. They're cute, intelligent, and fun to hang with. Everybody wants to know the blenny.

Bicolor blenny (Ecsenius bicolor)

This blenny has a front *(anterior)* half that is brown and a rear *(posterior)* half that is orange, hence the name. The bicolor is a shy species of fish that lives in small holes and caves. It's a pleasure to watch. When feeding, it darts from its home to catch food and quickly returns to the safety of its den by backing in. Like the midas blenny, the bicolor will readily accept a variety of foods and is compatible with invertebrates.

>> **Distribution:** Indo-West Pacific

>> **Size:** 3 inches

>> **Food:** Omnivorous

>> **Tank level:** Lower level

>> **Minimum tank size:** 30 gallons

Midas or Persian blenny (Ecsenius midas)

Like most blennies, this fish needs plenty of nooks and caves to hide in. After they're acclimated, the midas blenny is quite animated, perching itself on rocks to observe the rest of the aquarium. This yellow–hued fish swims like an eel, and its healthy appetite for all types of food makes it an ideal beginner's fish for the fish–only and reef tank.

>> **Distribution:** Indian Ocean, Red Sea

>> **Size:** 3 inches

>> **Food:** Omnivorous

>> **Tank level:** Lower level

>> **Minimum tank size:** 30 gallons

Butterflyfishes (Chaetodontidae)

The butterflyfishes in general aren't suitable for the inexperienced aquarist because they can be difficult to maintain. However, a couple of species are popular in the aquarium trade and can fare quite well if water quality is properly maintained.

Threadfin butterflyfish (Chaetodon auriga)

The threadfin butterflyfish is named for the threadlike extension that develops on the dorsal fin of the adult. It consumes a variety of aquarium foods and particularly enjoys live brine shrimp. Similar species include vagabond butterflyfish (*C. vagabundus*), Klein's butterflyfish (*C. kleinii*), and raccoon butterflyfish (*C. lunula*).

>> **Distribution:** Indo-West Pacific, Red Sea

>> **Size:** 8 inches

>> **Food:** Omnivorous

>> **Tank level:** Middle and lower levels

>> **Minimum tank size:** 100 gallons

Wimplefish, pennant coralfish, or black and white heniochus butterflyfish (Heniochus acuminatus)

This peaceful butterflyfish is easy to keep, easy to feed, and may be kept in groups of two or three if your aquarium is large enough. The front rays of the dorsal fin on the wimplefish are extended and grow with age. The wimplefish is often called the Heniochus butterflyfish, longfin bannerfish, or poor man's moorish idol. Young of this species have been known to act as cleanerfish (see Chapter 2). Similar species include the schooling bannerfish (*Heniochus diphreutes*).

>> **Distribution:** Indo-West Pacific, Red Sea

>> **Size:** 6 inches

>> **Food:** Omnivorous

>> **Tank level:** Middle and lower levels

>> **Minimum tank size:** 60 gallons

Gobies (Gobiidae)

The gobies remind me of the blennies, except their heads are little bigger. They, too, are animated, which makes them fun to watch. Gobies are the proverbial worker bees of the fish world, cleaning the substrate, the rocks, and even the other fishes.

Lemon goby (Gobiodon citrinus)

The lemon goby typically spends much of its time perched on aquarium decorations, quietly observing the rest of the tank. Its beautiful yellow coloration with blue streaks is a nice addition to any tank. This peaceful fish shouldn't be kept with large fishes because of its size, but it does well in a reef tank. After it's settled, the lemon goby will accept most foods and has a particular fondness for live brine shrimp.

>> **Distribution:** Indo-West Pacific

>> **Size:** 2 inches

>> **Food:** Carnivorous

>> **Tank Level:** Lower level

>> **Minimum tank size:** 10 gallons

Neon goby (Elacatinus oceanops)

The neon goby is a popular fish both in the wild and in the aquarium. It's well known for the cleaning services (removing parasites) that it offers to other fish. Although it tends to fight with other neon gobies, this critter is one of the few marine aquarium fishes that breeds in captivity. Unfortunately, it's short-lived, living only between one and two years in the average aquarium.

>> **Distribution:** Western Atlantic, Caribbean Sea

>> **Size:** 2 inches

>> **Food:** Omnivorous

>> **Tank level:** Lower level

>> **Minimum tank size:** 10 gallons

Randall's shrimp goby (Amblyeleotris randalli)

This colorful goby readily accepts a variety of meaty foods, including brine and frozen shrimp. Like many gobies, it likes to dig into the substrate, so a sandy bottom is required. Randall's shrimp goby makes a nice addition to a reef tank. Similar species include the orange-spotted shrimp goby (*Amblyeleotris guttata*).

>> **Distribution:** Indo-West Pacific

>> **Size:** 4 inches

>> **Food:** Omnivorous

>> **Tank level:** Lower level

>> **Minimum tank size:** 10 gallons

Yellow prawn goby (Cryptocentrus cinctus)

This is a peaceful goby that accepts a variety of meaty foods, including brine and frozen shrimp. Like many gobies, it likes to dig into the substrate, so loose coral rubble or a sandy bottom is required. It isn't aggressive toward other fish, but it's territorial with other gobies.

» **Distribution:** Western Pacific

» **Size:** 4 inches

» **Food:** Carnivorous

» **Tank level:** Lower level

» **Minimum tank size:** 30 gallons

Wrasses (Labridae)

Many of the wrasses grow quite large, something to take into account before you purchase one. In general, juveniles are peaceful, hardy fish that accept a variety of marine foods, but they do grow up, so be careful.

African clown wrasse or queen coris (Coris formosa)

This wrasse also changes colors as it matures, with its white stripes changing to blue-green. The African clown wrasse is a bottom-feeder that prefers live marine invertebrates, such as brine shrimp, as well as other meaty foods. Keep this wrasse as a single specimen in your tank, because these fish tend to quarrel among themselves. The African clown wrasse is generally safe with small fishes while a juvenile, but it may become more aggressive as it ages. This and other wrasses aren't well suited for the reef tank. Similar species include the clown wrasse or yellowtail coris (Coris gaimard).

» **Distribution:** Indo-West Pacific, Red Sea

» **Size:** 8 inches

» **Food:** Carnivorous

» **Tank level:** Lower level

» **Minimum tank size:** 180 gallons

Canary or yellow wrasse (Halichoeres chrysus)

With its bright yellow body and characteristic black spots, this wrasse is a beautiful addition to the beginner's aquarium. It's a hardy, peaceful fish that readily accepts a variety of frozen and live marine foods and will eat parasites off tank mates.

- **Distribution:** Indian Ocean
- **Size:** 4 inches
- **Food:** Carnivorous
- **Tank level:** All levels
- **Minimum tank size:** 50 gallons

Six line wrasse (Pseudocheilinus hexataenia)

Named for the six blue lines on its body, this wrasse is a beautiful addition to any saltwater aquarium. It's a hardy fish, but it can be aggressive toward other wrasses. It accepts a variety of frozen and live marine foods and will eat unwanted pests from live rock, like bristleworms.

- **Distribution:** Indo-Pacific Ocean
- **Size:** 3 inches
- **Food:** Carnivorous
- **Tank level:** All levels
- **Minimum tank size:** 30 gallons

Spanish hogfish (Bodianus rufus)

Hogfish are colorful wrasses with a funny name. Young Spanish hogfish are known to clean other fish. As the fish matures, depending on the locality of capture, the coloration changes and red becomes more predominant. Larger hogfish will make a meal of smaller aquarium inhabitants, so you may need to remove them when they grow too large. In other words, you may need to kick some wrasse (out of the tank). Similar species include the Cuban or spotfin hogfish (*Bodianus pulchellus*).

- **Distribution:** Western Atlantic
- **Size:** 8 inches

» **Food:** Omnivorous

» **Tank level:** All levels

» **Minimum tank size:** 150 gallons

Angelfishes (Pomacanthidae)

Angelfishes can grow large and have a tendency to become aggressive and territorial as they get older. Unless you plan on keeping large, boisterous fishes in a high-capacity aquarium, the dwarf angelfishes of the genus *Centropyge* are the right angelfish for the beginner. Specifically, this group includes the African pygmy or orangeback angelfish (*C. acanthops*), the coral beauty (*C. bispinosa*), the lemonpeel angelfish (*C. flavissima*), Herald's or yellow angelfish (*C. heraldi*), the flame angelfish (*C. loricula*), and the cherub angelfish (*C. argi*).

Unlike the larger species, many of these angels associate in pairs and can be kept with members of the same species. These fishes enjoy a variety of marine foods. An added advantage of these angelfish is that they're compatible with many marine invertebrates, should you decide to establish a reef tank. However, they have been known to pick on corals as they mature. Provide many aquarium decorations in which these species can seek refuge.

» **Distribution:** Western Atlantic, Indo-West Pacific

» **Size:** 3 to 5 inches

» **Food:** Omnivorous

» **Tank level:** All levels

» **Minimum tank size:** 55 gallons

Damselfishes (Pomocentridae)

The damselfishes, or damsels for short, comprise a charismatic group of aquarium fishes. This bunch has a lot of personality — in some cases, too much. Damsels can be like party guests that don't know that the party ended two hours ago, but some can be mellow.

Azure damselfish (Chrysiptera hemicyanea)

This two-toned blue and yellow fish is easy to maintain and very popular with beginners. It readily feeds on a variety of flake and frozen foods. It can be semi-aggressive and territorial when larger but does well with other azure damsels.

- » **Distribution:** Indo-West Pacific, East Indian Ocean
- » **Size:** 3 inches
- » **Food:** Omnivorous
- » **Tank level:** Middle levels
- » **Minimum tank size:** 30 gallons

Blue green chromis (Chromis viridis)

This is another peaceful, colorful damselfish that can be kept in a group. The green chromis is an active fish that may be finicky at the start but will consume a variety of chopped meaty foods after it has acclimated to the aquarium. Its bright coloration looks like blue-tinted green chrome, hence the name.

- » **Distribution:** Indo-West Pacific, Red Sea
- » **Size:** 2 inches
- » **Food:** Omnivorous
- » **Tank level:** Middle levels
- » **Minimum tank size:** 10 gallons

Clark's anemonefish (Amphiprion clarkii)

These hardy, peaceful community fish live happily without an anemone, but more than one may not get along. Its coloration can vary according to locality of capture, and it will eat a variety of foods including flake, live foods, and green foods. Similar species include the tomato clownfish *(Amphiprion frenatus)*.

- » **Distribution:** Indo-West Pacific
- » **Size:** 3 inches
- » **Food:** Omnivorous
- » **Tank level:** Middle and lower levels
- » **Minimum tank size:** 10 gallons

Common clownfish (Amphiprion ocellaris)

The common clownfish is the most popular anemonefish in the aquarium trade. Thanks to Hollywood, it has become even more popular in recent years. Clownfish are one of the few species reared in captivity, so it's best to find a tank-reared Nemo because wild-caught specimens are pretty hard to keep alive. This species doesn't live well when alone and should be maintained in pairs. It will readily accept a variety of finely chopped frozen foods and can be coaxed into accepting flake. Clownfish are adapted to living with an anemone (see Chapter 2), so they're well suited for the reef tank. The anemone isn't mandatory, though, so clownfish can be kept in the fish-only community tank, as well. A similar species is the orange clownfish (*Amphiprion percula*).

» **Distribution:** Indo-West Pacific

» **Size:** 2 inches

» **Food:** Omnivorous

» **Tank level:** Middle and lower levels

» **Minimum tank size:** 10 gallons

Sergeant major (Abudefduf saxatilis)

This damselfish is named after its black and yellow banding pattern that looks like military epaulettes. This is an active shoaling species that can be kept in groups. The sergeant major is considered an ideal marine tropical for the beginner because it is hardy and accepts a wide variety of marine foods. In addition, the sergeant major is less territorial and pugnacious than other damsels. Other damsels, including the blue damselfish (*Chrysiptera cyanea*), the humbug or whitetail damselfish (*Dascyllus aruanus*), the yellowtail damselfish (*Microspathodon chrysurus*), and beaugregory (*Stegastes leucostictus*), are also considered fine fish for the beginner because they're extremely hardy and easy to feed. However, these fish can be quite territorial and may create problems for the other fishes in your tank.

» **Distribution:** Indo-West Pacific, western Atlantic

» **Size:** 2 inches

» **Food:** Omnivorous

» **Tank level:** All levels

» **Minimum tank size:** 10 gallons

Sweetlips (Haemulidae)

In general, the sweetlips are hardy but shy fishes that feed on meaty marine foods. The colors on the yellow sweetlips *(Plectorhinchus albovittatus)* change with age, as well, and they become drabber with size. The beautiful yellow stripes of the yellow sweetlips fade, and the fish becomes browner as it gets larger. This species requires a lot of space and can be reclusive if kept with boisterous tank mates, but it's ideal for a peaceful fish-only or reef tank.

>> **Distribution:** Indo-West Pacific, Red Sea

>> **Size:** 4 inches

>> **Food:** Carnivorous

>> **Tank level:** Middle and lower levels

>> **Minimum tank size:** 100 gallons

Dottybacks (Pseudochromidae)

The strawberry gramma *(Pictichromis porphyreus)* is a brilliant purple dottyback that's easy to feed and hardy in captivity. Like many dottybacks, however, it can be aggressive toward similar species or similar-looking species. Therefore, it's best kept singly. It will accept most marine frozen, live, and flake foods. Similar species include the flash-back gramma *(Pictichromis diadema)*.

>> **Distribution:** Indo-West Pacific

>> **Size:** 2 inches

>> **Food:** Omnivorous

>> **Tank level:** Lower levels

>> **Minimum tank size:** 30 gallons

Sea basses (Serranidae)

Belonging to the family of sea basses, the lyretail anthias or sea goldie *(Pseudanthias squamipinnis)* is unlike many of its relatives in that it's a schooling species that doesn't become overly large and predatory. It can be kept in groups and adapts well to a peaceful fish-only tank. The wreckfish is carnivorous, so it requires live or meaty foods. These colorful fish are an attractive addition to the aquarium that can also be kept with invertebrates.

- >> **Distribution:** Indo-West Pacific
- >> **Size:** 4 inches
- >> **Food:** Carnivorous
- >> **Tank level:** All levels
- >> **Minimum tank size:** 50 gallons

Rabbitfishes (Siganidae)

The one spot foxface (*Siganus unimaculatus*) is a common rabbitfish kept in captivity. It's characterized by a large black spot on its bright yellow body. This fish is an algae eater, so an aquarium with lush algal growth is preferred. It will, however, accept a variety of foods as long as vegetable matter is presented. The one spot foxface can be aggressive toward its own kind, so it should be kept singly.

- >> **Distribution:** Western Pacific Ocean
- >> **Size:** 8 inches
- >> **Food:** Herbivorous
- >> **Tank level:** Middle and lower levels
- >> **Minimum tank size:** 70 gallons

Pufferfishes (Tetraodontidae)

The spotted sharpnose pufferfish (*Canthigaster solandri*) is the smallest and most beautiful of the common pufferfishes. This species differs from the others in that it's a small fish that won't outgrow the tank. It's a peaceful fish that should be kept away from its own kind and will accept a variety of finely chopped seafood. I don't recommend it for the reef tank.

- >> **Distribution:** Indo-West Pacific, Red Sea
- >> **Size:** 4 inches
- >> **Food:** Carnivorous
- >> **Tank level:** Middle and lower levels
- >> **Minimum tank size:** 50 gallons

Identifying the Wrong Fish for the Beginner

Many species of fish aren't well suited for the beginner's aquarium for a number of reasons.

>> Some may be highly sensitive to fluctuating water quality conditions characteristic of the new aquarium.

>> Others may have special needs, like special water or lighting conditions. The beginner typically isn't ready to provide this type of habitat without acquiring some experience.

>> A number of species aren't socially compatible with the peaceful tank. This group includes large carnivorous fish that eat smaller fish, territorial fish that don't tolerate trespassing, and mature fish that display aggression and combative behavior.

>> Some species of marine fishes exude poison when threatened. In a closed aquarium, this can have deadly consequences.

WARNING

At times, the pet store may offer or pet dealers may even promote aggressive species because the fish are smaller juveniles that may be considered harmless. Don't be fooled by this argument: Large predatory fish generally grow fast and develop aggressive behavior early in life. Also, don't be convinced to buy fish without doing a little homework. You may end up with a pet that requires special aquarium conditions. Oh, it may live for days or weeks in your tank, but chronic stress will set in, its immune response will fail, and the fish will ultimately die due to disease.

TIP

Don't rush into a purchase. As you develop your talents as an aquarist, you'll expand your capabilities and be able to keep some of the more sensitive species of fish. You may even want to establish an aquarium of compatible aggressive species. However, at this stage of your aquarium-keeping career, concentrate on maintaining water quality with a few compatible and rugged species of fish.

The following sections list those species that you should avoid in your tropical marine aquarium when you're first getting started. These fish are those that you're most likely to encounter in the aquarium store. I include some basic reasons why these fish aren't suitable for the beginner.

Surgeons and tangs (Acanthuridae)

Sometimes it's best not to have a surgeon in the house. Or a tang. Although not a lot of surgeonfishes are available to the average aquarist, your dealer may carry the following tangs that are difficult to keep:

>> **Achilles tang *(Acanthurus achilles):*** Delicate; not compatible

>> **Powder blue tang *(Acanthurus leucosternons):*** Aggressive; prone to marine ich; needs a lot of space

>> **Powder brown surgeonfish *(Acanthurus japonicus):*** Delicate; finicky eater

Triggerfishes (Balistidae)

Many species of triggerfishes are beautiful and fun to watch, but don't let that fool you. They can be predatory and aggressive, and nobody needs a hairpin triggerfish in his aquarium. Remember, they eat invertebrates, so avoid the following fish:

>> **Clown triggerfish *(Balistoides conspicillum):*** Large predator; aggressive; needs a lot of space

>> **Queen triggerfish *(Balistes vetula):*** Large predator; aggressive; needs a lot of space

>> **Undulate triggerfish *(Balistapus undulatus):*** Large; very aggressive; disruptive

>> **White-lined or boomerang triggerfish *(Sufflamen bursa):*** Aggressive

Blennies (Blenniidae)

The Blenniidae may be a peaceful family, but every family has a few bad seeds that shouldn't be planted in your tank:

>> **False cleanerfish *(Aspidontus taeniatus):*** Predatory fish biter

>> **Redlip blenny *(Ophioblennius atlanticus):*** Territorial; harasses other fish

Butterflyfishes (Chaetodontidae)

Believe me, many new aquarists want to include butterflyfish in their aquarium. They're simply too beautiful to resist. But their beauty is a two-edged sword because they're also delicate and difficult to feed. As you become a seasoned veteran of aquarium-keeping, butterflyfishes will become part of your pet repertoire. What follows are a few examples:

>> **Banded butterflyfish** *(Chaetodon striatus):* Delicate; incompatible

>> **Chevron butterflyfish** *(Chaetodon trifascialis):* Delicate

>> **Copperband butterflyfish** *(Chelmon rostratus):* Delicate; difficult to feed; needs very high water quality

>> **Four-eye butterflyfish** *(Chaetodon capistratus):* Delicate

>> **Red-headed or hooded butterflyfish** *(Chaetodon larvatus):* Delicate

>> **Red tail butterflyfish** *(Chaetodon collare):* Difficult to feed

>> **Saddleback butterflyfish** *(Chaetodon ephippium):* Difficult to feed; incompatible with others

Porcupinefishes (Diodontidae)

The porcupinefishes are oddities that many aquarists are drawn to. But these fish outgrow their homes very quickly, and their predatory nature will quickly disrupt your tank. Also, if you have a large one, and it gets spooked and inflates — well, you get the picture. Here are the ones to avoid:

>> **Common porcupinefish** *(Diodon hystrix):* Large; messy eater

>> **Long-spine porcupinefish** *(Diodon holacanthus):* Large; predatory

>> **Spiny boxfish or striped burrefish** *(Chilomycterus schoepfii):* Large; predatory

Fairy basslets (Grammatidae)

One would think that with a name like fairy basslet, this fish is ideal for the new aquarium. Not really. Put away those images of Cinderella and wait until you have a little more experience before buying one of these critters. For example, the black-cap gramma (*Gramma melacara*) is highly territorial.

Squirrelfishes (Holocentridae)

Although an attractive fish, the common squirrelfish (*Holocentrus adscensionis*) is predatory and boisterous and will quickly outgrow your aquarium.

Wrasses (Labridae)

Although many species of wrasses are very attractive, the following can be disruptive to a peaceful tank, aggressive toward smaller fishes, or too large for the average aquarium:

- » **Birdmouth wrasse (*Gomphosus caeruleus*):** Boisterous
- » **Dwarf parrot wrasse (*Cirrhilabrus rubriventralis*):** Delicate
- » **Harlequin tuskfish (*Choerodon fasciatus*):** Large; predatory
- » **Moon wrasse (*Thalassoma lunare*):** Boisterous; large; aggressive
- » **Twin-spot wrasse or clown coris (*Coris aygula*):** Grows too large

Snappers (Lutjanidae)

Like many of its fellow family members, the emperor snapper (*Lutjanus sebae*) grows too large for the average home aquarium.

Filefish (Monocanthidae)

The long-nose filefish (*Oxymonacanthus longirostris*) is a delicate fish and not the best choice for beginners.

Moray eels (Muraenidae)

It's a simple fact that moray eels are cool. One of my first fishes was a moray eel. Huge mistake! These snakes of the sea grow large and eat fish. Enough said. Avoid the following:

- » **Reticulate moray (*Gymnothorax favagineus*):** Large; predatory
- » **Snowflake moray (*Echidna nebulosa*):** Large; predatory

Boxfishes (Ostraciidae)

This group includes the spotted boxfish *(Ostracion meleagris),* which is delicate and secretes poison. Living in poisonous water tends to make life difficult for other critters in the aquarium.

Angelfishes (Pomacanthidae)

Like the butterflyfishes, the angels are delicate, beautiful, and attractive to the new aquarist. Many species are offered by your dealer, but allow your aquarium-keeping talents to develop before you become the guardian of an angelfish. Steer clear of these fish:

>> **Bicolor angelfish** *(Centropyge bicolor):* Delicate; territorial

>> **Blue-face angelfish** *(Pomacanthus xanthometopon):* Delicate

>> **French angelfish** *(Pomacanthus paru):* Aggressive; nippy when young; grows large

>> **King angelfish** *(Holacanthus passer):* Very aggressive; grows large

>> **Koran angelfish** *(Pomacanthus semicirculatus):* Grows large; territorial

>> **Purple moon or Arabian angelfish** *(Pomacanthus asfur):* Aggressive; territorial

>> **Queen angelfish** *(Holacanthus ciliaris):* Aggressive and territorial as it grows large

>> **Regal or royal angelfish** *(Pygoplites diacanthus):* Delicate; shy; difficult to acclimate

>> **Rock beauty** *(Holacanthus tricolor):* Very aggressive; finicky

>> **Three-spot angelfish** *(Apolemichthys trimaculatus):* Delicate; territorial; difficult to acclimate

Damselfishes (Pomacentridae)

Although it sounds funny, on more than one occasion I've been nipped by a dam-sel while diving in the tropics. That's because these little bullies are territorial and the size of the intruder doesn't matter when it comes to defending their turf, so avoid these damsels:

>> **Blue devil** *(Pomacentrus caeruleus):* Aggressive

>> *Dascyllus* **species:** Territorial; aggressive

Dottybacks (Pseudochromidae)

Like many dottybacks, the false gramma or royal dottyback (*Pictichromis paccagnellae*) can be aggressive.

Lionfishes (Scorpaenidae)

When you're tired of looking at all those beautiful small fish in your aquarium, introduce a lionfish and the balance of power will quickly shift. You'll then have an aquarium with only one fish. Oh, another neat feature of this critter: It has venomous spines. Get the point? Keep away from these fish:

>> **Lionfish (*Pterois* species):** Predatory; poisonous

>> **Shortfin turkeyfish (*Dendrochirus brachypterus*):** Predatory; poisonous

Sea basses (Serranidae)

If you want to keep a pet that you'll eventually fillet and serve for dinner, buy one of these basses and groupers. Simply stated, they grow big and they do so by eating small fish. Stay clear of these fish:

>> **Coral trout (*Cephalopholis miniata*):** Large; predatory

>> **Golden-stripe grouper or six-stripe soapfish (*Grammistes sexlineatus*):** Large; predatory

Seahorses and pipefish (Syngnathidae)

There is no doubt about it, the seahorses and their cousins, the pipefishes, are beautiful and graceful. But please don't run out and stock your new tank with them. The following fishes belong in a specialty aquarium where their special needs can be tended to:

>> **Banded pipefish (*Doryrhamphus dactyliophorus*):** Delicate

>> **Lined seahorse (*Hippocampus erectus*):** Delicate

>> **Yellow or spotted seahorse (*Hippocampus kuda*):** Delicate

Pufferfishes (Tetraodontidae)

The white-spotted puffer (*Arothron meleagris*) is a large, messy eater.

Chapter **4**

Looking Closer at Invertebrates

n Chapter 2, I discuss only the smallest portion of what makes up a natural coral reef: the fishes. Even though the number of fish species is in the thousands, that's nothing compared to the number of invertebrates. Did you know that biologists have described over a million species of animals, but only about 5 percent are vertebrates? The others are all invertebrates. Though many invertebrates live in the ocean, only a few, discussed in this chapter, are available to the marine aquarist.

REMEMBER

Aquariums with invertebrates are becoming more and more common because of better filtration systems, more sophisticated technology, and the wider availability of healthy invertebrate species. Invertebrates require special lighting and water of high quality. In Chapters 7 and 8, I discuss this equipment as it pertains to invertebrate tanks. In this chapter, I describe exactly what an invertebrate is and highlight species that are typically available to the home aquarist.

Perusing inside Invertebrates

As the name implies, *invertebrates* are animals that aren't vertebrates. The single unifying feature of invertebrates is that they lack a backbone.

TECHNICAL STUFF

However, although animals with a backbone are all lumped into the phylum Chordata, the invertebrates are so diverse that they comprise many different phyla. For example, insects are invertebrates and snails are invertebrates, as are jellyfish. But you know by looking at these critters that they are not closely related, except for the fact that they are invertebrates.

Describing the typical invertebrate is difficult because of the great diversity among the groups. However, in general, invertebrates do have special needs when compared to fishes. These animals are extremely sensitive to water quality, so advanced filtration systems are required. Other equipment, including protein skimmers and specialized lighting, are also essential. Chapter 7 helps you understand why a protein skimmer is important, but why would invertebrates need more light? Some invertebrates, like corals and anemones, have tiny algae in their bodies that capture light the way that plants do and provide energy for their hosts. Without intense light, these organisms and their hosts die. Some invertebrate species also require elevated water temperatures of 80 to 84 degrees F, so this must be kept in mind.

So the bottom line is that if you're going to keep invertebrates, make sure that you have the right equipment, discussed in Part 2 of this book.

Recognizing Common Aquarium Invertebrates

In the following sections, I discuss common invertebrates, starting with the most primitive and ending with the most complex.

Phylum Porifera

Members of the phylum Porifera are commonly known as *sponges*. The sponges are the most primitive of the multicellular organisms, lacking true tissues and organs. The fact that these critters don't even have a mouth led many early biologists to think they were plants.

The sponge in your kitchen sink is synthetic. However, for centuries, the sponges used by humans were the porous skeletons of animals harvested from the ocean and, in some parts of the world, they still are. Most of the more than 5,000 species of sponges are marine, found wherever there are rocks, shells, or coral to provide a suitable place for attachment.

TECHNICAL STUFF

The bodies of sponges are organized into a system of water canals and chambers lined with hairs, called *flagella,* that move to create the flow of seawater through the sponge. Feeding, gas exchange, and waste removal are dependent on this flow. Hence, sponges are filters.

More important to the aquarist, sponges are rarely drab colored. They typically exhibit bright colors of green, yellow, red, orange, or purple. They also come in a variety of interesting shapes, ranging from flat to heavily branched.

If you decide to add sponges to your aquarium, realize that they require high water quality and adequate flow that allows them to maintain healthy clean open canals and chambers. Also try to keep them out of direct lighting, which will enhance algal growth on their surfaces and literally choke them. Lastly, never remove sponges from the water: Doing so will kill them as air pockets form inside.

WARNING

A sponge that dies after being inadequately maintained can cause a significant toxic reaction, perhaps wiping out everything in the tank. Know this before considering them for your aquarium.

If you decide to maintain live rock in your aquarium, it's likely to be populated by very small sponges, which stay alive by filtering material from the water. Although larger aquarium varieties are available for purchase, many are toxic or difficult to keep in captivity. Common species include blue finger sponges (*Haliclona* spp.), orange ball sponges (*Cinachyra* spp.), and frilly sponges (*Callyspongia* spp.).

Phylum Cnidaria

This large group of invertebrates includes the jellyfish, hard and soft corals, sea anemones, sea whips, and sea fans. When you impress your friends with the funny name that these animals are called, make sure you don't pronounce the "c": ny-DARE-ee-ah.

These critters are all united by their *radial symmetry*; that is, their bodies are cylindrical. Unlike the sponges, cnidarians have a digestive cavity and a mouth surrounded by a circle of tentacles with stinging capsules, which aid in the capture and ingestion of food. These stinging capsules, called *nematocysts*, are a common feature of all cnidarians.

This phylum is composed of about 9,500 species and, with few exceptions, they are marine. Some cnidarians, like jellyfish, are free swimming, but most are *sessile*; that is, attached to the bottom.

Of all the invertebrates suited for the marine aquarium, cnidarians are the most popular. However, they're also the most delicate, requiring high water quality, optimal bright lighting conditions, and rigorous water flow.

There are three classes of cnidarians:

>> The Hydrozoa includes the hydras and hydroids.

>> The Scyphozoa are what people commonly call jellyfish.

>> The Anthozoa comprise the soft and hard corals, sea anemones, and sea fans.

Because this is an aquarium book and not an invertebrate biology book, I don't discuss the hydras and jellyfish in great detail because you're not likely to find them at the typical aquarium dealership. However, this doesn't mean that you won't have them in your aquarium, because the tiny stalked hydroids, which look like little plants, can be found on live rock with dozens of other invertebrate species.

On the other hand, the Anthozoans are the most popular invertebrates, and I want to highlight the groups that comprise this class.

Sea anemones

Pronounced "ah-NEM-o-nee," these beautiful tank additions of the order Actiniaria are common in the marine aquarium. My first anemone was purchased to house my first clownfish, which seeks refuge in a sea anemone's stinging tentacles. The sea anemone is one of the few invertebrates that may make its way into the fish-only tank for that sole purpose.

A sea anemone is a solitary animal known as a *polyp*. It differs from corals, which consist of a number of polyps connected together to form a colony. Sea anemones are often brightly colored as white, green, orange, red, or combinations of these colors, which can be spectacular. They inhabit coastal waters throughout the world, living attached to rocks, shells, or other bottom features.

TECHNICAL
STUFF

The body of the anemone consists of a column with a pedal disk that attaches to the substrate at one end and an oral disk with a slit-like mouth for feeding at the other. The latter is surrounded by one or more rows of tentacles, which vary greatly in size and number. The tentacles bear stinging cells that are used to stun prey and draw them to the mouth. Clownfish, *Amphiprion* species, are able to live among the tentacles of the sea anemone because something on their skin prevents the nematocysts from stinging. Clownfish have a mutualistic relationship with anemones, which means that they both benefit from living together, kind of like my wife and me, sort of. Other animals that are able to live on the anemone include cleaning shrimps, snapping shrimps, arrow crabs, and brittle stars.

WARNING

The reaction of people to these stinging tentacles ranges from nothing to mild inflammation and depends on the species and the location of the sting, so care must be taken when handling a sea anemone.

TIP

Like many forms of coral, some species of anemones house photosynthetic algae called *zooxanthellae* and, therefore, require intense aquarium lighting. Although seemingly immobile, the anemone can move about the aquarium and will find a spot that provides protection and adequate lighting and current.

Sea anemones (a *Heteractis magnifica* is shown in Figure 4-1) are capable of retracting their tentacles and oral disk to rid their bodies of wastes. They will also display this behavior when disturbed or under stress. Pay attention to your anemone. If it remains retracted for an extended period of time, it may be unhealthy, or the water quality in the tank may be poor.

Although anemones house algae that supply much of their nutritional requirements, they should be fed regularly every couple of days with small chunks of seafood, like fish, shrimps, clams, and scallops. Some aquarists prefer to feed inexpensive freshwater fish, like goldfish, to anemones on a regular basis. This practice should be discouraged because the fatty acid distribution in these fish is unlike that found in marine fish and can result in nutritional problems in the anemone.

Most sea anemones are captured in the wild, which has resulted in the complete loss of wild populations in some areas. If you intend to house a sea anemone, make an extra effort to obtain one that was bred in captivity or harvested in a sustainable way. Remember, you don't need an anemone to keep clownfishes healthy.

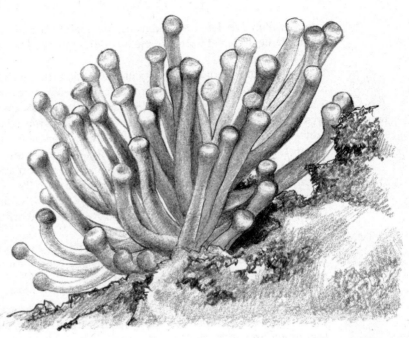

FIGURE 4-1:
The sea anemone
is a popular
cnidarian.

Common aquarium anemones include the following:

>> **Clownfish host anemone (*Entacmaea quadricolor*):** Also known as the *rose anemone, bubble tip anemone,* and *bulb anemone,* this pink and green species has swollen tips on its tentacles. As the name implies, clownfish are readily attracted to this species. This species is also readily available because it is reared in captivity, which is great for the environment.

>> **Gelam and Malu anemones (*Heteractis* spp.):** These closely related species are actually quite different in appearance. Gelam anemones typically have shorter tentacles with swollen tips. For this reason, they are also sometimes called bubble anemones. Their small size and vivid coloration make them nice additions to the aquarium. The Malu anemones, which come from Indonesia, are ideal for the invertebrate aquarium because they are readily available, attractive to clownfishes, and easy to maintain. They are typically larger than the Gelam anemones and have longer-tapered purple-tipped tentacles.

>> **Long tentacle anemone (*Macrodactyla doreensis*):** This is another Indo-Pacific species that is readily accepted by clownfish. Its coloration is typically red or pink with pink or purple-tipped tentacles. Also known as the corkscrew anemone, this is an important species that may be over-harvested in many areas, and not the most environment-friendly choice.

>> **Pink-tipped or Condy anemone** *(Condylactis gigantea)*: Also known as the Caribbean giant anemone, this long-tentacled anemone is one of the most common in the trade. Its body is white, brown, or pink and the tentacles are white or pink with an intense pink tip. Originating in the tropical Atlantic Ocean and Caribbean Sea, the pink-tipped anemone doesn't naturally house clownfish, which prefer Indo-Pacific anemones. In the wild, this species grows to 6 inches high and 12 inches across. Although inexpensive, this anemone needs a well-established aquarium and excellent water quality.

WARNING

Long-term survival of many anemones in captivity is poor. Aquarists should read up on their species of interest before making the commitment.

Polyps

Members of the order Zoanthidea are small anemone-like animals that are sometimes referred to simply as *polyps.* These critters can be either solitary, like the anemone, or colonial, like coral. They are typically small, short, and button-like with a short fringe of tentacles surrounding a broad oral disk.

Species of the genus *Zoanthus* are the most common in the aquarium trade. These polyps are found in clusters and come in various shades of green and brown. Like all invertebrates, they require high water quality and excellent lighting, but they are easy to keep.

Mushroom anemones or polyps of the genera *Discosoma* and *Rhodactis* are sort of a cross between anemones and corals. They are colonial but lack the skeleton common to the corals. They, too, have photosynthetic algae and are popular with marine aquarium hobbyists. They are typically flat with broad oral disks. Coloration can be red, green, or brown with radiating stripes. Periodic feedings to supplement their algae are recommended.

WARNING

Species of Zoanthid coral (including *Zoanthus* species) can contain a highly toxic and potentially lethal substance known as Palytoxin. You can be exposed to Palytoxin by direct contact with your skin or eyes or by inhaling aerosols from the aquarium. To minimize exposure, handle corals minimally, always wear latex gloves, and don't remove them from the water.

Stony corals

Moving your way through the class Anthozoa, you come to the close relatives of the anemones, the animals of the order Scleractinia, called the *stony* or *hard corals.* The foundation of diversity and beauty of the natural coral reef community is the hard calcium carbonate skeleton of the coral animals.

Like anemones, coral animals are polyps with a columnar body and tentacles. However, individual coral polyps are connected to one another to form a colony of animals. Unlike anemones, stony corals are not only colonial, but they also produce a calcium carbonate skeleton. Individual coral polyps are usually small, averaging one to three millimeters, but coral reef colonies can become large, covering huge sections of the ocean floor.

Over the last decade, a lot of acronyms have emerged in the saltwater aquarium hobby, including LPS and SPS, which are used to classify stony corals into two general categories: large-polyped stony coral or large-polyped scleractinian (LPS) and small-polyped stony coral or small-polyped scleractinian (SPS). This classification is broadly based on the size of the corals' polyps. So, of the corals listed here, a good example of LPS is *Euphyllia* and SPS is *Acropora*. Many species are marketed under these general categories, and LPS are generally more well-suited for beginners and SPS are more demanding in terms of water quality, lighting, and water movement, which means that only experienced hobbyists should stock them.

You need to know that grouping corals into LPS and SPS species is somewhat arbitrary because not all corals can be easily assigned to one of these categories. Also, some so-called SPS corals are relatively easy to keep while some LPS aren't. Some hobbyists want to remove these categories because they can be misleading. The bottom line: Don't rely on these acronyms and do your homework on each species before adding it to your tank. Most people who are familiar with stony corals think of the hard skeleton (called an *exoskeleton*) that is left behind when the animals die. In fact, the shapes and structure of this skeleton are typically used to classify species. Some corals are highly branched, while others resemble large boulders. If you're familiar only with dead coral and want to know what the live animal looks like, imagine the coral skeleton covered with a fine layer of interconnected tiny anemones.

As coral colonies grow in the wild and, as a result, reefs build up, the animals add new layers of calcium carbonate exoskeleton on top of the old. To do so requires calcium, which is readily available in the ocean. However, in the closed system of the aquarium, stony corals can easily use up the calcium, so you must add supplements (see Chapter 13).

Many species of corals have tiny photosynthetic dinoflagellate algae (see Chapter 14) within them called *zooxanthellae*. These algae, which require bright lighting and excellent water quality, provide the coral with much, but not all, of their nutritional needs. Therefore, it is necessary to supplement the coral every now and then, however, with microplankton and bits of seafood. Also, many species of corals can extend their tentacles and are capable of stinging and killing other corals, so keep corals separated.

Because it is illegal to harvest stony corals from the Caribbean, all wild corals available to you originate in the tropical areas of the Indo-Pacific. However, many hard corals are now grown in captivity, which is a much more environmentally friendly source.

TECHNICAL STUFF

The captive rearing of hard corals involves a process called *fragging*, during which the coral is fragmented into smaller pieces, which are then cultivated and grown to larger sizes. Think of it as cloning coral. The process results in the production of hard corals well-adapted to captivity and, therefore, better for your aquarium. You're also saving those in the wild from being harvested. Fragging is now becoming popular among aquarists as a means of expanding corals in their aquarium.

The following are those that you will find easy to maintain and are most likely to encounter:

>> **Acan Lords (*Micromussa lordhowensis*):** Often called *Acans,* these stony corals have many different color combinations (see Figure 4-2). In the reef aquarium, this coral is very hardy and fast growing, and it tolerates a wide variety of conditions. They're also cultured in captivity.

FIGURE 4-2:
Hard corals like Acan Lords have a calcareous skeleton.

© John Wiley & Sons, Inc.

- » **Brain corals (*Leptoria*, *Favia*, and *Favites* spp.):** These stony corals are familiar to most people because they are aptly named after that which they resemble, the brain. These corals can be massive, but stick with smaller specimens for your home aquarium. Coloration can vary depending on species from shades of brown to vivid green to purple and pink.

- » **Bubble corals (*Plerogyra* spp.):** This genus is aptly named after the bubble-like sacs that cover the mouths and tentacles of the colony. These tan or pearl-colored corals are loaded with zooxanthellae algae but should be fed pieces of seafood once a week.

- » **Plate corals (*Fungia* and *Heliofungia* spp.):** These flat corals with long tentacles are readily confused with anemones. Like anemones, some species are solitary animals that are mobile, moving about the aquarium. These species fend well when placed directly on the substrate, where lighting is good and flow is moderate. The tentacles of these corals make them easy to feed.

- » **Staghorn and elkhorn corals (*Acropora* spp.):** Corals of the genus *Acropora* are so named because of their distinctive shapes. These are relatively fast-growing stony corals that are heavily branched, ranging in coloration from yellowish or purplish brown to cream colored with paler tips. Although commonly available, these corals are difficult to keep.

- » **Vase and frog spawn corals (*Euphyllia* spp.):** This genus of coral has pronounced tentacles that resemble those of sea anemones. Vase corals have round tentacles, whereas those of frog spawn coral resemble a mass of frog eggs.

Soft corals

Not all corals have calcium carbonate skeletons. Those belonging to the order Alcyonacea are called soft corals because they have a soft skeleton comprised of spiny elements called *sclerites*. These animals form soft fleshy or leathery colonies that are irregularly shaped and quite large. The colonies of soft coral can have finger–like projections, as well. Soft corals are generally more hardy than their stony counterparts.

TECHNICAL STUFF

The order Alcyonacea now contains the gorgonians, which includes the sea whips and sea fans. These animals were formerly in a separate order called Gorgonacea. Sometimes referred to as the *horny corals*, the gorgonians have a body that contains a central axial rod composed of an inorganic substance called *gorgonin*. Like some other corals, gorgonians possess photosynthetic algae. These colonial animals are flexible, swaying gently in the currents of your aquarium.

TIP

Gorgonians should be placed perpendicular to the flow. You can anchor them in your aquarium with marine epoxy that's designed for aquarium use. Here are the ones I recommend:

>> **Finger or colt corals (*Alcyonium* spp.):** These tree-like branched soft corals are easy to maintain in captivity and are ideally suited for a beginning invertebrate aquarist. Coloration is brown to soft white. These fast-growing corals can be trimmed when they become overgrown.

>> **Leather, mushroom, or toadstool corals (*Sarcophyton* spp.):** Widespread throughout the Indo-Pacific, the leather corals are so named after their texture and brown coloration (see Figure 4-3). Leather corals can be mushroom-like in shape, but other forms can be finger-like as well. The polyps of these species are conspicuous when the animal is feeding, but retract when disturbed. This is a hardy group of soft corals that grows rapidly and is well suited for the beginner.

FIGURE 4-3:
Soft corals lack the calcium of their cousins.

© John Wiley & Sons, Inc.

>> **Pulse or waving hand corals (*Anthelia* and *Xenia* spp.):** So named after the rhythmic pulsing of their polyps, the pulse corals appreciate a good current in your aquarium. Pulse corals consist of a cluster of feathery or branch-like polyps that join at the base like a tree trunk and anchor the coral to the substrate. These corals are easy to keep, growing rapidly in the marine aquarium of even the most inexperienced aquarist. However, these corals are sensitive to rapid pH changes, so be careful when adding aquarium buffers.

>> **Sea fans (*Gorgonia* spp.):** As the name implies, sea fans grow in a flat plane that resembles a fan. Although their lacy appearance is attractive, they require a strong current and can be difficult for the beginner to maintain. Most species come from the Caribbean.

>> **Sea whips (*Muricea* spp.):** The sea whips are similar to the sea fans, but possess finger-like projections that extend in all directions. Like sea fans, sea whips require plenty of circulation and may be best suited for the advanced aquarist.

Phylum Platyhelminthes

Commonly referred to as *flatworms*, members of the phylum Platyhelminthes are aptly named because they are flat. Although there are three major classes of flatworms, only one, the Turbellaria, is not parasitic. Turbellarians range in size from microscopic forms to species that are more than 2 feet long. They are primarily aquatic, and most are marine bottom-dwellers that live in sand and mud. Flatworms are considered the most primitive animals that possess bilateral symmetry, that is, two sides that are identical.

Flatworms aren't common in the aquarium trade, but some kinds may be imported as hitchhikers on live rock. In some cases, flatworms can become a pest for the reef aquarium. Although they don't harm corals, they can block coral from getting enough light if they grow in numbers. Some wrasses are known to naturally feed on flatworms in the aquarium, but there are also commercially available tank remedies to get rid of this nuisance.

Phylum Mollusca

The group of invertebrates called mollusks is one of the most familiar because we like to eat them. Clams, oysters, scallops, mussels, squids, snails, and octopuses all belong to this group and have been part of the human diet for millennia. There are over 100,000 known living species of mollusks.

Mollusks are much more complex than the invertebrates in the preceding sections. Members of this group are united by several anatomical features. The body consists of three regions: a head with sense organs, a mouth, and a brain; a visceral mass containing most of the internal organs surrounded by a body wall; and a foot, the muscular lower part of the body on which the animal creeps. In addition, mollusks secrete a calcareous shell and possess a feeding organ called a *radula*. In some mollusks, like snails, these parts are pretty obvious, but in others, like squids, some of these features are reduced or absent.

Some species of mollusks, like snails, adapt well to the marine aquarium, and their scavenging habits make them easy to feed. However, many species of mollusks are filter feeders. That is, they actually filter food particles and small critters from the water when they feed. You probably already know that your aquarium should be well filtered in order to maintain healthy animals, so, you may have a problem with filter feeding critters. In general, the water in your aquarium is too clean for them. Therefore, filter feeding invertebrates are difficult to maintain in captivity, and I don't recommend them for the beginner.

There are seven classes of living mollusks, and the following are some of those that are most suitable for the marine aquarium.

Snails

The class Gastropoda consists of more than 75,000 species of mollusks that we call snails. These critters live not only in fresh and saltwater, but they have adapted to life on land, as well. You probably remember finding slugs under rocks in the garden. Snails, in general, have a shell and a muscular foot that they use to move about. However, some species have lost their shells, like the terrestrial slugs.

With so many different kinds of snails, it's difficult to single out a few species for the marine aquarium. However, in general, snails are scavengers that will consume algae, grazing it from the fixtures and glass. And that is a good thing. Snails that graze on algae need a lot to remain healthy. Therefore, don't add more than a couple of snails to your aquarium — too many and they will starve to death.

Some species of snails aren't suitable for your aquarium because they grow too large, like queen conches, or they are predatory of other invertebrates, like whelks.

Many snails are available to the aquarist. Here are some examples:

>> **Cowries (*Cypraea* spp.):** These gastropods have a highly polished domed shell with decorative patterns, but the shell is often concealed by a fleshy mantle that's drab in coloration. Some feed on algae, a few are omnivores, and some are predatory with feeding preferences toward soft corals and other invertebrates. Read up on the particular species you plan to obtain.

>> **Nudibranchs (*Aplysia* and *Chromodoris* spp.):** Sometimes called sea slugs or sea hares, these are snails without shells (see Figure 4-4). Although brightly colored, nudibranchs can be very difficult to maintain in captivity because many are predatory and difficult to feed. In general, avoid them.

>> **Top or star snails (*Astraea* spp.):** These snails have high conical shells often lined with ridges. They are also excellent algae grazers and are considered excellent additions to the reef aquarium.

FIGURE 4-4:
A nudibranch is pretty but not worth the trouble.

© John Wiley & Sons, Inc.

Clams, scallops, mussels, and oysters

These animals belong to the class Bivalvia because their bodies are housed in two shells that close like valves to protect them. There are about 15,000 species of bivalves and more than 80 percent of them live in the sea.

These invertebrates are well adapted to burrowing in the substrate with their wedge-like shape, but many species also live on top of the bottom. Most bivalves are filter feeders, and they can be difficult to keep in the average aquarium. It is possible to purchase liquid food preparations that are specifically designed for filter feeders, but this is best left to the experienced aquarist.

Most species of clams, scallops, mussels, and oysters shouldn't be kept by the beginner because of their specialized feeding mode.

Nonetheless, the most common bivalve in the marine aquarium is the giant clam of the genus *Tridacna* (see Figure 4-5). Although these species are known to grow to over 200 pounds, smaller specimens are farm raised for the aquarium trade. Despite what you may have heard, these clams don't trap people in their shells in an attempt to eat them. In fact, these clams harbor photosynthetic algae that help sustain them (but they still need to be fed live or cryogenically preserved phytoplankton). And they must be provided with excellent lighting.

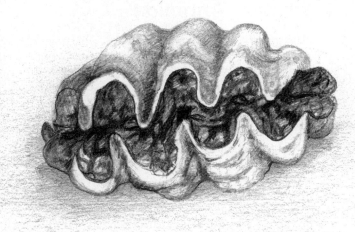

FIGURE 4-5:
The giant clam is not likely to eat your fish.

© John Wiley & Sons, Inc.

Squids and octopuses

As I move through the phylum Mollusca, the complexity of the animals has been increasing and the general body plan has been changing from the standard molluscan form. The squid and octopus belong to the class called Cephalopoda, which is the most specialized and complex group of mollusks. In fact, these critters are considered the most intelligent invertebrates.

Cephalopods have moved away from the substrate, and the body is adapted to a mobile life in the water column. The head of cephalopods bears a crown of arms and tentacles that they use for movement and feeding. In addition, feeding is aided by the presence of a parrot-like beak, which is used to tear apart and kill prey. Unlike their cousins the snails and bivalves, most cephalopods have no hard external shell.

There are only about 800 living species of cephalopods, and they are among the largest of the mollusks, ranging from just a couple of inches to more than 40 feet in length.

It will be tempting to keep squids and octopuses in your new marine aquarium because they are so beautiful and intriguing. But these invertebrates are best left for advanced aquarists who are able to properly care for them. Cephalopods are sensitive to water quality, they are expensive and highly predatory, and they typically require their own space. I don't recommend them for a beginner.

Phylum Annelida

This group is commonly known as the segmented worms, which includes the most popular worm on earth, the earthworm. But not all worms live on or in dirt. In fact, of the 9,000 species of segmented worms, nearly two-thirds live in the marine environment and belong to the class Polychaeta.

TECHNICAL
STUFF

In general, segmented worms have a more advanced body plan than the mollusks. As the name implies, they all have an elongated body that is segmented. In addition, most annelids have well-developed circulatory, nervous, and excretory systems. Some forms have gills for respiration.

The marine polychaetes come in two forms: those that move about and those that are sedentary, inhabiting tubes or burrows. The former can be predators, grazers, or bottom-dwelling detritus feeders, whereas the sedentary forms typically have large gills and tentacles for filter feeding.

Although these worms come in a variety of colors and sizes, not all are suitable for the typical aquarium. Some smaller forms may find their way into your aquarium on live rock, but you will hardly know that they are there scavenging marine detritus. The most common segmented worms kept in the home aquarium are the sedentary tubeworms of the following species:

» **Christmas tree worms (*Spirobranchus* spp.):** Like featherduster worms, these creatures live in a tube, but the tube is calcareous and typically embedded in coral. In addition, these colorful worms with heads of yellow, red, blue, or white have two sets of spiraling tentacles. These plankton feeders are difficult to keep alive because they require a regular supply of food. Like fan worms, they should only be kept by seasoned veterans.

» **Fan or featherduster worms (*Sabellastarte* spp.):** These sedentary worms are imported from the Indo-Pacific for the aquarium trade. They live in a parchment tube that's buried in the substrate. The feathery head is typically colorful and it is extended for feeding (see Figure 4-6). When startled, the feathery tentacles are withdrawn within a fraction of a second back into the safety of the tube. These invertebrates are not particular about lighting and can be fed brine shrimp. Unfortunately, these critters need a lot of planktonic food and tend to starve slowly in the typical aquarium. If your fan worms lose their feathers, it can be a sign that they aren't being fed well enough.

FIGURE 4-6:
Fan worms
need a lot of
planktonic food.

© John Wiley & Sons, Inc.

Phylum Arthropoda

The phylum Arthropoda is by far the largest group of animals on the planet. There are over one million species of arthropods, but over 900,000 of these are insects, which I don't include here (ants can't swim).

Instead, I direct my attention to the class of marine insects called Crustacea. This group comprises more than 67,000 species and includes many familiar creatures, like shrimps, crabs, and lobsters, that you encounter not only in the aquarium but also in the kitchen.

Being arthropods, crustaceans have a hard encasement called an *exoskeleton*, which provides protection. Like the annelids, arthropods are segmented with joints in the exoskeleton that permit movement. It's tough to grow with a hard exoskeleton, so arthropods must periodically shed or molt their exoskeleton to get bigger.

Unlike the annelids, the segments of arthropods are not alike, and the body is divided into parts called the head, thorax, and abdomen. In the order Decapoda, which includes the shrimps, crabs, and lobsters, the head and thorax are fused to form the *carapace*.

The order Decapoda, which means ten feet, is named after the five pairs of legs that these critters all have. Many species of crustaceans are scavengers, but some can be predatory, as well. This means that not all crabs, shrimp, and lobsters are right for the marine aquarium.

Crabs

The crabs are decapod crustaceans that are more flattened than the others, have heavier legs, and an abdomen or tail that's folded under the body. So, take a lobster and flatten it, shrink its tail, and fold it under the body, and you have a crab.

Some crabs can be crabby, so it's best to choose smaller species like the following:

>> **Anemone crabs (*Neopetrolisthes* spp.):** Clownfish are not the only critters that can make a home out of an anemone — so can the anemone crab. This small (1-inch) crab will gladly accept any kind of anemone. This genus has a number of species that come in a variety of spotted color patterns. Although they will scavenge a bit, they also rely heavily on filter feeding, which makes them difficult to keep well fed.

>> **Arrow crab (*Stenorhynchus seticornis*):** With its triangular head and body and long legs, this odd-looking crab is a neat addition to any tank. The arrow crab is easily maintained and is a carnivore that can be fed bits of seafood. They will also consume the noxious bristleworm, which is good. Unfortunately, arrow crabs also eat tubeworms and other small invertebrates, so take care when choosing tank mates.

>> **Hermit crabs:** There are hermit crab genera from all over the world that make nice additions to your aquarium. Unlike their cousins, hermit crabs have a soft abdomen that's protected by a snail shell that the crab steals or finds uninhabited. They can be ideal scavengers in the aquarium and excellent algae grazers. However, some species are large and predatory, causing

damage to the average invertebrate aquarium. Take care when choosing a hermit crab for your tank. Smaller species, like the blue-leg hermit *(Clibanarius tricolor)* and the scarlet hermit *(Paguristes cadenati)*, are preferred.

» **Horseshoe crab *(Limulus polyphemus)*:** This common species, shown in Figure 4-7, is not a crustacean and actually belongs to its own class, known as the Merostomata. I include it here because it is typically marketed as a crab. Although this species grows to over 20 inches, smaller specimens can be entertaining. Much of their time is spent half buried in the bottom, and they can be fed small pieces of seafood. They require deep sand beds and tend to do a lot of digging, so they aren't suited for beginning aquarists.

FIGURE 4-7: A horseshoe crab needs deep sand beds for digging and is not for beginners.

Lobsters

In general, lobsters are not recommended additions to the invertebrate tank. One is shown in Figure 4–8. They are boisterous, aggressive scavengers that are well known for rearranging and disrupting the aquarium. They can be predatory of other invertebrates and even fish, so they should be kept only with larger fish.

Nonetheless, there are exceptions to this generalization, and the smaller species of lobsters are less noxious.

» **Flame lobsters *(Enoplometopus* spp.):** Resembling a crayfish, this small brightly colored lobster is typically less than 5 inches. It is less boisterous and predatory than its cousins and will gladly accept most meaty seafoods.

» **Purple spiny lobster *(Panulirus versicolor)*:** This is one of the spiny lobsters, which means that it lacks large claws, but has two long antennae. These colorful lobsters are fine for the aquarium when less than 5 inches long, but they become predatory when larger. Spiny lobsters are efficient scavengers that readily feed on small pieces of seafood.

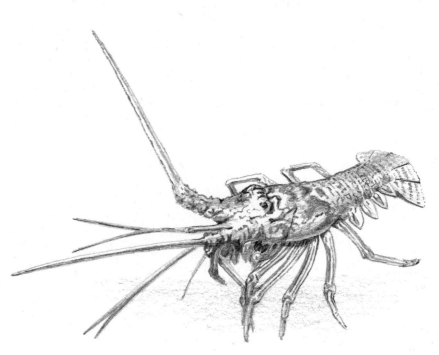

FIGURE 4-8:
The lobster can disrupt your aquarium.

Shrimps

The shrimps are the close cousins of the lobsters, without the attitude. They are much smaller and more delicate than lobsters, as well, making them attractive additions to the invertebrate and mixed species tank (see Figure 4-9).

The following shrimp species are best for the beginner. Most come from the Indo-Pacific, but some Caribbean species are also available. Shrimps are efficient scavengers that feed on many aquarium foods. Take care to avoid aggressive shrimp, such as mantis shrimp, which are predatory with powerful arms that can spear their prey.

» **Anemone or commensal shrimps (*Periclimenes* spp.):** If you know that the cleaner shrimp are like cleanerfish, and you guessed that anemone shrimp are like anemone fish, you're right. They live among the stinging tentacles of the anemone, which provides them with protection. These are generally small shrimp, rarely larger than 1 inch, and are almost clear in coloration with white, brown, or purple spots. Although some bond with a coral host, unless you're keeping an anemone, you shouldn't keep anemone shrimp.

» **Banded coral shrimp (*Stenopus hispidus*):** Another common aquarium shrimp, this species has bands of white and red, as well as a pair of long claws. This larger species, which grows to over 2 inches, should be kept singly; it can be aggressive with other shrimps. This shrimp is also called the boxing shrimp or the coral-banded shrimp. A number of other species of this genus are also available.

» **Blood or fire shrimp (*Lysmata debelius*):** This beautiful decapod is vivid red with white spots. Although considered by some to be shy, they aren't really. They're just nocturnal.

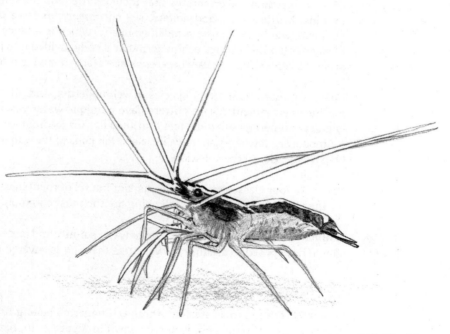

FIGURE 4-9:
Shrimps are like lobsters without the attitude.

© John Wiley & Sons, Inc.

- » **Candy or camelback shrimps (*Rhynchocinetes durbanensis*):** Sometimes called the camelback shrimp because of the hump on its tail, the candy shrimp is also named for its red and white striped coloration. These shrimp grow to just over an inch. They are a common species in the aquarium trade, readily available but not necessarily great for the beginner. They eat an awful lot of polyps of various species and thus are only safe for the largest reef tanks.

- » **Cleaner shrimps (*Lysmata* spp.):** These are by far the most popular shrimps for the marine aquarium. As you can imagine, these critters are named after their propensity to clean parasites and damaged skin from many species of fish (and comically so, when they are cartoons — see *Finding Nemo*). In return, fish will generally not feed on them. Cleaner shrimp are colorful, with various combinations of red and white stripes and long white antennae. They can also be kept in groups of four or five.

Phylum Echinodermata

This is a group of invertebrates that includes the familiar starfish as well as sea urchins, brittle stars, sand dollars, sea cucumbers, and sea lilies. The group is characterized by *pentamerous radial symmetry,* which is a fancy (and shorter) way of saying that the average echinoderm has a body divided into five parts arranged around a central axis like a wheel. Look at a starfish, and you will see this clearly.

There are more than 7,000 species of echinoderms, and all of them live in the marine environment. These critters have a unique water vascular system, which operates numerous tiny tube feet that they use for locomotion and feeding. Some echinoderms, like starfish, have little suction cups at the end of the tube feet that help them cling to the substrate.

There are four classes of echinoderms, but not all of them have members suitable for the marine aquarium. The following are the most common.

WARNING

Echinoderms are extremely sensitive to water salinity and under no circumstances should be exposed to a salinity lower 1.024 (salinity is covered in Chapter 13).

Sea stars (Starfish)

Generally referred to as starfish, these echinoderms belong to the class Asteroidea. Sea stars, like the peppered red shown in Figure 4-10, have a central mouth on their underside and, in some cases, they extend part of their stomach to digest their prey. Many sea stars are carnivorous, eating other invertebrates, like clams, using their tube feet to pry them open.

FIGURE 4-10: You can shoot for the sea stars, but aim for some experience first.

WARNING

The tube feet and vascular system of the starfish are sensitive and easily damaged. Take care when purchasing a starfish to be sure that the animal is in good condition. Also, rapid changes in salinity will damage the vascular system. Beginners should know that most sea stars have specialized food requirements and generally die of malnutrition in captivity after several months to a year.

>> **Blue sea star *(Linckia laevigata)*:** This species is another popular and colorful addition to the marine aquarium. So named for its brilliant blue coloration, this species is readily available and easy to maintain.

>> **Brittle stars (*Ophiactis* and *Ophiocoma* spp.):** These are not your typical starfish. Like most sea stars, they have a central disk, but their arms are long and thin and help them move quickly around the aquarium. Brittle stars are imported from the Caribbean, as well as the Indo-Pacific region. Although they tend to be drab colored and nocturnal, they are excellent scavengers and are easy to maintain.

>> **Orange or elegant sea star *(Fromia monilis)*:** Imported from Indonesia, this colorful orange and red species is a common addition to the invertebrate aquarium. The orange starfish is not a large species, rarely growing to more than 3 inches. It will feed readily on small pieces of seafood, but it also needs special dietary items, like live sponges, so it is not a species that a new aquarist should be keeping.

Sea stars are well known for their ability to regenerate their limbs when they are damaged or lost. In some species, not only does the star regenerate the limb, but the limb can regenerate the star!

Sea urchins

Although related to the sea stars, sea urchins and their cousins the sand dollars belong to a different class of echinoderms called the Echinoidea. Like the sea stars, they are radially symmetrical, but they lack arms. Instead, sea urchins have a calcium carbonate skeleton, called a *test*, with movable spines, which you can see in Figure 4-11. If you've ever been to a tropical beach, it's not unusual to find the dried tests of sea urchins.

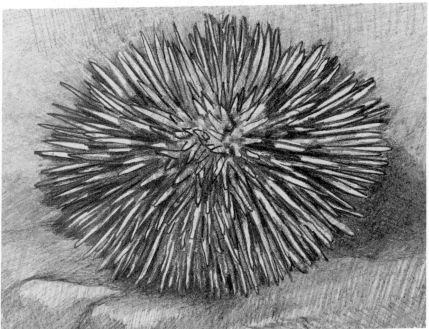

FIGURE 4-11:
Sea urchins are attractive but difficult to handle.

© John Wiley & Sons, Inc.

Like sea stars, sea urchins have a mouth on their underside and tube feet. However, the mouths of sea urchins have a toothed beak-like organ called *Aristotle's lantern.* This is used to gnaw algae and scavenge organic matter off the reef. In the aquarium, sea urchins will scavenge as well.

Some sea urchins are also equipped with poison glands, which makes handling them a bit of a problem. The venom is not likely to cause death, but it will cause pain and infection.

>> **Common or short-spine sea urchins (*Echinometra* spp.):** Members of this genus are sometimes called *black sea urchins* because of their coloration. They typically have shorter and blunter spines that can still penetrate your skin. Growing to about 4 inches, these sea urchins are easy to maintain.

>> **Long-spine sea urchins (*Diadema* spp.):** Found throughout tropical seas, members of this genus are favored by many aquarists. They have long, thin spines that are extremely sharp and sometimes poisonous, but they are easy to maintain. Coloration is generally black, but some species and smaller sea urchins may have banded spines.

>> **Pencil urchins (*Heterocentrotus* spp.):** These species of sea urchins have thick blunt spines that don't pose a threat. Unlike most sea urchins, which are typically drab colored, the pencil urchin can be more colorful and, therefore, a more attractive addition to the aquarium. Although readily available, they tend to be expensive and predatory, as well.

Sea cucumbers

Members of the class Holothuroidea are generally called sea cucumbers because of their shape. These echinoderms are elongated, with a mouth at one end and an anus at the other. They are related to sea stars and sea urchins because they have tube feet.

The mouth of the sea cucumber is surrounded by tentacles, which may be finger-like, stalked with a button-like tip, or branched. The tentacles are actually modified tube feet: parts of the water vascular system that are used for feeding. While some sea cucumbers filter feed, most scavenge organic matter from the bottom, gobbling up the substrate and straining it through their bodies.

In general, sea cucumbers aren't recommended for the new marine aquarist because some species can extrude toxins, when disturbed, that will poison your aquarium.

Nonetheless, a couple of species are readily available and relatively easy to maintain in captivity.

>> **Knobby black cucumber (*Stichopus chloronotus*):** Although aptly named for its dark drab coloration, the black cucumber is enjoyed by some aquarists because it swallows mouthfuls of unfiltered substrate, scavenging detritus and providing a useful service.

» **Sea apple *(Pseudocolochirus axiologus)*:** Don't let the name fool you, this is indeed a sea cucumber and not a sea fruit. This is one of the most popular aquarium species because of its striking pink, orange, yellow, and red coloration. One is shown in Figure 4-12. With feathery tentacles, the sea apple is a filter feeder that will position itself in the current of your tank. It is difficult to feed, but small pieces of seafood, brine shrimp, and rotifers will satisfy this critter. This is a species not to be kept with fish.

FIGURE 4-12:
The sea cucumber will not pickle in your aquarium.

© John Wiley & Sons, Inc.

» Taking the trip home

» Introducing your new pets to their
new abode

Chapter **5**

Going from the Dealer to Your Home

Most of your new tropical marine fish and invertebrates come from the farthest reaches of the world (see Chapter 2 for more information). (The Indo–Pacific probably isn't around the corner for you.) With some exceptions, fish and invertebrates are collected, double-bagged, and boxed for shipment, which can take days. That's a long trip, but professional collectors and importers are good at what they do. They don't stay in business long if they deliver dead fish, so they take great care to ensure that a healthy marine animal is delivered to your dealer.

Although most aquarium fish are still collected from the wild, several common aquarium species are bred in captivity. These include some species of angelfishes, clownfishes, dottybacks, blennies, and gobies, to name a few.

It's no secret that marine species are more expensive than their freshwater counterparts. So, it's important to protect your investment from the moment you make it! The process of buying fish and invertebrates, getting them home, and introducing them into your new aquarium isn't complicated, and this chapter helps you keep it that way.

Understanding Why Quarantining Your Fish Is Essential

Any time a living creature is abruptly removed from its environment, whether from the wild or a captive breeding program, and introduced into a new one, the critter is going to experience a stress. How many times, after all, have you stressed out just commuting to work? Of course, the stress is even greater if the animal is boxed or bagged up and transported halfway around the world. Stress in any animal can lead to disease and death (as I discuss in Chapter 17), whether it's an anemone or an anemonefish. So, after that long trip from the tropics, your pets need to acclimate to their new home and settle down a bit. This settling down period is often referred to as the *quarantine period.*

In general, your new pets will have two quarantine periods:

>> When they get to your dealer

>> When they get to your home

The best way to ensure that your new saltwater fish survive in your new aquarium is to set up a quarantine tank. This type of tank prevents the spread of disease, which can only come from new additions, spreading rapidly and, in some cases, wiping out entire aquariums. Don't let the concept of a quarantine tank spook you — it need not be big or expensive, but it's worth every single penny. A quarantine tank is a simple aquarium, usually about 10–20 gallons, with an internal box, sponge, or external power filter, a heater, and some simple decorations. (Chapter 9 covers how to set up a quarantine tank.)

REMEMBER

You need to routinely test the water quality of the quarantine tank because you don't want to add your new pets to an unhealthy environment. The quarantine tank should be set up at the same time as the main aquarium and well before you go to the dealer to purchase fish.

TIP

When fishes arrive from distant places, they should be allowed to adjust to captivity and settle down from the trip in quarantine for at least a week before you consider buying them. You also want to make sure the fish is feeding before you purchase it.

Working with a Reliable Dealer

You want to establish a good working relationship with your aquatic dealer because you need someone to advise you during the setup and maintenance of your system. You want somebody who maintains a good, clean business, has healthy fish in his or her aquariums, and is always willing to answer your questions and spend time with you. A good dealer gives you invaluable information on new and reliable products. He or she is motivated by the desire to help you to maintain your system correctly — not solely by money.

TIP

Choose someone with the right attitude: someone who will be consistently available to help. Try to avoid dealers who don't take the time to explain details to you or find the specific fish that you desire. I prefer the pet shops that cater to the needs of all levels of enthusiasts, are willing to special order supplies, and would rather send you elsewhere than sell you an improper choice.

The right dealer has a consistent supply of healthy fish and invertebrates. The right dealer also lets you know where they come from, when they arrived, and how well they're doing in captivity.

WARNING

If your dealer doesn't communicate, you need a different dealer.

If you've worked successfully with a freshwater aquarium dealer in the past, this would be the logical place to start with your marine interests.

TIP

Acronyms are becoming very common in the aquarium trade. Many online aquarium resources typically refer to your dealer as an LFS or local fish store, for what it is worth.

Choosing Healthy Fish: The How-To

Your goal is to have healthy fish and invertebrates in your marine aquarium, and your dealer's goal is, you hope, to provide them to you.

Your first fish should be a hardy one that's easy to maintain. (See Chapter 3 for my suggestions on fish to add to your aquarium.) I recommend captive-bred or Floridian and Caribbean fishes because they've traveled the shortest distance and tend to be in better condition when they arrive. Some examples include captive-bred clownfish and cardinalfish.

REMEMBER

Tropical marine fish are more costly than their freshwater counterparts. Spend wisely and walk before you run.

Here are some tips for choosing healthy animals:

>> Buy fish only from healthy-looking aquariums with clear water, a clean tank, and no dead fish.

>> Make sure that the fish you want is healthy looking (see Chapter 18). If the fish has any cuts, scrapes, or fin problems, don't buy it. Watch for possible symptoms of disease, such as white granular spots, cottony white patches, frayed fins, or dull skin. The stomach of the fish should be rounded and not pinched in, and the fish's eyes should be clear.

>> Watch the behavior of the fish. Healthy fish swim horizontally in a lively manner and aren't shy. Jerky movements or scratching against tank fixtures could be early signs of disease.

>> Watch the fish feed before you buy it to make sure it has recovered from the stress of shipping and has acclimated to life in an aquarium.

REMEMBER

Furthermore, I recommend that you purchase captive-bred fish as your first option. Buying captive-bred fish definitely has some of the following distinct advantages:

>> Doing so is better for the environment because fewer wild fishes need to be harvested.

>> They've always been in captivity so they're already adapted to captivity, which makes them hardier than fish collected from the wild that are exposed to high levels of capture, storage, and transport stress.

>> They tend to be free of disease because they're exposed to fewer pathogens in captivity.

When at all possible, try to choose and buy captive-bred species.

Going Home with Your Fishy Friends

When you're satisfied with your choice, your dealer will net the fish or invertebrate and place it in a bag containing water from the aquarium. A properly bagged fish will have water in about two thirds of the bag and air in the remaining space.

The air space is very important. It provides a supply of oxygen for the water in the bag. Some aquarium dealers have newer aquarium bags that actually breathe. That is, air passes through the bag material and into the water. If your dealer uses one of these bags, it won't contain an air space.

TIP

If you have a particularly long trip home or you need to keep your new pet bagged longer than 2 hours, don't add more water and sacrifice air space. Instead, ask your dealer for a larger bag.

Some invertebrates, corals, live rock, and algae are bagged without water. Don't worry: This is how they're transported from distant seas, and they'll be fine.

At the checkout counter, your bagged fish should be placed in a paper bag for the trip home. After you're in the car, keep the bag in a stable place and, if possible, have somebody hold it — not you if you're driving! Don't put your new pets in the trunk because you can't control the temperature there. Basically, make every effort to keep the bag from jostling too much and don't expose it to radical changes in temperature. Keep the fish away from direct exposure to sunlight and the car heater or air conditioner.

REMEMBER

Water loses heat more slowly than you may think, so for a short trip home, you don't need to keep your car at 75° F to 79° F. On the other hand, a heavily air-conditioned car will slowly cool your fish if your trip home is long.

Taking the Plunge — Acclimating Your New Pets to Their New Surroundings

When you get home, take the time to acclimate your new pets to their new home. Don't unpack your groceries or take the dog for a walk; instead, tend to your fish immediately. This is a relatively simple process and one that I find to be pretty exciting.

REMEMBER

The water chemistry from your dealer isn't likely to be identical to that in your quarantine tank or main aquarium (this is particularly true for salinity), so take the time to properly acclimate your fish to the new conditions. If you don't, it can go into shock and die.

There are a several ways to acclimate the fish to its new home. The key is to minimize stress, and the best way to do that is to minimize handling and slowly transition the fish from the water in the bag to the water in the quarantine tank. The simplest and most common method is as follows:

1. **Float the unopened plastic bag (with your new fish inside) in your tank for at least 15 minutes (as in Figure 5-1).**

   Let it sit in the tank so that the temperature in the bag can acclimate to the temperature in the aquarium.

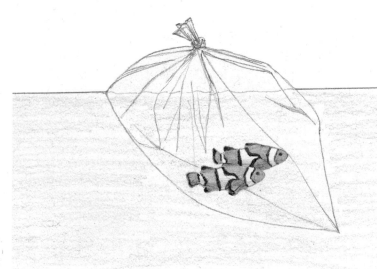

FIGURE 5-1:
Float the bag with the fish in the aquarium so it can acclimate.

2. **Open the bag and let air in.**

   To ensure that the fish won't be shocked by the aquarium water, make sure that both have a temperature within a degree of each other.

3. **Add a cupful of water from your aquarium to the bag and let it sit for another 15 minutes.**

4. **Repeat this process two more times, removing water from the bag as needed to prevent the bag from filling.**

5. **Add the fish to the tank by simply and gently inverting the bag and letting the fish out (refer to Figure 5-2).**

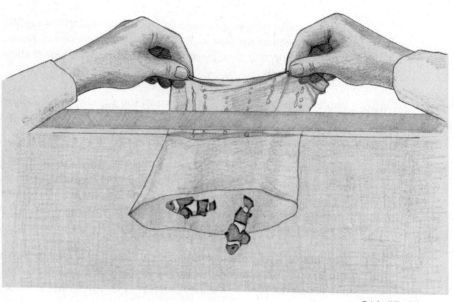

FIGURE 5-2:
Gently turn the
bag upside-down
and let the fish
swim out.

Some aquarists commonly follow these steps with a couple of modifications. For example, they prefer to acclimate their fish in a separate container, like a bucket, while slowly adding aquarium water with a cup or through air tubing (also known as the *drip method*).

WARNING

If the bag water is cloudy or you suspect there have been disease issues at the dealer, don't add the bag water to your aquarium. Instead, pour off as much water as possible into a sink or bucket and then add the fish to the quarantine tank. This method can be used to add invertebrates to your tank as well, but make sure the *salinity* (the amount of salt in your aquarium water) in the bag is extremely close to that in the quarantine tank for delicate species.

Keeping a Sharp Eye on Things

Quarantine your new fish for at least two weeks. Some aquarists actually prefer 30 days. During that time, closely inspect your fish for parasites or signs of disease (as I discuss in Chapter 17), monitor the fish's behavior, and feed the fish small meals a few times each day. If all goes well during this period, you can then transfer the fish to the main aquarium using the same method I describe in the previous section.

Although you may be tempted to stock your aquarium rapidly, introduce fish to the main aquarium one at a time every month or so. Doing so is particularly important for your newly established aquarium because it allows fish to acclimate to each other.

REMEMBER

Don't stock your saltwater aquarium too rapidly. Also, follow the tank capacity guidelines that I outline in Chapter 6.

Your new tank inhabitants are definitely worth watching. Their behavior probably won't be normal in the beginning as they acclimate to their new surroundings and new tank mates. You may see aggression between the new arrivals and the tank inhabitants, which have set up territories. Don't worry; some aggression is to be expected, so don't let a little nipping bother you. However, if it persists for several days, you may want to reconsider your choice of tank mates.

TIP

New arrivals typically require several hours to acclimate to their surroundings, and I don't recommend that you feed them during this period. They aren't likely to feed, so the food will only burden your filtration and pollute your aquarium.

2

Setting Up Your Aquarium

Plan the perfect location for your new aquarium, choose the best tank size and shape, top the tank with the right cover, and add the proper support with an aquarium stand.

Get to know why you need filtration to keep your aquarium water clean, take a serious look at all the filter systems available for your aquarium, and choose the optimal filters that will work for your saltwater aquarium.

Understand how to maintain the most comfortable temperature and light levels for your saltwater pets and how to choose the best water heater and optimal lighting.

Build an aquascape in your aquarium with the right decorations, suitable substrate, and well-balanced saltwater, and get the tools you need to test and maintain water quality.

Explore the option of setting up a brackish water aquarium and choose the unique fishes and plants that are optimal for this environment.

Follow all the right steps to get your new saltwater aquarium up and running, from the placement of the stand to turning it all on and adding the fish.

IN THIS CHAPTER

» Contemplating tank size

» Recognizing your different tank choices

» Covering your aquarium

» Supporting your aquarium

» Figuring out where to put your aquarium

Chapter 6

Selecting the Best Aquarium That Meets Your Needs

I n this chapter, I discuss one of the most important parts of the aquarium system: the aquarium itself, the stand, and the hood. You can probably get away with leaving one or two aquarium components out of the system and having your fish survive. They may live only one day, but they'll live nonetheless. However, without the aquarium tank itself, you and your marine friends don't have a chance. Fish and invertebrates simply don't deal well without water, in a box or permanently in a bag: They need a tank to live in. Not just any container sold at a pet store will do.

WARNING

For marine creatures, the old-fashioned goldfish bowl isn't a comfortable option. I liken it to forcing someone to live in a closet without ventilation. Keep away from goldfish bowls, Siamese fighting fish bowls, small rectangular plastic ornamental tanks, or homemade wooden contraptions. I can guess what you're thinking: Who would use such things? I'll keep the names to myself, but it has happened before. Simply put, the aquarium tank, the stand, and the hood, aren't pieces of equipment that you decide to save a few bucks on.

As you may expect, you have quite a few options. Aquariums come in many shapes, sizes, and styles. They can be glass or acrylic, tall or short, rectangular or multi-sided. What you choose depends on several factors, which include the amount of space you have available, the amount of money you want to spend, the number of fish you want to hold, and, last but not least, what tickles your fancy. This chapter helps you sort through those options.

Purchase your tank, stand, and hood as a package built by the same manufacturer. Doing so ensures that aquarium components won't be mismatched, and the package may be less expensive than buying separate components.

Considering Tank Size

The general rule is to buy the largest aquarium you can afford and accommodate in your home. The reason for this is straightforward: Would you rather live in a one-room apartment or a five-room suite? Fish and invertebrates require space to swim and sufficient oxygen to live, and both are limited by the size of the tank. Also, when choosing a tank, consider the kinds of fish and invertebrates you plan to keep in your aquarium. Small, coral-dwelling fishes, like clownfishes, will be fine in a smaller tank, whereas large, open ocean fishes, like tangs, require quite a bit more space.

If you plan to set up a reef tank with corals, they require intense lighting, so you should avoid deeper tanks. As a general rule, tanks deeper than 2 feet aren't ideal for corals.

The oxygen content of water is related to the surface area of the tank. *Surface area* is the amount of area on the surface of the tank that's exposed to air. The more surface area a tank has, the more room for gas exchange at the surface, and the more oxygen enters the water and toxic gases, such as carbon dioxide, leave the water. Oxygen content is also related to the temperature of the water. Warmer water has less oxygen than colder water. Because most marine tropical fishes prefer water in excess of 75 degrees F, the amount of oxygen may be limited in the tank, so you have to increase your surface area. How do you do that? By choosing a tank that has a large area on top that's exposed to air.

When choosing a tank, the shape and size make a real difference when it comes to calculating surface area and the number of fish you can keep. In the following sections, you find out about the dimensions of the tank and how to provide enough room for your fish and invertebrates.

The dimensions

Tanks come in all sizes and shapes. Although two tanks may have the same volume, their shapes dictate the amount of surface area, which may be different. Tall, slender tanks don't have a lot of surface area relative to the volume of water, so you don't get a high rate of gas exchange with one of these. On the other hand, a short, wide tank has more surface area and is better for gas exchange.

For example, consider two 55-gallon tanks: One measures 48 inches long x 12 inches wide x 21 inches high, and the other measures 36 inches long x 12 inches wide x 28 inches high. You can calculate the volume of these tanks by multiplying length by width by height; the surface area is equal to just length times width. Both tanks have a capacity of 12,096 cubic inches, but the first tank has a surface area of 576 square inches, and the second has a surface are of 432 square inches. Clearly, the first tank is preferred.

In general, short and wide is better than tall and narrow because not only will your tank have more surface area, but it also will have more horizontal swimming space for the fish, more efficient light penetration for your invertebrates, and easier maintenance (you won't need 4-foot arms!). If your heart is set on a tall and narrow tank, go for it, but just realize that you'll need to increase water circulation, use more lighting, and buy longer tools to clean it. So don't be afraid to go to your dealer with a measuring tape and a calculator to help you pick out your optimal aquarium. You should already have a general idea of the size you want, given the space available in the spot you chose for the tank.

Room to move

When choosing your tank, factor the number of aquarium inhabitants that your aquarium can accommodate into your decision. If you put too many fish into your tank, you'll overcrowd it, the filtration system will be overwhelmed, and you'll have serious water quality problems. In addition, fish become stressed when they're crowded, and stress leads to disease and death. (Have you ever been in an overcrowded elevator?)

A few general rules for determining fish capacity are as follows: Most aquarium enthusiasts use maximum fish length and tank volume to estimate the number of fish that a marine aquarium can hold. Larger fish consume more oxygen and, therefore, require more aquarium space.

REMEMBER

You can probably accommodate 1 inch of fish per 4 gallons of water for the first six months. Gradually increase fish density to 1 inch per 2 gallons after this initial period.

For example, a 40-gallon aquarium should contain no more than 10 inches of fish for the first six months. These may be comprised of one 3-inch dwarf angel, two 1-inch clownfish, one 2-inch wrasse, one 1-inch bicolor blenny, and two 1-inch Beau Gregory's. After six months, additional fish may be added gradually to increase the total number of inches to 20. Keep in mind, however, that fish grow, so your 2-inch wrasse may grow to 3 inches in those six months. Also, realize that this general rule doesn't compensate for the shape of the fish. The width of a fish is called its *girth*. For example, the girth of an eel is much smaller than that of a grouper. The 6-inch eel is likely to require less space than the 6-inch grouper, so the general capacity rule doesn't apply. If you plan to keep heavier fish, be more conservative in your tank capacity calculations.

It's better to err on the side of too few fish than too many.

Bottom line

You may be saying to yourself, "If you leave it up to me, I'll buy the smallest and least expensive tank because I want to minimize my investment." This is indeed possible, but not the best approach.

A saltwater aquarium is a big investment in money and time, so don't go halfway. All the time in the world won't keep a very small tank from becoming a problem. The bigger the tank, the more water to dilute any minor water quality problems associated with overfeeding, contaminants, or dead fish. Buying the wrong tank will lead you to either buy the right one down the road anyway or will discourage you from becoming a long-term aquarium enthusiast, resulting in a waste of money either way. The bottom line is this: If you can't afford or accommodate an aquarium that's at least 30 gallons, don't make the investment.

Identifying the Different Types of Tanks

After you've decided on the appropriate size and shape of your aquarium, choosing the tank itself is largely a matter of personal taste. In my early years of aquarium-keeping several decades ago, plate glass tanks and goldfish bowls were the standard. In those days, many of these tanks were framed in metal and came in standard 10-, 20-, and 55-gallon rectangular sizes. Wow, how times have changed with the development of plastics! Modern aquariums now not only come in a variety of sizes, but also in a number of interesting shapes. Have you ever seen an aquarium table? It's out there. Both glass and acrylic tanks are available to you, and each has its distinct advantages and disadvantages. Both styles can be purchased *reef-ready,* as well. That means that the tanks have predrilled holes for equipment and plumbing, but this feature can be a bit more expensive. The following sections examine your two main options: glass or acrylic.

TIP

When choosing your tank, either glass or acrylic, be sure you select one with no scratches. Also check that no areas are devoid of silicone by closely inspecting the aquarium seams.

I don't recommend this if you're a beginner, but some enthusiasts build their own tanks. If you have some technical expertise in handling glass or plastics, go for it, but be sure to use nontoxic silicone cement to seal the seams.

Old school glass

Glass tanks, like the one shown in Figure 6-1, are sealed with a silicone rubber cement. Although the most common design is rectangular, glass tanks are also available in a variety of multisided shapes such as octagon and hexagon. The bow front aquarium has a really neat curvature to the front panel that I find particularly attractive.

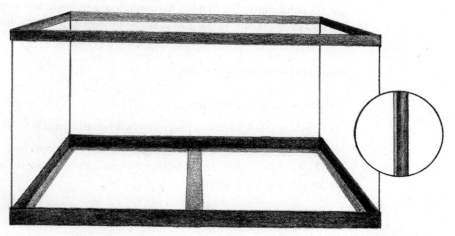

FIGURE 6-1:
A typical glass
aquarium.

© John Wiley & Sons, Inc.

Here are a few advantages to using a glass aquarium:

>> Glass is nontoxic. Glass aquariums are built for the sole purpose of housing living animals.

>> Glass also doesn't scratch as easily as acrylic does.

On the other hand, glass does have one main disadvantage: It's heavy, and the larger the tank, the thicker the glass. Keep this in mind when you're finding a good location for the aquarium. Most glass aquariums are equipped with plastic frames or rims that provide some stability as well as attractiveness. The frames come in a variety of colors and styles, so you can pick one that matches the drapes, if you so choose. If you don't like rims, rimless tanks are becoming more popular as glass and silicone strength has improved in recent years.

In today's aquarium market, the glass used in these tanks may be either *plated* or *tempered*. This book doesn't cover the specifics of how each glass type is made, but suffice it to say that plate glass won't shatter like tempered glass, and plate glass is more common than tempered, but not as strong. If you plan to drill holes in your glass aquarium for filter plumbing, make sure it's plate glass.

In general, glass aquariums are still preferred by many aquarists, but with each passing year I see more and more turn to acrylic.

Molded acrylic

Acrylic aquariums are molded as a single piece with few seams, which makes them more transparent, but you'll get some viewing distortion of the tank inhabitants at the corners.

Here are the advantages of acrylic:

>> Acrylic is lighter than glass.

>> Acrylic is offered in more shapes and sizes than standard glass aquariums.

>> Acrylic tends to be stronger than glass, so it doesn't break or shatter as easily. Some of the largest custom aquariums are built out of acrylic, and they're beautiful but expensive.

However, acrylic does have a couple of disadvantages:

>> Acrylic is more expensive than glass.

>> Acrylic scratches easily. Algae scrapers and tank decorations can also cause damage to the tank when not properly handled. You must use plastic scraping tools to clean the pesky coralline algae off the inner walls of an acrylic tank. Although not easy to repair, you can buff out scratches in the acrylic with special scratch-remover kits.

Putting a Cap on It

An essential item for any aquarium is a *hood* (also called a *canopy* or cover). This important piece of equipment performs many of these functions that will make your life and those of your friends in the tank easier.

>> **Protection from above:** It prevents unwanted items from entering the tank and injuring the fish. If your daughter Evie decides to throw the sand-covered Nerf ball in the house, it's nice to know that the ball, the sand, and little Evie won't end up in the tank.

>> **Protection from below:** It prevents overzealous fish from jumping out of the tank. No doubt about it: Fish *will* jump. Sometimes they're motivated by another member of the aquarium community; sometimes they're spooked by sudden vibrations or movement in the room. Other times, they simply run out of water while swimming toward the surface. When your buddy Rick comes over and knocks or raps on the aquarium, this can also cause skittish fish to jump. Remember, fish can't breathe air, and nothing is worse than finding your pet on the floor next to the aquarium in the morning.

>> **Protection of surroundings:** The cover prevents water from splashing to the walls and floor, causing damage to the aquarium surroundings and *salt creep*, which is caused by the bubbling of saltwater. You don't want to ruin your upholstery.

>> **Protection from evaporation:** The hood slows the rate of water evaporation from the tank. A properly working aquarium has a lot of water movement and bubbling from aeration and filtration. In most aquariums, the water temperature is over 75 degrees F. Water evaporates when it bubbles and when it's kept at a high temperature. Now when water evaporates from a seawater aquarium, the salts don't leave the tank but become more concentrated, thereby increasing the salinity. (I discuss salinity in Chapters 9 and 13.) This disturbs the fish and water quality if not carefully monitored. No matter what you do, you need to routinely add water to the tank. To reduce the amount of water required, you use an aquarium hood. Water condenses on the cover and reenters the tank instead of evaporating to the room.

>> **Protection from cooling:** The hood helps the aquarium to retain heat, thereby reducing the use of the heating unit.

>> **Protection from electrocution:** The hood keeps water from damaging the aquarium light and prevents a potentially dangerous electrical problem. Remember, water and electricity are both important for the aquarium, but you still want to keep them apart.

The hood is generally fitted to the dimensions of the tank and can be adjusted to allow for aquarium accessories. Make sure that it's composed of thick (⅛-inch) glass or plastic so that it can support the weight of other aquarium components if needed. In addition, it should be segmented or hinged so that the entire assembly need not be removed to feed the fish or work in the tank.

REMEMBER

In some units, the hood also houses the aquarium lights. These units are self contained and properly designed to keep water away from the lighting unit, to minimize danger, and to cover the entire tank thoroughly.

Offering More than a Little Support — Your Aquarium Stand

The best support for the heavy weight of the aquarium and all its components is a commercially manufactured *aquarium stand.* This type of support is built to hold a full aquarium (hundreds of pounds). Homemade stands and common household furniture may look sturdy, but they can fail under such a heavy load. The weight of the tank, all its components, and water (8.4 pounds per gallon) could reach 500 to more than 1,000 pounds, depending on its size. Stand failure can be costly to both the aquarist and the homeowner, not to mention the fish. Gallons of water can wreak havoc on a room, so don't try to save money on your aquarium stand — unless you're thinking you might also like an indoor pool.

Of course, if your aquarium is very large, you can place it directly on the floor. But even with a tall tank, you'll still have to look down to enjoy the action, and that can be a pain in the neck, literally.

The most common commercially built aquarium stands are made out of iron or wood. Which one you buy depends on your personal preference.

Iron

Wrought-iron and angle-iron stands are the simplest and least expensive to buy. The design of these stands is open, which doesn't provide much room to hide aquarium components, but they're extremely sturdy.

Wood

If you're willing to spend more for something more decorative, buy a wooden cabinet stand. The aquarium sits on a cabinet that can house aquarium supplies and equipment behind doors on the front. These cabinets come in a variety of styles and finishes that will likely match your room decor, if that's important to you.

The most expensive aquarium stand is the aquarium *enclosure*. This is really a cabinet stand that includes a canopy that covers the top of the tank. The canopy may or may not be attached to the cabinet as one piece. These stands can be quite elegant, making the aquarium a handsome addition to your room.

WARNING

Be careful to stay away from cabinet stands made of particleboard because they'll come apart after long-term exposure to water.

TIP

If you decide to use a piece of furniture for an aquarium stand, place under the tank a 5/8-inch sheet of plywood and a half-inch sheet of polystyrene cut to the dimensions of the tank. These layers will even out any imperfections in the supporting surface and distribute the load of the tank. Homemade stands aren't uncommon, but if you go this route, make sure that you use materials that can hold hundreds of pounds level.

Selecting the Perfect Location for Your New Aquarium

After you set up your aquarium system, you're not going to move it unless you take it completely apart. So choosing a permanent site for the aquarium is something you don't want to take lightly. (In fact, you want to decide this during your planning process.) This section shares a few tips and reminders.

Fish watching

I think I can assume that you're not setting up an aquarium for exercise. Instead, you, like me, find marine critters fun, beautiful, peaceful, and exciting. So, you need to place your aquarium in an area of the house where you can enjoy it most and where you're likely to spend a lot of time. (That doesn't mean the garage if your other hobby is working on cars.) Generally, the living room or den is a great place to put it. Well-used living areas provide an excellent setting for your aquarium because the fish acclimate to people entering and leaving the room. Poorly used areas will render fish skittish and timid when people enter or approach the tank.

Don't, however, choose the busiest room in the house. Too much activity can spook your tank inhabitants or cause damage to your tank. For example, the kids' playroom may be a fun place for the aquarium, but jumping children and flying objects don't blend with a peaceful aquarium.

Aquariums can be fun, but they also require some attention. Routine system checks are easy if the aquarium is in a place where you can spend a lot of time watching fish. You don't want to be forced to make a special trip out to the aquarium room in the very back of your house, past the dog that really doesn't like you.

Windows and doors and floors

You may have the perfect room for your aquarium picked out because you spend a lot of time there. But a few other factors may change your mind. Suppose the spot you chose is right next to a huge picture window, behind a swinging door, on the third floor of a house built in 1850. Good location? Not! Here's why:

>> **Windows:** Although windows illuminate the room and the aquarium, they cause problems for your little ecosystem. Light and temperature are two very important parameters that you need to keep an eye on in your aquarium (see Chapter 8). You don't want either of these to change greatly from day to day. An aquarium too close to windows will be illuminated by direct sunlight, causing changes in water temperature and promoting extensive growth of algae. Algae can be good, but too much is not.

>> **Doors:** Similarly, doors let in drafts and sunlight, causing light levels and temperature to fluctuate. In addition, a swinging door may hit your aquarium, and a cracked aquarium is a disaster.

>> **Floors:** The strength of your floor is also important. Make sure the part of the house you have chosen can hold your aquarium when it's chock-full of water, gravel, rocks, coral, and equipment. Keep in mind that saltwater weighs 8.4 pounds per gallon, so a 50-gallon tank weighs at least 420 pounds and that's without the other system components. The floors in older homes may not be able to support this kind of weight.

Hot and cold

Bearing in mind that you have to maintain a relatively constant aquarium temperature, you can see why room heaters and air conditioners can cause problems. If you live in an area with hot and cold seasons, all your rooms have some kind of heat source. I don't expect you to remove it for the aquarium, and you shouldn't. The room heater actually helps the aquarium heater to keep the water in your tank at the right temperature. (If you didn't have a heat source in the room, the aquarium heater would be running almost constantly.) On the other hand, if the room's heat source is too close to the aquarium, it may overheat the tank, causing water-temperature problems.

Much of this information is also true for room air conditioners, which can cool aquarium water.

Water and power

Now, when I think about water and electricity, I see a dangerous mix. But the fact of the matter is that when you set up an aquarium, you positively need both to make it work. Normally, placing electric motors and gadgets in and around a tank full of water is a no-no. (So parents, don't let your children set up the aquarium alone!) More than once, I've felt the odd sensation of 110 volts being conducted through my body because I wasn't paying attention. This wasn't pleasant and was potentially lethal. Keep in mind (and teach your children) the dangers of electricity. I can't overemphasize the importance of following the proper steps when setting up an aquarium.

REMEMBER

All electrical equipment for your aquarium should be plugged into connectors with *ground fault interruption* capability. These types of outlets are inexpensive, easy to install, and go a long way in preventing electrocution. Also, if you plan to have a very large aquarium, consider the potential power draw and make sure you don't have a lot of other devices on that circuit.

When you choose the final place for your aquarium, you must have access to water and power. Moving buckets of water through a living room loaded with antique furniture may not be the greatest idea. Running extension cords across the room to power as many as ten electrical components doesn't sound good, either. Instead, find a spot with easy access to a water source and a power source.

TIP

Keep in mind that all the planning in the world won't keep an area from getting wet from the aquarium and its maintenance. You may not want to set the tank above your favorite Oriental rug. Choose an area that can tolerate a little moisture from time to time. I find that tile or concrete are the best surfaces. Set your tank so that you have easy access on all sides for cleaning and maintenance.

TECHNICAL STUFF

Marine tanks suffer from *salt creep*, which is caused by the bubbling of saltwater. When water is bubbled or splashed, the water evaporates, leaving the salt deposit on the tank glass, filter unit, and just about everything the water contacts. You can reduce salt creep with an aquarium hood (and I talk about that in the "Putting a Cap on It" section of this chapter), but you must have access to all sides of your tank so you can clean it.

Chapter **7**

Figuring Out Filters

The most important requirement for healthy fish is clean water. Just as air is to humans, water is to fish and marine invertebrates. Imagine how you would feel if you were literally forced to inhale bad air, like car exhaust, all the time. Fish in the natural marine environment live in an open system where products of respiration (breathing) and digestion are readily swept away and naturally filtered. The sheer volume of water keeps problem substances at low levels unless environmental pollution impacts the area.

On the other hand, fish housed in the aquarium live in a closed system where products of respiration and digestion remain until they're removed. The primary piece of equipment that removes toxic substances from the aquarium is the filter. An aquarium without a filter is like living in a house without plumbing. Ugh!

In Chapters 12 and 13, I discuss the chemistry of water and how it affects your fish. You don't need to read those chapters before reading this one and making some important decisions on filtration, however. Basically, all you need to know is that fish and invertebrates are living creatures that, like all living things, take substances from the environment and give substances back to the environment.

Breathing and Eating

Like most living creatures, fish and invertebrates need to breathe oxygen to produce energy and stay alive. When they remove oxygen from the water using gills, they put back carbon dioxide, which is called *respiration*. Humans respire as well, only not underwater. So, not only do fish need oxygen in the water, but they also change the chemistry of the water by releasing carbon dioxide.

Fish and invertebrates in your aquarium also need energy to live and to grow, and this comes from the food you feed them. Just like other living creatures that eat food, these animals process it internally, taking away important nutrients and disposing of wastes. These wastes, which break down into ammonia, need to be removed from the water, as well.

The inhabitants of your aquarium aren't the only ones that put substances into your aquarium water. So do you. Not all the food that you feed your pets is consumed, and those morsels that aren't consumed become aquarium waste that breaks down into its chemical components like carbon, nitrogen, and hydrogen.

As you can read more about in Chapter 12, ammonia and other compounds with nitrogen are harmful to fish and invertebrates, so they need to be removed from the aquarium. This is the job of the filter.

Cleaning Your Water — The Different Types of Filtration

Just as the name implies, the filter is a piece of equipment that filters the water in your aquarium. When the aquarium water is filtered, certain substances are either removed from the water and retained in the filter or converted to less harmful compounds and returned to the aquarium. This process is called *filtration*. Substances that are retained in the filter need to be disposed of when the filter is cleaned.

Not all filters are the same, and no filter removes all the harmful substances from the water. So, although filters help you clean the water, they don't do all the work for you. You still need to make partial water changes to remove some substances, and you also need to clean your filter (see Chapter 15).

Not all filters perform the same kind of filtration. The part of the filter that actually does all the work is the *filter medium* (more than one medium is *media,* and some filters have several kinds of filter media). For example, the typical power filter has synthetic floss in it, which filters the water by removing debris but also provides a lot of surface area for bacteria to grow. These bacteria act to filter the water as well. Therefore, some mechanical filters really provide two kinds of filtration.

There are three different kinds of filters: mechanical, biological, and chemical. Some filters provide only one kind, whereas others provide all three. It's like having ice cream that's just vanilla or ice cream that's vanilla, chocolate, and strawberry. For your saltwater aquarium, you want all three flavors (of filtration that is, not ice cream).

Mechanical filtration

Filters that provide mechanical filtration physically remove suspended materials, like uneaten food and waste, from the water by passing it through a fine filter medium, which sifts out these particles. Typical filter media include floss, fiber pads, sand, gravel, and screens. Most of the filters that you find at the dealer provide at least some degree of mechanical filtration. You can think of mechanical filtration as being very similar to skimming debris from the surface of a pool, only the debris isn't only from the surface of the water but from the entire aquarium.

If not removed, the particles that are suspended in your aquarium eventually break down into smaller molecules that mess up your water chemistry. Getting them out when they're larger saves your aquarium a lot of potential trouble. However, you need to remove this waste from the mechanical filter before it breaks down into dissolved nutrients that can go back into your aquarium. So, these types of filters need to be cleaned frequently.

Obviously, smaller molecules aren't removed by mechanical filtration, so they need to be removed by other means. External power filters and canister filters provide rapid mechanical filtration and work well with smaller aquariums. Larger systems, and particularly reef tanks, need more sophisticated filtration systems, like a sump, which has some mechanical filtration incorporated.

Biological filtration

Biological filtration uses the most abundant form of life in the world — bacteria — to break down and remove harmful molecules, such as ammonia, from the water in your aquarium. Although when you think of bacteria, you probably think of nasty little buggers that cause problems, in all honesty, humanity would be in serious trouble if we didn't have bacteria in our lives. In an aquarium, bacteria drive the *nitrogen cycle*, which is the conversion of a harmful nitrogenous substance, like ammonia, into a less harmful substance, like nitrate. In Chapter 12, I discuss the nitrogen cycle in detail because it's critical to the successful maintenance of your aquarium. For this chapter, suffice it say that the bacteria that live in a filter or filter media provide biological filtration of your aquarium water, thereby removing molecules that mechanical filtration can't. Without biological filtration, your aquarium will fail!

In the 1970s, the most common example of a biological filter was the undergravel filter, which draws water through the aquarium substrate. The *substrate* is the stuff that you put on the bottom of the aquarium — the gravel or sand, which actually acts as your filter media because it contains the necessary bacteria to convert nitrogenous wastes to nitrate. Over the last few decades, the old under-gravel filter has been replaced by more organic filtration methods, namely live rock, live sand, and a protein skimmer.

Chemical filtration

The removal of dissolved organic compounds from the water is referred to a chemical filtration. In the marine aquarium hobby, a number of chemical filtra-tion methods are now available, but the most common involves the addition of activated carbon (or activated charcoal) to your filter. In doing so, the filter is using a chemical treatment to remove toxic substances from the aquarium. Some aquarists consider chemical filtration to be another form of mechanical filtration, but at the molecular level. If you think of mechanical filtration as the removal of debris that's suspended in the water, think of chemical filtration as the removal of substances that are dissolved in the water.

For example, activated carbon in your power filter absorbs dissolved molecules from the water by trapping them. Other filter media, like *zeolite* and *ion-exchange resins,* similarly remove toxins from the water by taking advantage of their molec-ular shape. You can turn a filter that provides mechanical filtration, biological filtration, or both into one that also provides chemical filtration by adding one of these media to the filter. Many of the commercially available filters on today's market allow you to do this, primarily with activated carbon.

REMEMBER
Chemical filters get used up over time and need to be replaced. Whereas some mechanical and biological filter media can be rinsed, chemical filter media like activated carbon should be thrown out every month or so (see Chapter 15).

Adding a Sump

Imagine what your aquarium would look like if it weren't cluttered with equipment and simply showcased your beautiful marine critters. Also imagine that all your equipment was in a separate tank that was easily accessible without disturbing the peace and tranquility of your pets. If your imagination is running wild, then you're thinking about an aquarium sump. Although some experts feel that the sump is an essential part of the saltwater aquarium setup, in my opinion it's well-suited for larger, more complex aquarium systems.

The sump is a small tank (10 to 20 gallons) that sits below your main aquarium and houses everything from your heater, to your protein skimmer, and even your biological filter in a section called the *refugium* (see the "Refugia" section in this chapter). The sump is compartmentalized for each function, typically with baffles. Water flows from the main aquarium into the sump, then progressively into each chamber where it's heated and filtered before being pumped back up into the display tank.

A sump is an all-in-one system and includes all three types of filtration:

>> **Mechanical filtration:** Filter rollers, filter cups, or filter socks provide mechanical filtration as it enters the sump.

>> **Chemical filtration:** Chemical filtrations comes from the protein skimmer.

>> **Biological filtration:** In the refugium, a deep sand bed containing bacteria or a bare-bottom with macroalgae provides biological filtration.

Sumps not only loosen up space in your aquarium, they also actually expand the capacity of your aquarium so you can add more critters. Commercial sumps are available online and at your local dealer, and many experienced aquarists like to build their own. If you're considering the addition of a sump to your aquarium setup, speak to your dealer about the best options available to you.

Considering Your Filter Choices

Most commercially manufactured aquarium filters provide all three kinds of filtration (mechanical, biological, and chemical), but they do so to different degrees of effectiveness. For example, an external power filter mechanically removes particles, chemically removes toxins (if it contains activated carbon), and biologically converts nitrogenous wastes via the nitrogen cycle in its filter media.

However, you must match the filter with the aquarium. For example, imagine that you're shopping for a vacuum cleaner. A lot depends on what kind of floor you're cleaning and on how big the room is. You're not going to need a really powerful vacuum for wood floors, but a mini-vac may be too small for a living room. The same is true for aquarium filters. The extent to which you need to clean your water is dependent on the type of aquarium you're planning. Size your filtration system to your aquarium — a good dealer can assist you in doing so.

Invertebrate and reef aquariums need to have the highest possible water quality for their inhabitants. Invertebrates like corals, sponges, and anemones are sensitive to even the smallest amounts of harmful substances such as ammonia. On the other hand, if you're the owner of a fish-only aquarium (no invertebrates), you don't need to keep sensitive invertebrates alive, so the filtration system can be less efficient and perhaps a little less expensive.

Some of the filters available to the aquarist include internal box filters, external power filters, canister filters, undergravel filters, trickle filters, live rock, fluidized bed filters, protein skimmers, and complete external water management systems. In addition, water-sterilization techniques are also available in the form of ultra-violet (UV) sterilizers and ozonizers. Choosing the right system for your new aquarium can be a bit confusing given all the different kinds and manufacturers. For the marine aquarium, I thoroughly recommend multiple filter systems, which include all three types of filtration discussed in the preceding section. The simplest filtration system depends heavily on biological filtration using live rock, chemical filtration with a protein skimmer, and some mechanical filtration with an external power filter.

In the following sections, I describe each filter type, give you an idea of what kind of filtration it provides and for what kind of saltwater aquarium it applies, and offer some specific recommendations so that you don't leave this chapter overwhelmed by the options. I include some older style filters, which are still on the market, but not necessarily optimal for the saltwater hobbyist. By doing so, I don't want to confuse you, I only want you to be familiar with all types of filters so that you're ready when an aquarium dealer tells you that you "must" buy a particular system.

Inside box filter

Also known as a *corner filter*, an *internal box filter* is one of the most basic forms of aquarium filters. Usually relegated to the corner of the aquarium, this small, clear plastic box is filled with filter floss and activated carbon, working its little heart out to keep the aquarium clean. Air is driven from an external air source down into the center of the box, creating a vacuum as it exits and drawing water into the filter. The water pulled in is filtered through the floss mechanically and through the carbon chemically (see Figure 7-1). If the filter is allowed to mature over time, the floss provides a substrate or medium for bacterial colonies to establish, providing biological filtration. Sounds great, right?

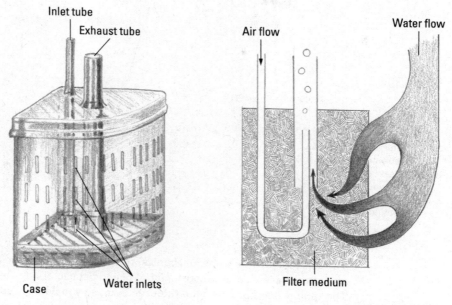

FIGURE 7-1: The internal box filter, also known as a corner filter, is an old-school type of filter.

Wrong! Although very inexpensive (less than $10), the box filter is by far the most primitive filter — I haven't had one since my famous freshwater guppy tank of 1971. It's simply too small and inefficient to handle the wastes and debris that accumulate in the saltwater aquarium. That doesn't mean that there's no place for the box filter in certain saltwater aquarium systems. Some aquarists use the simple box filter to keep their smaller quarantine tanks clean (see Chapter 5). Box filters are maintained by replacing the activated carbon and the filter floss, although some of the latter should be retained for the bacteria that they harbor.

Sponge filter

Sponge filters, like the one shown in Figure 7-2, have rapidly replaced box filters in most small saltwater aquarium tanks, such as a quarantine aquarium (see Chapter 5). As the name implies, the filter is composed of a sponge material that's highly porous. Like the box filter, the sponge filter sits in the aquarium and sticks out like a sore thumb. Air is driven into the sponge from an external air pump, and water is pulled into the filter as the air escapes.

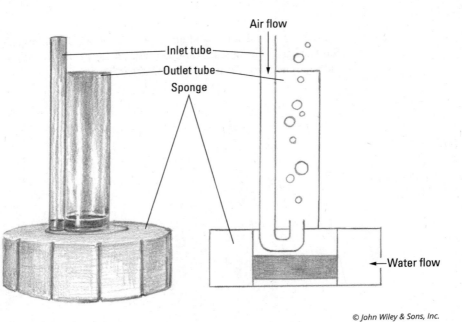

Air flow

Inlet tube

Outlet tube

Sponge

Water flow

FIGURE 7-2:
The sponge filter is an update to the box filter, but it's probably not up to the task of filtering your saltwater aquarium.

© John Wiley & Sons, Inc.

These filters provide some mechanical filtration, but more importantly, they have enough surface area to support a lot of beneficial bacteria for biological filtration. The sponge itself provides the filter medium, so you don't need additional media. These filters provide no chemical filtration. Sponge filters are easy to maintain (simply rinse), are inexpensive (less than $10), and come in sizes that can filter tanks up to 125 gallons. Although they're simply too inefficient to be the primary filter for a typical saltwater aquarium, adding one or two to your aquarium or sump will increase biological filtration, and they're ideal for smaller quarantine tanks.

Undergravel filter

Undergravel filters are the old workhorses of the saltwater aquarium hobby. For many years, they were considered the most efficient filters for saltwater aquaria, and no successful tank was found without one. Although times have changed, and more advanced filtration systems are now available, the undergravel filter is still considered by some to be an effective filtration choice. Although this filter has evolved, and improvements have increased its filtration efficiency, fewer and fewer aquarists use the undergravel filter as newer technology becomes more readily available. Nowadays, undergravel filters have been relegated to smaller tank setups and the occasional quarantine tank.

A basic undergravel filter consists of a perforated plastic plate that rests on the bottom of your aquarium tank under your gravel. At each rear corner of the plate is a lift tube that extends up into the aquarium. Air is pumped to the bottom of each lift tube, and bubbles that come right back up the tube create a water vacuum. More recent models pump water with powerheads through the tubes to increase efficiency. In both cases, aquarium water is pulled down through the substrate and the filter plate and out the lift tube. Therefore, you get water circulating from the aquarium down through the gravel.

In an undergravel filter, your gravel acts as the filter media. Particles and debris get trapped in the gravel providing mechanical filtration. More importantly, excellent biological filtration is provided when the gravel becomes the home of millions of bacteria that break down harmful ammonia. For this reason, certain kinds of gravel are required for this filter, and a longer setup time is necessary to establish bacterial colonies. Most undergravel filters are covered by two grades of gravel: fine gravel on top of coarser gravel, separated by what is known as a *gravel tidy*. After a healthy filtration system is established, this filter can be used for months without intense maintenance and cleaning.

A basic undergravel filter, however, has its share of these problems:

>> Debris accumulates in the gravel and needs to be routinely vacuumed so that the filter doesn't get clogged. Cleaning can be difficult if too many corals and rocks are sitting in the tank, and that's why they aren't well suited for the reef aquarium.

>> Most undergravel filters don't provide chemical filtration, but carbon cartridges that fit on the lift tubes are available.

>> Although air-driven undergravel filters provide aeration, they tend to be noisy and may not be strong enough to provide for adequate water circulation, particularly as the gravel clogs.

TIP

How do you avoid clogging the gravel in an undergravel filter? Reverse the flow of water through it and instead of pulling water through, push it. This way, the filter media doesn't get as heavily clogged, and the efficiency of the filter is maintained. There are a couple of ways to reverse the flow of water through the filter:

>> The most common way involves adding another filter to the process. By pumping water from the output of a canister filter down the lift tube of the undergravel filter, you can easily reverse the flow of the entire system. You won't have the mechanical filtration of the gravel, but the canister filter does that for you. (I discuss canister filters in more detail in the "Canister filters" section, later in this chapter.)

>> You can also use powerheads to move water more efficiently through the system. The reverse flow gravel filter provides excellent *biofiltration* (biological filtration) without some of the problems associated with the basic system.

As a major improvement to the undergravel filter, *powerheads* can replace the less efficient air-driven system. The powerhead sits on top of the lift tube and literally pulls water through the gravel from the aquarium (see Figure 7-3), which improves filter efficiency and also increases water circulation.

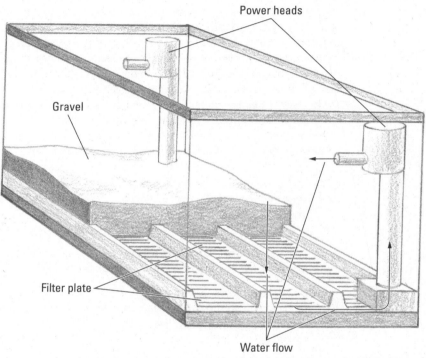

Power heads

Gravel

Filter plate

Water flow

© *John Wiley & Sons, Inc.*

FIGURE 7-3:
The undergravel filter with powerheads replaces the less-efficient air-driven system.

REMEMBER

Undergravel filters are relatively inexpensive filters that provide good biological filtration for a fish-only aquarium. If you're going to use an undergravel system, reverse flow is the most efficient, either with powerheads or, preferably, with a canister filter for added filtration.

Power filters

A power filter is the one of the easiest and least complicated filter systems for you to employ as a beginner aquarist. The design is simple: Water is pulled into the filter media and pumped back to the tank. But, as is the case with most filter systems nowadays, power filters have improved over the years, and now a few kinds are available.

External power filter

An *external power filter* looks like a big square cup that hangs on the outside of the tank and is powered by its own motor. The filter generally contains filter floss or filter sponges and activated carbon as filter media. Water is drawn into the filter by a U-shaped intake tube, flows through the filter media, and is pumped back to the tank either through a tube or a spillway. The filter media provide mechanical and chemical filtration; biological filtration is established as the filter matures and bacteria colonize it. Therefore, these filters provide all three kinds of filtration and are specifically designed to turn over large amounts of water. The power filter also circulates the water, providing valuable aeration.

These filters are easy to maintain — most have simple cartridges that can be routinely replaced. However, retain some of the used filter floss or use a sponge-type media so that you can hang onto helpful bacteria.

REMEMBER

External power filters are ideal for tanks that also have an undergravel filter system or live rock.

Biowheels

Some external power filters come with a nifty option called a *biowheel* (see Figure 7-4). The biowheel comes into contact with both the air and water in the filter. As water moves through the filter, the wheel spins, exposing millions of bacteria that live on the wheel to the air and the water. Because these bacteria need air to efficiently convert ammonia, this system provides enhanced biological filtration in your power filter. Also, the biowheel allows you to retain these bacteria even though you have to replace the internal filter media. Biowheels aren't available only on external power filters but are also offered as separate units that hang on the back of your aquarium and are powered by a powerhead or canister filter.

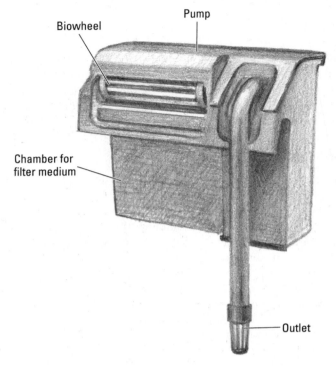

Biowheel

Pump

Chamber for
filter medium

Outlet

FIGURE 7-4:
An external
power filter with
a biowheel is a
nifty option.

Internal power filters

I mention *internal power filters* not because they're an improvement to the external
power filter but because they're currently available on the market. These filters
are similar to the external power filter, but sit inside the tank, taking up valuable
space and obstructing the view. However, some newer models are neatly disguised
as aquarium decorations. Although most models provide mechanical, chemical,
and biological filtration, I don't recommend them as a permanent filter system.

Canister filters

A canister filter (see Figure 7-5) is really just an external power filter that doesn't
hang on the tank but sits on the floor or under the aquarium. I'm treating it separately because the canister filter is a different category of power filter that's much
more efficient. The canister filter is a self-contained, high-pressure pump that
draws water from the aquarium with an intake tube and returns it with an output
tube that can be directed anywhere the aquarist desires (preferably back to the
tank). As I discuss in the earlier "Undergravel filter" section, output from a canister filter can be directed to increase circulation in the aquarium or at another
filtration system, such as a reverse flow undergravel filter or a biowheel.

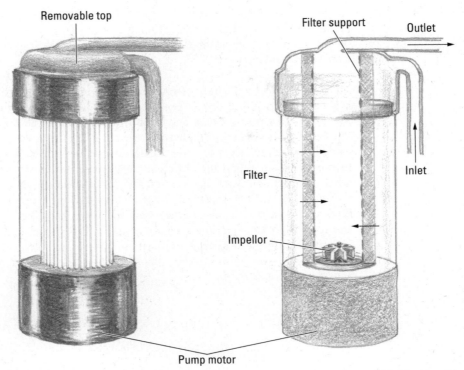

Removable top

Filter support

Outlet

Filter

Inlet

Impellor

Pump motor

© John Wiley & Sons, Inc.

FIGURE 7-5:
The canister filter doesn't take up space inside the aquarium.

The filter itself contains compartments with various kinds of filter media, such as activated carbon, filter sponges, filter floss, and ceramic bodies. Water is pumped over all the media layers, providing mechanical, chemical, and biological filtration. These filters are more expensive, yet provide excellent efficient filtration at a high rate. They don't need to be cleaned frequently, and the use of multiple filter media allows valuable bacteria to be retained when the filter is cleaned every three or four months.

REMEMBER

If you intend to have more than a fish-only saltwater aquarium, the high efficiency of a canister filter makes it one of my recommended filter options.

Trickle filters

Trickle filters, also known as *wet-dry filters,* have become a popular choice for saltwater aquarists over the last decade, although they were once reserved for those who built their own filter systems. Now, many companies commercially manufacture a number of styles and sizes for home aquariums. In essence, the theory behind the trickle filter is to maximize the exposure of the aquarium water to bacteria and air at the same time (like a biowheel does) so that bacterial conversion of ammonia is most efficient.

An overflow box on the back of your tank delivers water from the aquarium to the large acrylic trickle filter box. Some tanks are predrilled with overflow boxes in the tank, and water exits the aquarium through a bulkhead into the trickle filter. The filter box is generally divided into two compartments. The main compartment contains multiple layers of filter media for mechanical, biological, and chemical filtration. This compartment is mostly dry except for the lower few inches. The other compartment contains a pump and other optional equipment. Water from the aquarium is sprayed or trickles evenly over the first compartment through the filter media where it collects at the bottom, moves into the other compartment, and returns to the aquarium (see Figure 7-6). This filtration and the sump that I discuss earlier have several similarities. Indeed the wet portion of the trickle filter is often referred to as the sump. However, the modern day sump doesn't have a dry compartment.

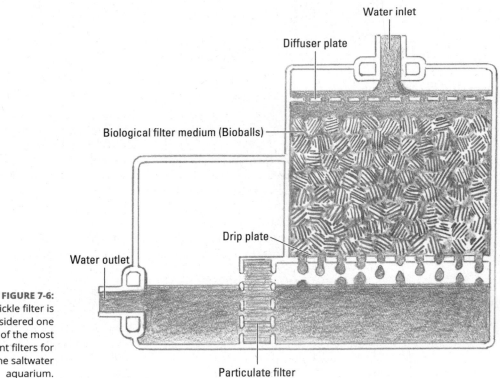

FIGURE 7-6: The trickle filter is considered one of the most efficient filters for the saltwater aquarium.

© John Wiley & Sons, Inc.

This flame angelfish, like most dwarf angelfishes, is a stunning addition to almost any marine aquarium.

The bicolor blenny, like most blennies, is an ideal fish for the peaceful community aquarium.

These featherduster worms have extended their tentacles to feed on plankton.

With its unique paint job, the Picasso triggerfish is popular, but like most triggers, it eats invertebrates.

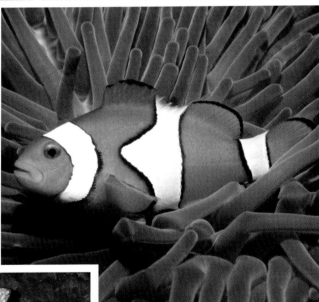

The clownfish is the celebrity of the damselfishes and lives well both with and without an anemone.

The sergeant major is a hardy damselfish for the beginner that can be kept in groups.

The neon goby is a popular cleaner goby that removes parasites from other fishes.

Although beautiful, groupers, like this coral hind, will eat smaller tankmates.

The sweetlips is a colorful addition to any peaceful aquarium, but its colors may fade with size.

With poisonous spines and a large size, the lionfish is not ideal for the beginner.

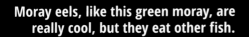
Moray eels, like this green moray, are really cool, but they eat other fish.

With its beak-like mouth and stunning coloration, the parrotfis is tempting, but grows too large for the average aquarium.

The graceful seahorse is delicate and needs a quiet aquarium.

The yellow tang is one of the most colorful and common species for the home aquarium and ideal for the beginner.

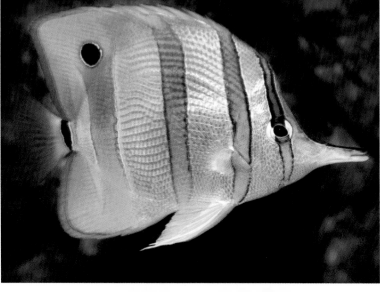

Like many butterflyfishes, the copperband butterflyfish is beautiful but delicate and demands very high water quality.

Sea anemones are common aquarium invertebrates that require excellent water quality.

Stony corals have a hard skeleton covered by a colony of soft polyps.

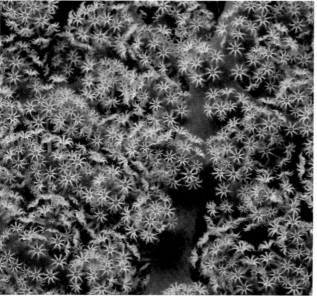

The colorful soft corals lack the calcium-based skeleton of their stony counterparts.

The colorful nudibranch is a snail without the shell.

The most common bivalve in the aquarium trade, the giant clam, needs excellent lighting.

The pajama cardinalfish is a peaceful fish with large eyes for nocturnal feeding; it can be kept in groups.

The colorful cleaner shrimp is one of the most popular invertebrates for the marine aquarium.

Sea stars can be magnificent to look at, but difficult to feed.

Sea urchins graze on aquarium algae, but care should be taken when handling them.

The filter is called a *wet-dry filter* because of a basic division of bacterial labor in the system. The dry part involves the multiple layers of filter media above the wet part. These media include coarse and fine matting for mechanical filtration and plastic spheres known as *bioballs* for bacterial colonization. Bags of activated carbon are typically placed in the sump for chemical filtration. In the dry part of the filter, water dripping through the system has maximum exposure to air and bacteria for efficient conversion of ammonia to nitrate. The wet portion of the filtration in the sump involves the further conversion of nitrogen compounds (nitrate) to less harmful nitrogen gas. The bacteria that do this don't need oxygen, and the wet portion of the filter allows this to happen. Unfortunately, in most trickle filters, the dry part works very well (up to 20 times better than an undergravel filter) but the wet part isn't as efficient, so nitrates must be removed by other means. I discuss this in greater detail in Chapter 12.

Trickle filters offer great advantages over other filter systems relative to filtration efficiency and effectiveness. They're ideal for fish-only tanks that don't have live rock. In addition, some trickle filters on the market today allow you to add other aquarium components to the second compartment (sump) of the filter. These include heaters and protein skimmers (see the following section).

Live rock and live sand

The use of *live rock* and/or *live sand* as a filtration method is now considered the gold standard for saltwater aquarium filtration and has become very popular in the aquarium trade. Live rock is coral rubble or reef rock that is permeated with organisms (see Chapter 9 for more on live rock). The kinds of life that can be found on live rock include bacteria, many kinds of algae, corals, sponges, snails, clams, bryozoans, sea squirts, crabs, barnacles, shrimps, starfish, and worms. Many aquarists rely solely on live rock, an external filter (power, canister, trickle), a protein skimmer (see the section, "Protein skimmers"), and powerheads for water circulation. Bacterial colonies housed on and in the live rock provide biological filtration at very high levels. The other filter augments the live rock and provides mechanical, chemical, and additional biological filtration. Live rock is easy to maintain, keeping aquariums clean for months to years with very little maintenance.

Live rock was once considered essential for only reef tanks, but now it's becoming the filter of choice for all types of marine aquariums. Although some species of fish in fish-only tanks will pick at and consume critters living on the live rock, this does not affect the beneficial bacterial colonies providing biological filtration. Aquarists who use live rock don't have to deal with the problems associated with the function, maintenance, and cleaning of an undergravel filter system. This means less tank intrusion, less accumulation of waste, and better water quality.

Like live rock, live sand is a natural substrate that's loaded with lots of critters and bacteria that work in your favor and provide a lot of biological filtration. I personally find sand to be the most natural looking substrate, but that's my preference. Both live rock and live sand can be purchased online or from your dealer.

TIP

Although I mention all kinds of filter options in the previous sections, the saltwater aquarium keeper is best served by a combination of filters comprising live rock and/or sand and an external filter system.

Perusing Filters' Helpers

This section contains information about those kinds of filters that help the primary filter system to maintain water quality. I separate these filters from the previous section to emphasize the fact that these filters need to be matched with others for a complete system. Think of these filters as components of a stereo system. The receiver may work beautifully, but you need speakers to make it a complete set.

Fluidized bed filters

The *fluidized bed filter* is considered one of the most efficient biological filters. The operation of this filter is quite simple. The unit consists of a media-filled chamber, typically sand, that either hangs on or sits under your aquarium. An inlet port directs water into the filter and outlets return water to the aquarium. In the filter, your aquarium water comes into contact with millions of sand grains populated by beneficial bacteria for extremely efficient biological filtration.

Some manufacturers claim that these units have 20 times the biological filtering capacity of the same volume trickle filter. The problem is, that's all they do. Therefore, if you intend to have a fluidized bed filter, you need some other filter, like a canister filter or external power filter, for mechanical and chemical filtration and aeration. Fluidized bed filters also need some kind of pump to move water through them. Therefore, you must purchase a powerhead or a similar pump in addition to the filter.

REMEMBER

The efficiency of a fluidized bed filter makes it a perfect candidate for a reef aquarium, but other filters are required to provide additional biological filtration as well as mechanical and chemical filtration.

In-line filters

I briefly mention in-line filters here because they can be used in conjunction with fluidized-bed filters to provide mechanical and chemical filtration. *In-line filters* are just chambers that contain cartridges with filter media. Water must be supplied to the filters via a powerhead or similar pump.

Protein skimmers

At one time used only in the advanced marine aquarium, the protein skimmer is now considered an essential piece of equipment for all saltwater enthusiasts. This piece of equipment utilizes *foam fractionation* to remove dissolved organic wastes from the water. What does that mean? Basically, the protein skimmer is a tube that hangs in the back of your tank or sits in a sump. Air is delivered to the bottom of the tube by an external source, generating a cloud of fine bubbles that flow to the surface. Proteins and other wastes adhere to the bubbles, travel to the surface, and collect in a removable cup that's emptied. This is really just a form of chemical filtration, but unlike other filters, wastes are actually removed from the water and not converted to something else, so the protein skimmer takes a lot of burden off the other filters.

With so many protein skimmers on the market, keep in mind that their effectiveness depends on how long the air bubbles are in contact with the water of the aquarium. In general, the different types of protein skimmers carry out this process in a couple of different ways, which I discuss in the two following subsections.

Counter-current

Counter-current is just a fancy way of saying that the water in the protein skimmer moves in the opposite direction of the air flowing through it. Therefore, in these units, water is pushed down the skimmer cylinder by a powerhead or water pump, and air supplied by an air pump to a wooden airstone rises from the bottom of the cylinder. These units typically hang in the tank, thereby obstructing your view and taking up valuable aquarium space. A counter-current skimmer is shown in Figure 7-7.

The effectiveness of this kind of protein skimmer depends on the height of the cylinder, which is limited by the height of the tank. The longer the skimmer column, the more air-water contact and the better the cleaning efficiency. Keep this in mind when you select your protein skimmer.

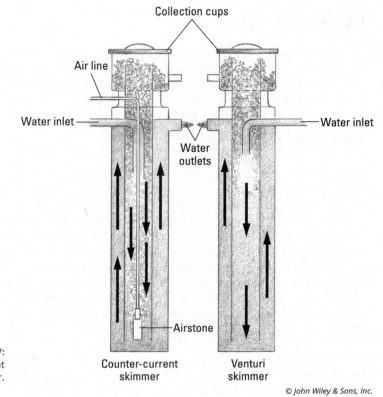

Collection cups

Air line

Water inlet

Water outlets

Water inlet

Airstone

Counter-current skimmer

Venturi skimmer

FIGURE 7-7:
A counter-current protein skimmer.

© John Wiley & Sons, Inc.

Venturi

These units allow water and air to be injected into the skimmer at the same time by the same water pump. They're situated outside the tank and can be kept out of sight. Although they tend to cost more, you don't have to worry about a separate air supply, wooden airstones, and noise from the air pump.

REMEMBER

You can add protein skimmers to your sump — several models are designed for that application. So if you plan on having a sump, you probably want to consider a protein skimmer that will fit into it and be kept out of sight.

TIP

No matter what kind of saltwater aquarium you have, I strongly recommend that you outfit it with a protein skimmer. This minimal investment will save you and your filtration system a lot of time and trouble. Your fish and invertebrates will like it, too.

Refugia

Nowadays, you hear the word *refugium* (plural is *refugia*) used quite a bit in the saltwater aquarium world. Although every expert has his interpretation of what a refugium is, it's always considered some kind of separate tank or container that shares water with your main display aquarium and provides biological and chemical filtration. In your sump (refer to the "Adding a Sump" section earlier in this chapter), for example, you can place deep sand, live rock, or macroalgae (if the refugium has a light) in a refugium compartment to remove excess nitrate from the aquarium water. A refugium can also provide a safe space for tiny critters, like small copepods, to proliferate. These are ideal food for some aquarium fishes. I have also heard of aquarists using refugia, if large enough, to temporarily house injured or bullied specimens as long as you don't treat them.

As the complexity of your aquarium increases, you should consider the addition of a refugium. I suggest you add one in association with a sump, which can also contain other aquarium equipment.

Diatom filters

This unique aquarium filter system takes advantage of technology that has been deployed by swimming pool filters for decades. *Diatoms* are tiny single-celled algae that are encased in tiny shells composed of silica. Diatom filters use powder-like filter media comprising these tiny skeletons, which have tiny pores capable of filtering the smallest particles.

Diatom filters are mechanical filters that are actually too efficient, because they remove even the beneficial free-floating tiny animals that your aquarium invertebrates feed on. They are so efficient that they clog rapidly if used for more than an hour. Therefore, diatom filters aren't good for permanent filtration and are best suited to short-term water "polishing" after the bottom is stirred up.

Denitrators

Denitrators are designed to reduce the nitrate load in your tank. Nitrate is the end product of the nitrogen cycle (see Chapter 12) and is usually removed with frequent partial water changes. The denitrator (the name sounds like a killer robot) uses bacteria to break down nitrate, providing biological filtration and reducing the need for partial water changes. Most denitrators consist of a simple airtight chamber filled with substrate for bacterial growth, but more recent models use sulfur-based reactions to reduce nitrate and balance water chemistry. Although they can fit nicely into the sump, some models can be placed in the aquarium as well.

Denitrators aren't essential pieces of aquarium equipment at this stage of your saltwater hobby. If your budget allows for the purchase of one, or if one comes with your trickle filter, fine. Otherwise, consider this piece of equipment optional.

Complete water-management systems

For your new aquarium, you can buy a complete water-management system that incorporates the biological filtration of trickle filters with chemical and mechanical filtration, heaters, aerators, denitrators, and protein skimmers. These units can be very expensive, but they represent the state-of-the-art water-quality management in home aquariums. Before you purchase your aquarium components, at least look into one of these new systems.

Disinfecting Water

Two common methods for disinfecting water are commercially available to the home aquarist: ultraviolet sterilizers (UV) and ozonizers. Although some authors recommend one or both of them for the marine aquarium — and, therefore, I discuss them in this section — I don't think they're necessary because they can cause more problems than they're worth.

UV sterilizers

Ultraviolet sterilizers are self-contained units that kill some microorganisms that may be harmful to your fishes. Water is passed from your power filter or canister filter to the UV unit, where it's exposed to ultraviolet light before being returned to the tank. However, the effectiveness of this method depends on many factors, and its usefulness for the home aquarist has been questioned. I recommend UV disinfection only if you intend to maintain delicate species of fishes and only to treat severe outbreaks of disease.

Ozonizers

Ozonizers produce ozone, a compound consisting of three atoms of oxygen, that kills microorganisms in the aquarium. However, the chemistry of ozone in seawater is poorly understood, and ozone can be harmful to humans. Therefore, I don't encourage the beginner to use ozonizers for water disinfection.

Knowing Which Filter System Is Best for You

With all these filters that I present in this chapter, I can imagine that you're sitting there thinking, "Thanks for the laundry list, Greg, but which filter is best for me?" The simple answer to your question is: Use a combination of filters and put the best filtration system into your aquarium that you can afford.

In the old days, an undergravel filter was a must, and it was generally combined with an external power filter. Nowadays, the undergravel filter is going extinct. The live rock/sump filter combination has replaced it as the best filtration available. Many aquarists use large amounts of live rock combined with internal powerheads and an external power filter or canister filter to keep their aquariums in top running condition.

If you really can't afford a trickle filter/sump system, don't want to get into live rock, or perhaps you inherited your Uncle Greg's old aquarium equipment, you can use the undergravel filter system, but you should combine it with an external power filter or canister filter. Ideally, powerheads or a reverse flow undergravel system is best if you decide to go this route.

Be mindful that the type of aquarium you intend to keep will also dictate the kind of filtration you provide. The undergravel system is fine for the simple fish-only tank, but you should bite the monetary bullet and invest in a more advanced system for any aquarium that houses invertebrates (reef tank). That's because this type of aquarium requires the most efficient filtration and lots of water movement.

REMEMBER

Regardless of the filtration system, always add a protein skimmer to your list of essential aquarium components.

Aerating and Circulating Oxygen

Your fish and invertebrates need oxygen. The process in which you add oxygen to the water is called *aeration,* pronounced "air-AY-tion." Of course, you're really just adding air to the water, but when you do so, oxygen diffuses into the water, and your pets love you for it. Aeration and circulation go hand in hand. Adding oxygen is one thing, but it must be distributed throughout the tank. Circulation facilities gas exchange at the surface and is particularly critical for reef tanks because it not only delivers oxygen but also sweeps away wastes, delivers food, and helps the animals' own internal circulation.

By keeping the water moving in the aquarium, you're also evenly distributing the temperature of the water. What good is a heater if it heats only one corner of the tank? (See Chapter 8 for the lowdown on heaters.)

With the exception of live rock, most of the filter systems that I discuss in this chapter aerate the water in some way, shape, or form. The undergravel filter with venturi powerheads, for example, provides circulation and aeration. Input piping from a canister filter or trickle filter provides circulation and some aeration. Additional circulation and aeration doesn't hurt in either case.

In contrast, live rock provides excellent filtration, but no circulation or aeration. In fact, it's critically important that circulation and aeration be added to keep live rock healthy and to maximize biological filtration.

You can't have too much oxygen in your aquarium, so I recommend adding equipment that will increase circulation and aeration, which includes the use of air pumps, airstones, powerheads, and wavemakers.

Air pumps and airstones

I used to think that the best way to add oxygen to the aquarium was through the use of an air pump attached to an airstone, but I was only partially correct. (An *airstone* allows air to pass through it, splitting the airstream into tiny bubbles.) Bubbles coming from airstones don't actually diffuse to any great extent directly into the water. Instead, the major site of gas exchange and, therefore, water oxygenation is at the water's surface.

What an air pump actually does is increase circulation in the tank, promotes oxygen exchange at the surface, and increases the escape of carbon dioxide, carbon monoxide, and free ammonia from the tank. In addition, this increase in circulation acts to mix all the aquarium levels so that a uniform temperature is maintained throughout the tank.

The two general air pump designs (as shown in Figure 7-8) are as follows:

>> **The diaphragm type:** The *diaphragm pump,* also known as the *vibrator pump,* is the more common of the two and generally provides enough maintenance-free usage for most aquariums. It can, however, be a bit noisy.

>> **The piston type:** The *piston pump,* however, is more powerful and should be used in larger aquariums, particularly if an undergravel filter and multiple airstones need to be powered. In this air pump, air is generated with a piston mechanism.

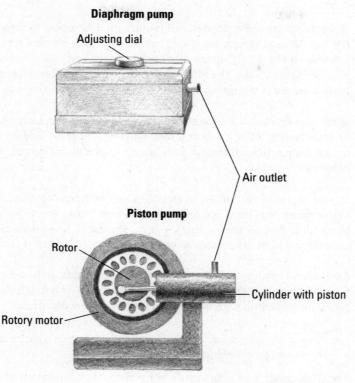

Diaphragm pump

Adjusting dial

Air outlet

Piston pump

Rotor

Cylinder with piston

Rotary motor

FIGURE 7-8:
Diaphragm and
piston pumps are
two types of air
pumps.

© John Wiley & Sons, Inc.

REMEMBER

The size and power output of air pumps vary. Although many are meant to correspond to the size of the aquarium, buy one based on what you're going to do with it. If you plan on air-powering a protein skimmer and an undergravel filter in your 30-gallon tank, you need a high-capacity air pump. However, this would not be the case if you simply want to run air to a mermaid ornament in your 90-gallon tank; you can buy a smaller one.

An *airstone*, also known as an *air diffuser*, is generally made of porous stone or perforated wood that allows air to pass through it, splitting the airstream into tiny bubbles. Too fine a mist will cause bubbles to adhere to various tank decorations and to fish. You want the bubbles to travel slowly to the surface and agitate the water. Airstones come in a variety of sizes and shapes, and the ones you choose depend on how much you need to aerate and on your personal preference. Some airstones on the market today can create dramatic effects.

REMEMBER

Be sure to keep a watchful eye on your airstones because they'll degrade and clog over time, making your air pump work harder and increasing wear and tear. Airstones are relatively inexpensive, so replace them when the bubbles they generate become inconsistent.

Your air pump and airstones will require *air-line tubing* to form the link between the two. This is plastic or rubber tubing that delivers air from your pump to the airstone. It should fit snugly at all joints so that air doesn't escape from the system. Air leaks reduce the efficiency of the system (filter, airstone) and may ultimately burn out the pump.

WARNING

Make sure the tubing is manufactured for use in the aquarium; other grades may be toxic to fish. Also, air-line tubing will degrade over time, so if it starts kinking or cracking, replace it to save your air pump and maintain the efficiency of the air delivery.

If you intend to run multiple airstones or additional devices, like filters, from a single pump, you need one or more air valves. These enable air flow to be directed to multiple devices from a single pump. The use of several air valves allows you to turn on and shut off devices as you see fit.

Air pumps, tubing, and airstones are fine for small, fish-only systems and well suited to augment existing circulation from filter systems. However, pumping air into your aquarium with airstones does have a few downsides:

>> They aren't as efficient or effective as powerheads in creating water movement and promoting gas exchange.

>> They create a lot of salt spray, which produces salt deposits on your aquarium equipment, called *salt creep*.

>> They need routine maintenance because they clog, wear out, and stop doing their job.

Powerheads

However, reef tanks with live rock and invertebrates really need a lot of circulation, and I mean a *lot* of circulation. The better option for aerating and circulating the water in this type of aquarium is with powerheads.

I've spent countless hours diving on coral reefs and can tell you that turbulent water movement from currents and tides is never lacking in this marine environment and is actually quite critical to reef survival. To create this same scenario in your home aquarium, use powerheads. Powerheads improve the efficiency and performance of an undergravel filter, as well as water circulation and aeration. But you don't need an undergravel filter to add powerheads to your aquarium.

If you plan on keeping a reef tank, powerheads (see Figure 7-9) are strongly recommended as the best way to increase circulation and aeration. I suggest that aquarium owners with tanks in excess of 20 gallons use at least two powerheads, one in each corner. To reproduce the same turbulent conditions in a natural reef ecosystem, point the outflows from the powerheads so they crash into each other or into the aquarium glass or some of the aquarium decorations, like live rock.

FIGURE 7-9:
Powerheads move water throughout the aquarium. The left illustration shows one out of the tank, and the right illustration shows one in action in a tank.

© John Wiley & Sons, Inc.

Other options

Some reef aquarists use an electronic *wavemaker* to turn powerheads on and off in an alternating pattern. The resulting rhythmic movement of water in the tank actually simulates the motion of the ocean, creating a natural setting for the invertebrates in your aquarium.

The latest and greatest way to increase circulation in your aquarium is called a *gyre*. This mounts inside your aquarium and circulates water in a way that creates flow evenly throughout the aquarium. They are thought to be more efficient and less bulky than multiple powerheads.

Circulation is the key to a healthy reef aquarium, so I suggest you add a wavemaker or gyre if you plan to have a reef tank.

Chapter **8**

Heating and Lighting Your Aquarium

In the ocean, fish and invertebrates are surrounded by saltwater and, with very few exceptions, their body temperature is the same temperature as the surrounding water. Their bodies have, therefore, evolved to operate at very specific water temperatures. The same is true for light levels. The amount of sunlight differs around the globe, and marine animals require certain levels of light to survive, which is especially true for many marine invertebrates, like corals, that rely on photosynthetic algae.

In the captive environment of the aquarium, maintaining the correct temperature and optimal light levels for your pets is critically important. To do this, you need to purchase an aquarium heater and lighting. In this chapter, I tell you about this essential equipment and how to choose the right ones.

Understanding Temperature in Relation to Your Wet Pets

The oceans of the world aren't uniform in temperature and light levels. If you've been to tropical areas like, for example, the Caribbean, you know that the water is warmer, crystal clear, and bright with sunlight. In contrast, waters off northern areas like New England have temperatures and day lengths that fluctuate seasonally. In these natural environments, which differ dramatically, the animals living in each of these regions are well adapted to local temperatures and light levels.

Most fish and invertebrates are cold-blooded animals. That means their body temperature is the same as the temperature of the waters in which they live. In general, their bodies function best at specific water temperatures and, therefore, all fishes have temperature preferences that are tightly linked to where they originate.

Fishes can be grouped into the following general categories based on where they live and water temperature.

REMEMBER

Temperature can be reported in either degrees Fahrenheit (F) or Celsius (C). Don't let this confuse you — it's simply a difference in scale. Throughout this book, I use Fahrenheit. If you want to convert from Fahrenheit to Celsius, simply apply the formula in Chapter 22.

Temperate

These types of fish include many species that inhabit cooler northern waters. If you set up a coldwater aquarium, it will likely contain temperate fishes. They're also well adapted to the low light levels and shorter days in these areas.

Tropical

The most common fishes in the marine aquarium are tropical coral reef species. The term *tropical* refers to natural habitats where the waters are warm throughout the year. It should come as no surprise, therefore, that you must heat your aquarium water to a specific temperature range. This is the job of an aquarium heater. This essential piece of equipment maintains your aquarium water at a constant temperature, regardless of the room temperature.

In their natural home, tropical fishes typically experience very little variation in water temperature. So, in your aquarium, you want to mimic the natural environment and maintain as constant a temperature as possible.

If you live in a warm place, like Florida, year-round, you may be thinking that you don't need an aquarium heater. Not true. In Florida, the outside air temperature isn't always constant: It too fluctuates and this influences water temperature. It creates problems for your pets if you don't have an aquarium heater because fluctuations of even a few degrees can stress your animals and possibly kill them. This is further complicated if you have air conditioning, and I don't know many Floridians who don't!

Tropical marine fish and invertebrate species require that the aquarium temperature be maintained at 76 to 80 degrees F. However, this range is entirely dependent on the species you choose, so consult your local pet dealer or one of the many fish encyclopedias (see the appendix) for the temperature requirements of your specific pet. Make sure that you don't mix species that have very different temperature preferences.

Identifying Types of Heaters

As you can expect, a lot of heaters are available on the market for today's home aquarium. Some designs are clearly better than others, but the most popular aquarium heaters work off the same principles and have many parts in common.

With the exception of some specialized heater designs that are relatively uncommon, a basic aquarium heater looks like a big test tube with a bunch of wiring in it and an electrical cord coming out of it. This wad of wiring is actually a heating coil contained in a glass tube that gets submerged in your aquarium. (The extent to which it's submerged depends on the type of heater.)

Of course, the heating coil has to be turned on and off, and that's the job of the *thermostat,* the mechanism that usually dictates the quality of the heater. You set the thermostat with the control knob, and an indicator light fires up when the heater is operating. (I discuss thermostats in the "Considering Your Heater Options" later in this chapter.)

Based on these basic parts of a heater, it's much easier to explain the differences between the various following types to help you choose the right one.

Submersible heaters

A *submersible heater* (shown in Figure 8-1) is the preferred choice for the saltwater aquarium. Also known as an *immersion heater,* the submersible heater is placed fully in the aquarium in any location that you desire. This means that you can put it near the bottom, out of the way of the aquarium's inhabitants, out of your view, and in a more efficient location for heat dispersion. You can even put the submersible heater in your sump (see Chapter 7), keeping it completely out of the way of the aquarium.

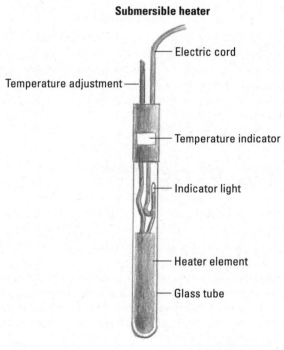

Submersible heater

— Electric cord

Temperature adjustment —

— Temperature indicator

— Indicator light

— Heater element

— Glass tube

FIGURE 8-1:
A submersible heater is the best choice for a saltwater aquarium.

© *John Wiley & Sons, Inc.*

In addition, most submersible heaters have advanced thermostat controls that make temperature selection and control easier. Although glass was the primary affordable heater option available, now there are unbreakable fully submersible heaters made of titanium or covered in a protective plastic sheath.

Hanging heaters

A *hanging heater* is also referred to as the *clamp-on, clip-on,* or *semi-submersible* heater. This is the oldest style of aquarium heater and has been around since my early aquarium days, way back in the 1970s. As you may expect, the hanging heater is so named because it hangs on the upper part of the aquarium clamped to the rim of the tank. The glass body of the heater is submerged in the aquarium, but the controls remain out of the water.

Although these heaters are the least expensive, they also tend to be the most primitive, and I don't consider them to be the best choice for the saltwater aquarium. First, their placement at the top of the water column isn't the most efficient location for heat exchange. This location also makes them extremely vulnerable to being disturbed by both you and the tank's inhabitants. The more either of you bang into the heater, the higher the chance that it will be damaged (the glass body can crack). These heaters also tend to have less efficient thermostats for controlling their operation.

In-line heaters

The *in-line* or *external heater* is installed in the intake or output lines of the aquarium's filter system. This heater doesn't take up any space in your aquarium, and it's generally kept out of sight. These heaters heat the water of the aquarium more evenly, but they're more expensive and they do require an external source of water flow, like a canister filter — no flow, no heat.

Considering Your Heater Options

Whether you choose a hanging heater or a submersible heater, look for the following features.

Thermostat

The switch that controls the operation of your heater is the *thermostat,* and it comes in a variety of styles. Most heaters have a built-in thermostat, but others have a separate one. The external thermostat is placed on the side of the tank or has a separate probe that's placed in the water. Although this style isn't common, it offers excellent temperature control because it is electronic, and digital temperature displays are more accurate. The following sections point out the two types of thermostats.

Bimetallic strip

The most common aquarium heater is regulated by a built-in thermostat. Older models have a mechanical thermostat called the *bimetallic strip.* As your aquarium cools, the strip contracts until the circuit is closed and the heater is turned on. This system is the old workhorse of the heater thermostat world, but it has flaws.

Bimetallic strips tend to lose efficiency with time and ultimately fail to function properly. If you do purchase a heater with a bimetallic strip thermostat, be sure it has magnetic contacts. These close the circuit more effectively, decreasing wear and tear on the unit.

Electronic

Although heaters equipped with bimetallic strip thermostats tend to be less expensive, heaters with electronic thermostats are better. An electronic thermostat operates more efficiently than an older mechanical thermostat. These units usually detect water temperature more accurately from the glass body of the heater, instead of from the air inside the glass body. In addition, more advanced electronic heaters are designed to fail in the off position, so that your fish aren't cooked if the heater has a problem. This gives you time to detect the problem, which is why you want to keep a watchful eye on your aquarium water temperature every day.

Temperature control

All heaters have some kind of temperature control that you use to set the proper temperature. The knob that controls the operation of the heater is closely related to the thermostat. I treat it separately because you use this part of the heater to set its operation. Now, some heaters are user-friendly and others aren't.

Older-style heaters with bimetallic strip thermostats have control knobs that you use to set the temperature, but you need to calibrate the heater using the knob and a thermometer. Although a fancy-sounding word, *calibrate* really just means that you set the heater to operate at a desired temperature, usually about 78 degrees F.

How do you do that? After your tank is filled and long before you add animals, you place the heater in the tank and then plug it in. Your thermometer will tell you the temperature, and you hope that it's close to 78 degrees F. If it's cooler, adjust the control knob just until the point that the heater turns on and the indicator light is on. If the temperature is too high, adjust the knob until the heater is off. Over the next several hours, repeat these steps until the temperature stabilizes at 78 degrees F. Perhaps you can see why these heaters aren't very convenient.

On the other hand, you can avoid having to calibrate the heater by buying one of the more advanced electronic heaters. These units usually have a control knob that lets you select the desired temperature. Therefore, all you have to do is set the control dial to 78 degrees F without any adjustment.

I recommend that you double-check the temperature even with an electronic heater after initially setting it up, just to be sure that it's operating correctly.

Thermal protection

Consider this: You're putting a glass tube with electrical elements inside of it into a tank full of water and a bunch of live animals. To most people, that spells an accident waiting to happen. And believe me, any time you put water and electricity together, you're going to have an element of danger. That's why some protective options are available in heaters.

Fish are inquisitive creatures and are bound to investigate your heater. If the heater is hanging on the side of the tank or just lying on the bottom, it's only a matter of time before your wet pets push it into the wall of the tank or on a piece of coral — and it cracks.

Make it a point to buy a heater with suction cups, which keep the heater in one location and buffer it from occasional strikes from both you and your fish. If your heater doesn't come with suction cups, purchase them separately.

You can also protect the glass body of the heater itself. I know of at least one manufacturer that markets a plastic protective guard for the heater to protect both the heater and the fish. Some heaters also have protective finishes on the glass body of the heater. These protective coatings include titanium, ceramic, Teflon, silicone, and even stainless steel. They may cost more, but the health of your fish is worth it.

One Size Doesn't Fit All — Knowing What Size Heater to Purchase

You may have selected a type of heater, but now you need to know what size to buy. Size depends on a few of the following factors.

Water and wattage

Aquarium heaters come in a variety of sizes based on their power output. This is measured in wattage (just like light bulbs) and ranges from 25 to over 200 watts. Buying the right size heater for your aquarium setup is extremely important.

REMEMBER

The general rule is 5 watts per gallon of water up to 50 gallons. Because larger aquaria tend to hold heat better, three watts per gallon is enough power for tanks greater than 50 gallons. So, for example, a 30-gallon tank would require a 150-watt heater while a 60-gallon tank would require a 180-watt heater.

Not only the size of the aquarium dictates the size of the heater, but you should also take into account how hard the heater has to work. In other words, how cold is the room that the aquarium is in, and more importantly, what's the difference between the room temperature and the aquarium temperature? For example, some folks prefer to keep their room temperature at 55 degrees F, yet a tropical aquarium should be at 75 degrees F. That means that the heater must work hard to maintain the aquarium temperature 20 degrees F above the room temperature. On the other hand, a warmer room would allow the heater to work less.

With this in mind, some heater manufacturers and aquarists size the heater not only to the aquarium, but also to this room-aquarium temperature difference. Basically, if your room temperature is just a little cooler than the aquarium, you can buy a smaller heater than the general rule dictates. If your room is much colder, you need to go bigger. Table 8-1 guides you through the selection. For very large tanks in very cold rooms, I recommend two heaters, and this is indicated by a (2) next to the wattage.

TABLE 8-1   **Heater Size Selection**

Heater Size by Difference in Room and Aquarium Temperature			
Aquarium Size (gal.)	10° Difference	20° Difference	30° Difference
15	50W	75W	150W
20	75W	100W	200W
30	100W	150W	250W
40	150W	200W	300W
55	200W	250W	200W (2)
65	200W	250W	250W (2)
75	250W	300W	300W (2)

More than one

In Table 8-1, you see that larger tanks require more than one heater if the room temperature difference is large. But you don't need to have a large room temperature difference to have two heaters. Here's why: If your single aquarium heater fails or malfunctions, your fish and invertebrates can potentially die.

If, however, you have two heaters, the other heater can pick up the slack if one fails. I only recommend this for larger tanks because hiding *one* heater can be difficult, let alone two.

TIP

If you opt for more than one heater, simply divide the recommended power by two. For example, instead of a single 200W heater for a 55-gallon tank, you can use two 100W heaters. You may want to put one in your aquarium and one in your sump. A little backup heater power is a sound investment.

Depth and length

Aquarium heaters come in a variety of lengths ranging from 6 to 15 inches. In general, heaters that are more powerful are longer. This is not a problem for the fully submersible heater, but hanging types should be at least 3 inches shorter than the tank height to account for gravel and other ornamentation.

Reminding You of Some Important Basic Heater Tips

When choosing and using a heater for your aquarium, keep these tips in mind:

WARNING

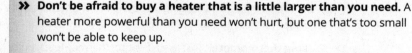

» **Don't be afraid to buy a heater that is a little larger than you need.** A heater more powerful than you need won't hurt, but one that's too small won't be able to keep up.

» **Be careful with a damaged heater.** A damaged heater is a dangerous electrical appliance for all living things near it. Remember, electricity and water don't mix!

» **Don't be a cheapskate.** After you've made such a significant investment in your aquarium, don't jeopardize the success of the entire system by saving $20 on a cheap heater. Many of your tank's inhabitants are worth more than the amount you'll save.

- » **Place your heater close to an area of high circulation so that heated water can be rapidly and evenly distributed throughout the tank.** This is usually near the filter system, the filter input from an external filter, or the powerheads (see Chapter 7). For instance, place the fully submersible heater at the bottom of the tank so that heating convection can be optimized. The filter sump is also a great place, because water is always moving through it.

WARNING

- » **As with all electrical components, handle your heater with extreme care.** Don't plug your heater in until it's submersed in water regardless of what kind of heater it is. A hot heater will readily burn you, can potentially start a fire, and will crack if you suddenly submerse it in cool water. As a matter of course, keep all your electrical components unplugged until the tank is completely set up and full.

WARNING

- » **Never remove your heater from the aquarium unless it's unplugged.** Also allow it to cool even after unplugging it before you take it out of the water.

Choosing a Thermometer

You should think of the thermometer as something that measures the amount of heat in your aquarium, hence a *thermo meter*. This is an essential piece of equipment that I recommend even if your electronic heater has a temperature probe or sensor. A standard thermometer is a minor investment that assures you that your heater is operating properly.

A number of kinds are on the market today, and some are more accurate than others. Here are your options, starting with the simplest:

- » **Floating thermometer:** This style has been around for decades. It floats in the aquarium, but it tends to wander about in the currents if it's not restrained in one area. Finding and reading a floating thermometer can be a hassle, particularly if you have to lift the hood (see Chapter 6) to retrieve it.

- » **Sticking thermometer:** Just like a floating thermometer, but it has suction cups that adhere it to the inside glass of the aquarium. A bit easier to read, but it's something for your fish to play with.

- » **Hanging thermometer:** This glass thermometer is attached to a stainless steel bracket that hangs on the inside of your aquarium. It stays in place, but it may interfere with your aquarium hood and, again, is something for your fish to bump into.

- » **Sinking thermometer:** This is really just a floating thermometer that's weighted and sinks to the bottom. It drifts about the aquarium if not secured and provides a toy for your fish, which isn't good.

- » **Thermometer-hydrometer:** This is a thermometer that's inside your hydrometer and floats in the aquarium. The hydrometer is used to measure the amount of salt in your water, which is called *salinity*. I discuss salinity and hydrometers in Chapter 9.

- » **Liquid crystal thermometer:** This thermometer sticks to the glass wall of your aquarium on the outside. There's nothing for your tank inhabitants to interfere with, and they're very easy to read but not as accurate as other thermometers. After one is in place, it's difficult to move.

- » **Digital thermometer:** A digital thermometer is a bit more expensive, but it provides the most accuracy for your aquarium. These are external units that have a temperature probe that goes into the tank. Most also tell you room temperature, and some have a built-in alarm that alerts you when the temperature is too hot or too cold.

- » **Temperature controller:** This unit integrates with a heater and actually controls your aquarium water temperature electronically. They're less expensive than they used to be and best suited for large systems.

TIP

Thermometers are inexpensive (less than $2), so buy a couple, perhaps a liquid crystal stick-on and a floating or hanging type. You can keep the latter out of the aquarium and use it to double-check the temperature or to check the temperature of water that you're adding to the tank. Ideally, a digital thermometer or temperature controller is the best yet most expensive, but I recommend them if you can afford the investment.

The Lowdown on Lighting

When you think of the tropics, what comes to mind? Bright sunshine and crystal-clear, warm, turquoise waters teeming with colorful living creatures, right?

Well, sunshine, clear waters, and colorful creatures go hand in hand. In the tropical waters of the world, the water is clear, and sunlight is able to penetrate deeper than in more northern temperate waters. Over time, this allowed for coral reefs to develop in the areas with the right combination of light and water depth. And with the coral reefs came a huge diversity of invertebrates and fishes.

Did you ever notice that where there is no intense light, there is no coral? Coral isn't a plant. It's an invertebrate animal that actually houses tiny plant-like organisms in its body that feed it. Therefore, corals need light and a lot of it. Tropical fish need light as well, but not as much of it. They need to see what they eat, and their lives are adapted to changes in light intensity over the course of a day and over the course of a year.

Lighting is important in your aquarium, just as it is for you in your life, and these sections explain just what you need to know about lighting your aquarium.

The importance of light

Daily changes in light dictate rest periods for fish. Consider these two classifications:

>> A *diurnal* fish is active during the day and rests at night.

>> A *nocturnal* fish does the opposite.

In addition, monthly changes in light intensity stimulate spawning in many tropical reef fishes and invertebrates. So light is extremely important in the natural environment.

Now, here's the challenge: Bring enough light into your aquarium so that your reef creatures live and act naturally. Is it possible? Yes. Even though it's highly unlikely that you'll get them to spawn, you'll be able to mimic natural lighting so that they resume their diurnal or nocturnal habits.

TECHNICAL
STUFF

Oh, by the way, a light in your aquarium is good for you as well your fish. What good is an aquarium if you can't see what's in it? Light is classified based on its wavelength:

>> **Visible light:** This is the light with wavelengths that people are able to see. As visible light wavelengths decrease, the colors change from red to orange, yellow, green, blue, and violet.

>> **Infrared light:** Light with wavelengths longer than visible light is called *infrared,* but you can't see it without special equipment.

>> **Ultraviolet (UV):** Light with wavelengths shorter than visible light is called *ultraviolet* (UV), and you can't see it either. UV light can also be damaging to your skin and your eyes.

Before I'm through boring you to tears, I want to add one more bit of knowledge to this physics lesson. The shorter the wavelength of light, the deeper it penetrates in the ocean. Therefore, blue and violet light goes the deepest whereas red and yellow light are filtered out quickly by the properties of water. This is called *light attenuation,* and fish and invertebrates have adapted quite well to it.

What does all this have to do with aquarium lighting? Well, it turns out that reef invertebrates, like coral, are dependent on short wavelength light such as blue, violet, and even ultraviolet. This light is important because these animals have photosynthetic algae living in them. These algae are called *zooxanthellae,* and they're able to take wastes from the coral, harness the energy of the sun, and convert it to energy for their host. What does that tell you? If you plan on having a reef aquarium, you need to increase the intensity of your lighting and include light from the blue side of the spectrum.

REMEMBER

Fish, on the other hand, don't have such special needs for high-intensity lighting. Thus, a fish-only marine aquarium shouldn't have high intensity lighting because it promotes excessive growth of algae in the tank, and most fish don't prefer it.

Watt is power

The intensity or power of a light bulb is measured in watts. Depending on the type of light, aquarium lighting can be as powerful as 400 watts.

Although power is rated in watts, the color of light is rated in degrees Kelvin. I'm not going to get into the specifics of why, because I think you've had enough physics already. Suffice to say that aquarium bulbs can range from 5,400 to 20,000 degrees K, and the greater the number, the more blue light is produced. Typical reef aquarium lighting is about 10,000 degrees K because it produces a lot of blue light. I tell you this because when you're shopping for light bulbs, you'll encounter these numbers.

TECHNICAL
STUFF

The acronym PAR is becoming more common in the aquarium trade. This stands for photosynthetically active radiation and refers to those wavelengths that support photosynthesis, which is actually the same spectrum of visible light. In plain English, your corals need PAR to survive. Hobbyists with reef tanks now can measure PAR output from their lighting to be sure they have the right amount for their corals. These units are expensive, but some local fish stores and fish clubs will rent you instruments that measure PAR.

Another specialized term that you'll undoubtedly encounter is actinic lighting. *Actinic* light bulbs produce light at the blue end of the spectrum, near UV light. They're ideal for corals and other photosynthetic invertebrates, but they aren't full-spectrum bulbs, so additional lighting may be needed.

Your lighting fixture options

Aquarium lighting comes in two general types of fixtures:

>> **Strip lights:** These are simply long lighting fixtures that are either built into your aquarium hood, sit on top of your glass canopy, or hang suspended over your tank. A good example of a strip light is the standard fluorescent hood fixture.

>> **Hanging spotlights:** Most hanging fixtures are high-intensity lights that generate a lot of heat and can't be kept on top of the aquarium. Dome-shaped hanging fixtures are called *pendants,* and they deliver a concentrated spot of light.

TIP

Because aquarium fixtures come in a variety of styles, make your choice when you plan your aquarium. The type of lighting you choose depends on your tank's inhabitants and the visual effects that you want to achieve.

For example, high-intensity lamps that hang above your aquarium will create a much different lighting effect than a standard hood fixture that distributes light evenly. It will look like sunlight rippling through clear tropical waters, creating a truly dramatic natural look. However, if you're going to go with this type of lighting, you really don't want to buy a full plastic aquarium hood (see Chapter 6). Instead, use a glass canopy.

Lighting the Way — Selecting Lighting for Your Aquarium

You can find a number of choices for lighting your aquarium. In this section, I run through your options and give you an idea of the benefits of each type, including the qualities of the lighting, the initial expense, the amount of electricity a unit consumes, and the life of the bulb.

Natural light

Although natural sunlight is an ideal source of light for your aquarium, it's also the most difficult to harness in the right quantities. It's certainly inexpensive, and it does provide the entire spectrum of wavelengths, called *full-spectrum light.* Nonetheless, direct sunlight is difficult to control, it's not predictable, and therefore, it's not a logical source of aquarium light.

Tungsten

If you started with a 10-gallon freshwater setup a few years back, you may have had an incandescent light on top of it. This is also called *tungsten lighting*. The typical light bulb in your living room lamp provides tungsten light. Consider the following about this type:

>> **Quality of light:** Tungsten lights burn hot, they don't provide full-spectrum lighting, and they promote the growth of nuisance algae.

>> **Bulb longevity:** Tungsten light bulbs don't last long and require frequent changing.

>> **Expense:** The initial cost of these units is low, but they consume a lot of electricity.

>> **Recommendation:** Not for the saltwater aquarium.

Fluorescent

Considered by many to provide the optimum lighting for the aquarium, fluorescent lighting is popular for saltwater aquariums. If you think that you're unfamiliar with fluorescent lighting, think again. It's common in commercial office buildings, and more than likely you've used it in your everyday life. There was a time when the same type of lighting was used in the aquarium, but times and technologies have changed.

Now, fluorescent lights are made specifically for saltwater aquariums. The most common is the T5 fluorescent bulb, which produces a broad light spectrum that works well with corals. If you choose this type of lighting, make sure to buy it from your fish dealer. These fixtures usually come as full hood aquarium lights or may be purchased separately as a strip lights for glass canopies. (See Chapter 6 for more on hoods and canopies.) Consider the following about this type:

>> **Quality of light:** Fluorescent fixtures produce cool, bright light that spreads evenly from the light into the aquarium. This type doesn't allow for natural surface ripple effects, but it does distribute light evenly in the tank. Fluorescent bulbs or tubes come in a wide variety of choices and power outputs. Full-spectrum lighting is available and ideal for reef tanks. Multi-bulb fixtures are available so that light of different spectral qualities can be mixed. Fluorescent lighting is also pleasing to the eye.

>> **Bulb longevity:** Fluorescent tubes generally retain their spectral qualities until they fail. They are known to last from several months to two years, depending on the bulb.

>> **Expense:** Initial cost is less expensive than other aquarium lighting, they operate very efficiently, and they consume relatively low amounts of electricity. They're expensive to replace.

>> **Recommendation:** Excellent lighting for fish-only tanks and some kinds of reef tanks.

Power compact fluorescent

This type of lighting is really just a U-shaped fluorescent tube instead of a straight tube. However, it has a much higher light output than a standard fluorescent fixture. Power compact fluorescent lights are sold as strip lights, or you may purchase a retrofit kit for a standard hood. Consider the following about this type:

>> **Quality of light:** These fixtures have the same benefits of standard fluorescent lights, but they produce higher intensity lighting. Full-spectrum and specialty lighting are available and work well for deeper reef tanks. Multi-bulb fixtures are available so that light of different spectral qualities can be mixed. Like fluorescent lighting, power compact is also pleasing to the eye.

>> **Bulb longevity:** Power compact fluorescent tubes also retain their spectral qualities until they fail. They are known to last from several months to two years, depending on the bulb.

>> **Expense:** Initial cost is more expensive than standard fluorescent lighting, but they operate more efficiently and consume less electricity.

>> **Recommendation:** Excellent lighting for reef tanks.

Light-emitting diodes (LEDs)

LED fixtures are relatively new to the hobby, but they're quickly becoming the most popular. LED lighting for the aquarium is basically an array of small lights arranged to produce a bright light, having different intensities and different color options. LEDs are energy-efficient and tend to run cooler than other light sources. Fixtures for these lights come as full hood aquarium lights and strip or spotlights for glass canopies. Consider the following about this type:

>> **Quality of light:** This lighting offers a high degree of control for the aquarist with regard to light intensity, color balance, and lighting effects. Multi-bulb fixtures are available so that light of different spectral qualities can be mixed. Like fluorescent and power compact lighting, LED is pleasing to the eye.

>> **Bulb longevity:** Long functional lifespan of years. They also retain their spectral qualities until they fail.

>> **Expense:** Initial cost can be expensive, but they operate more efficiently and consume less electricity.

>> **Recommendation:** Excellent lighting for reef tanks, but will produce shadows that will hurt SPS corals over time.

Mercury vapor

This lighting uses mercury vapor to produce light from spotlights suspended above the aquarium. Consider the following about this type:

>> **Quality of light:** These fixtures provide spotlighting, which can create dramatic natural visual effects with water rippling. Although intense, the spectral quality of the light is lacking on the blue side of the spectrum, so they're not good for reef tanks without additional lighting. These lights produce heat, so they need to be ventilated.

>> **Bulb longevity:** Can be quite short with a significant loss of efficiency in less than six months. Bulbs need to be replaced frequently.

>> **Expense:** Expensive to purchase and operate.

>> **Recommendation:** Good for deeper saltwater tanks but not for reef tanks without additional blue lighting.

Metal halide

Like mercury vapor lighting, metal halide lights produce powerful spotlighting that penetrates deep and produces dramatic visual effects. Metal halide light bulbs look like standard light bulbs on steroids. Metal halide lighting is available in hanging lamps, hanging pendants, or ventilated canopy fixtures. Consider the following about this type:

>> **Quality of light:** Provides intense, deep-penetrating, full-spectrum light that's ideal for invertebrate tanks. Bulbs that favor the blue side of the spectrum are available for special reef lighting.

WARNING

The lights need to be suspended above the aquarium and ventilated because they run hot. Because they may produce ultraviolet light, they can be damaging to the human eye, so take care around them.

- **»** **Bulb longevity:** Need to be replaced every 8 to 12 months to maintain maximum efficiency.
- **»** **Expense:** Expensive to purchase and operate.
- **»** **Recommendation:** Ideal for reef and invertebrate tanks.

Combination

You can purchase lighting systems that offer a combination of lighting types. Most of them are offered as light strip fixtures that sit above your aquarium. The most common are metal halide fluorescent fixtures that include multiple light sources.

TIP

Although expensive, these systems offer the best of both worlds: high intensity light for photosynthetic invertebrates and soft fluorescent lighting for pleasant viewing.

Switching from Day to Night

An often overlooked component to a lighting system is also one of the most critical: the on/off time switch. Tropical marine fish and invertebrates come from regions where day length ranges from 10 to 15 hours, so you can't expect your pets to be exposed to 24 hours of light. Remember, some animals are diurnal and some are nocturnal, so you really need to simulate day and night in your aquarium.

REMEMBER

An inexpensive automatic timer will turn your lighting system on and off at the same time so that a consistent day length can be maintained. A 10- to 12-hour day is generally recommended for most aquariums.

Consider making an effort not to startle your fish with the sudden switching of lights. In nature, the sun doesn't drop like a rock, so neither should the one in your aquarium. You can mimic a more natural sunset and sunrise in a couple of different ways.

First, if you have more than one lighting fixture, you can have another automatic timer. Stagger the timing of the lights so that one shuts off and turns on about an hour before the other. If you don't have more than one light fixture, control the lighting in the room, instead. Simply put room lights on automatic timers or control them yourself so that lighting changes gradually. This little detail helps keep your fish happy and, therefore, healthy.

Chapter **9**

Decorating Your Tank — Fishy Furnishings and Finishing Touches

In the wilds of the ocean, the name of the game is simple: Eat or be eaten. Most of the small fish and invertebrates that you keep in your aquarium are the ones that often end up on the short end of the stick. In nature, these little critters are always wary of potential predators.

The coral reef ecosystem, however, provides hiding places, caves, and nooks for protection. Many species of fish even set up small territories that they defend. Thus rocks, sand, plants, macroalgae, and coral reefs are important structures that fish and invertebrates need to survive.

When you introduce your aquatic guests to their new home, they'll undoubtedly be looking for the same nooks and caves they left behind. To make them feel comfortable and keep them healthy, you need to decorate and *aquascape* (underwater landscape).

Your new pets need clean water, oxygen, heat, light, and housing. But there are a few loose odds and ends to buy in order to make your new aquarium complete. In this chapter, I discuss the basics of what you need to get your aquarium up and running and keep it running. That includes little things that you need on a daily basis to keep your aquarium clean and to take care of your new pets.

REMEMBER

Almost everything that you place in your aquarium, from gravel to cleaning equipment, can and will influence your water chemistry. That influence may be either positive or negative. Anything that contains toxic compounds, such as heavy metals, will negatively impact your water chemistry and potentially harm your pets. Throughout this chapter, I tell you how to avoid adding toxic compounds to your tank with each of your fishy furnishing.

Aquascaping Is a Matter of Taste

Just how you aquascape (that is, underwater landscape) your saltwater aquarium is entirely up to you as long as you take into account the following basic rules:

>> **Don't put anything into the tank unless you're positively sure it won't harm your fish and invertebrates.** The best way to ensure this is to avoid collecting your own decorations. Buy them instead from a reputable dealer.

>> **Make an effort to give your aquarium creatures some creature comforts, such as caves and crannies.** Most marine animals seek the comfort and protection of a hiding place during the day or night, depending on if they're diurnal or nocturnal.

>> **Don't overstuff your aquarium with decorations.** The most important element in the tank is water. Every piece of rock or coral you put in the tank will displace water and space, and your pets need both. In general, cover only about 50 to 60 percent of the bottom of your tank.

>> **Stick with *calcareous* ornamentation whenever possible.** This just means that the decorations are calcium-based, such as coral and dolomite. Doing so will help stabilize the chemistry of the water, which needs to be alkaline. I talk more about this issue in Chapter 13.

>> **When you stack rocks and other ornamentation, make sure the structure is stable.** Rocks, by definition, are heavy, and you don't want one changing the decor in your living room, if you know what I mean. A good rule is to make the base of structure as wide as it is high.

>> **Take the time before you buy to design the decor of your aquarium.** Sit down with a pencil and paper and draw it. Get creative, pulling ideas from books and public displays, and then try to make it a reality.

Going for the Natural Look

There is no such thing as a typical freshwater aquarium look because so many kinds of ornaments, gravel, plants, and weird toys are available to suit the many tastes out there. Remember the kid next door who had the purple gravel, bubbling skeleton, and plastic plants? Must have been the '70s.

On the other hand, the norm for the saltwater aquarium is the natural look. As you may expect, I'm a true believer in the use of natural-looking ornamentation. Corals, rocks, and dolomite not only look good, but they also help water chemistry and give your fish a more natural setting.

REMEMBER

Most freshwater decorations simply aren't for the marine aquarium. Of course, if your child wants to put a ceramic skin diver in the tank, go ahead and have some fun.

A WORD ON CONSERVATION

Marine fish, invertebrates, live rock, and corals are harvested from the wild largely for the marine aquarium trade. Many of them come from Pacific islands with small, rural, low-income areas that have few options for employment. Without proper management, these areas become quickly overharvested, and a great deal of natural habitat is destroyed. This doesn't happen everywhere, but the extent of the damage is really not known.

The marine aquarium trade is a billion-dollar industry that has a vested interest in staying alive. That's why industry leaders, conservationists, and dealers from around the world got together in 1998 to form the Marine Aquarium Council (www.marineaquariumcouncil. org/). The primary goal of this important international body is to transform the marine industry into one that's based on quality and sustainability. If all goes according to plan, you'll be able to walk into your dealer and buy a piece of live rock or a fish and know that it was harvested properly and in a way that didn't impact the natural ecosystem.

But the Marine Aquarium Council is a little ways off from getting to this level of control. In the meantime, the best thing you can do to ensure that your aquarium isn't set up at the expense of a piece of nature is to buy from a reputable dealer. In the United States, you can find several member associations of the Marine Aquarium Council.

Focusing on the Background

I don't know about you, but if I didn't have a background on the back of my tank, my guests would see not only all my aquarium wiring and tubing but also the wall behind it (which needs painting very badly).

The aquarium background masks these poor views and also provides a pleasing backdrop to the beauty of your aquarium inhabitants. I've always felt that the ideal aquarium background is one that blends with the aquarium and becomes barely noticeable. The wrong background pulls attention away from your pets. I tend to lean toward a darker background because it highlights the colors in the tank.

Of course, if you're using your aquarium as a room divider or as part of a wall and want to view it from both sides, you wouldn't want to use a background. Check out your background options in the following sections.

Painting

The least complicated background that I've seen is a paint job. That's right, many aquarists paint the rear wall of their aquariums to give them a uniform appearance. Painting isn't a bad idea if you choose the right color, but these backgrounds are somewhat permanent and don't lend themselves to spontaneous change. I've seen black and dark blue painted backgrounds, and both can be pleasing to the eye. If you go this route, clean the glass thoroughly and simply roll on a thin layer of latex paint . . . before you set up the tank.

WARNING

It should go without saying that if you paint, paint the *outside* of the glass. Paint in aquarium water would be a chemical disaster for your critters.

Sticking on stick-ons

Other backgrounds used today are mounted, glued, or self-stuck to the back of the tank. Underwater scenes are the most common, but solid colors and artwork are available at every aquarium dealer. Most of these can be purchased precut or can be cut to fit your tank.

You can either use nonpermanent adhesive, tape, or special mounting tabs to affix one of these to the back of the tank or buy one that's self-sticking with static cling. I prefer any method that affords me the option of changing my tastes. Many of these backgrounds are waterproof material, like vinyl, and two-sided so that you can reverse them when you want a change of scenery.

Adding dioramas

The most elaborate background involves the construction of a *diorama* behind the tank, which is basically a box behind the tank that has natural aquarium decorations and lighting. It's an extension of the aquarium without water in it. This gives your aquarium a remarkable 3-D effect that looks very natural. Aquarium dioramas that you can insert into the tank are available, but they take up space, can trap fish, and need occasional cleaning.

Dioramas are usually custom built or result from do-it-yourself endeavors. For this reason, they tend to be more expensive than the average aquarium background.

Unraveling the Gravel

The best place to start when furnishing the inside of your aquarium is literally from the ground up. The "ground" in the aquarium is called the *substrate* and is generally composed of gravel or sand. Some hobbyists prefer not to use any substrate for fish-only tanks, but I don't subscribe to that method. There's substrate in the ocean, and I think it belongs in the aquarium.

Unlike the gravel in a freshwater aquarium, the gravel in the saltwater tank must be of a specific type. Just as you use calcareous decorations in your marine aquarium, which act to keep the alkalinity in the aquarium high, your gravel should do the same. Calcareous gravels have proven to be the most suitable substrate for the marine aquarium. The most common are coral gravel, aragonite, crushed shell, and oolite. They all contain calcium carbonate, which is thought to help buffer the seawater and maintain pH levels.

The substrate is far more important to the health of the saltwater aquarium than it is in a freshwater system. Not only does it provide some buffering of the water when pH is high, it also harbors important bacteria that provide biological filtration and it provides a home for burrowing critters and a variety of beneficial macro-organisms.

TIP

Before using your gravel or sand, rinse it in freshwater. If possible, do this outside where it's easier. Simply place the gravel in a bucket and run water into it, mixing the gravel with your hands. The water will be cloudy gray for a while and then gradually clear up. The gravel doesn't have to be spotless, but this rinsing removes a lot of the dust and dirt.

Aragonite is the most common saltwater aquarium substrate on the market. Aragonite is composed calcium carbonate, which is exactly what the skeleton of coral is made of. It comes in a variety of grain sizes ranging from coarse gravel to sand. It's named after the place where it was discovered: Aragon, Spain.

When choosing your bottom substrate, you should consider the use of live sand, grain size, and the depth of the substrate, which I discuss as follows:

It's alive!

A close relative of *live rock* (see the "Live rock" section in this chapter) is *live sand*. Of course, the sand isn't moving, but it's alive with literally millions of little critters, including helpful bacteria. Live sand is good to add to your saltwater aquarium because it brings important bacteria to the system. If you increase the depth of your sand to 4 inches or more, you're creating a *deep sand bed* (DSB), which provides additional biological filtration. Many aquarists rely heavily on the filtration provided by the DSB.

The DSB in an aquarium harbors two kinds of bacteria that provide biological filtration (see Chapter 12 for more information):

>> Those living in the top layers use oxygen to convert ammonia to nitrate using the nitrogen cycle.

>> The deeper layers lack oxygen and provide habitat for bacteria that convert nitrate to nitrogen gas, which is also important.

If you use sand as a substrate, be careful if you have an undergravel filter because the sand will probably clog your filter.

Grain size

The grain size of your substrate is important and depends on your choice of filtration. If you decide to filter your aquarium with a traditional undergravel filter (as I discuss in Chapter 7), your choice of gravel is critical. Remember, this substrate will also be working as your filter media, so it must be the right size. The name of the game is surface area, and gravel that's between ⅛ and ¼ inch has a lot of it. Grains that are any smaller will clog your filter, whereas grains much bigger will trap debris and also clog your filter.

If you don't have an undergravel filter, you can use finer gravel or sand. These finer substrates are great for invertebrate tanks and reef tanks because they allow these little critters to burrow, which actually helps keep the substrate clean. If you plan to establish a DSB for natural nitrate reduction, use very fine sand. Finally, if your substrate has nothing to do with your filtration, choose the grain size of gravel that you find the most aesthetically pleasing. Just realize that coarser grains won't accommodate burrowing and will also trap waste and need frequent cleaning.

Depth

Like grain size, how much gravel you use depends on whether or not your substrate is linked to your filtration. The general rule for undergravel filters is 1 to 2 inches of gravel. Some hobbyists use two sizes of gravel (fine gravel on top, of course) separated by a plastic mesh or *gravel tidy*. Using two may allow for filtration while minimizing the amount of substrate that can become clogged. The gravel tidy also protects the filter from burrowing tank inhabitants.

If your aquarium has DSB filtration, use a minimum of 4 to 6 inches of fine sand. However, the DSB can consume a lot of space in a short and wide aquarium. For example, 6 inches of sand chews up 25 percent of the space in an aquarium that is 24 inches tall. When planning your system, keep this in mind. A DSB is an effective biological filter and can be pleasing to the eye, but nobody wants to look at just sand in an aquarium! If your substrate isn't used for filtration, you don't need to build a thick layer of gravel. Instead, I find 1 to 2 inches is the most aesthetically pleasing and doesn't result in dead zones that can mess up your water chemistry. If you plan to house burrowing invertebrates and fish, go with 2 inches of substrate.

Determining how much gravel to buy depends, of course, on the size and shape of your aquarium. A good place to start is about 1 to 2 pounds per gallon, depending on whether or not you're using it for biological filtration.

Buy a bit of extra gravel so that when you aquascape your tank, you have sufficient amounts to sculpture the bottom and provide some contouring.

Getting Rocked

After you've done the groundwork, it's time to get creative. Your choices at this point depend on the kind of marine aquarium you're planning. For example, fish-only aquariums don't require live rock for filtration. Also, standard fish medications may kill the rock. Therefore, some fish-only aquariums typically have dead coral, tufa rock, or lava rock.

On the other hand, a reef tank, by definition, has live invertebrates, including live corals and live rocks. Of course, you can use other kinds of rocks, too. In fact, other rocks are typically usually used to build a foundation for the reef. You don't want to pile live rocks on top of live rocks if you're building a nice terrace. There are other rocks for that.

Some people think they can go outside, dig around, and find some rocks for the aquarium. Not true! Please don't do this. Depending on where you live, the rocks around your house may be high in metals and, therefore, dangerous for your pets. Plus, a chunk of granite isn't exactly what I call a natural-looking saltwater decoration, on earth, at least.

There are several rocky options for your saltwater aquarium and they are as follows:

Tufa

Tufa is a natural addition to your aquarium that's composed of calcium carbonate and is, therefore, good for your water chemistry. Tufa is calcareous rock that's soft, porous, and easy to mold. It's ideal for a fish-only or reef tank because you can shape it, and algae and invertebrates readily colonize it. It's lightweight and porous, so it doesn't displace a lot of water. Tufa is a nice addition to any tank and is typically a lot less expensive than live rock. Some hobbyists use tufa as a base for live rock.

Lava rock

This isn't real lava rock, and that's good because volcanic lava is high in metals and toxic to your aquarium. Instead, lava rock is an attractive man-made material that, like tufa, is light with low volume displacement; it too becomes readily colonized by algae, invertebrates, and other beneficial critters (like bacteria). Although it can be expensive, lava rock is easy to handle and stacks well if you decide to build a centerpiece or terrace.

Dry rock

The use of dry rock is a much cheaper alternative to live rock. *Dry rock* is a calcium-based, highly porous rock that is mined or collected for use in the aquarium. Like tufa and lava rock, dry rock will become colonized by bacteria, algae, and other beneficial critters, and eventually become live rock. You can even purchase dry rock with bacteria that will activate when added to your aquarium, giving it a bit of a head start. In addition, you don't need to deal with the extensive curing process with dry rock, and you don't run the risk of adding the pests to your aquarium that can hitchhike on live rock. To save money, some hobbyists start with a combination of live and dry rock in their aquarium. Eventually, the former will help to populate the latter.

Live rock

I'm not talking about a rock 'n' roll concert in your tank. Live rock really isn't the best name for this type of rock because it's not actually alive. Live rock does, however, provide a home for all kinds of small living sea life, from bacteria to starfish. So it could be called "rock with living things on it," but that would be tough to market.

Live rock has now become a standard decoration in almost every saltwater aquarium because it's not only pleasing to the eye, it's also a natural biological filter that aquarists use as their primary means of keeping their aquarium healthy. I discuss the use of live rock as a filter in Chapter 7. By keeping live rock, you kill two birds with one rock by providing natural decor and excellent filtration.

TECHNICAL STUFF

Live rock is coral rubble or reef rock that's carpeted with living material. It's either collected from wild areas in the Indo-Pacific or cultivated in Florida or other areas. In the United States, it's illegal to harvest live rock from U.S. waters, but it can be cultured.

I recommend the use of cultured live rock because it's less damaging to natural reef systems. This rock is limestone that is mined, gathered, or manufactured from land materials and placed in the ocean for months to years so it becomes encrusted with life.

Understanding what is alive in live rock

A lot of people, including me, talk about live rock and say "Oh, it's covered with a lot of critters." What does that mean? Although I discuss invertebrates and algae in more detail in Chapters 4 and 14, here's a small list of the kinds of life that can be found on live rock:

>> Bacteria

>> Barnacles

>> Bryozoans

>> Clams

>> Corals

- Crabs
- Many kinds of algae
- Sea squirts
- Shrimps
- Snails
- Sponges
- Starfish
- Worms

Although most of these critters are great for the tank, some, such as mantis shrimp and bristleworms, can be a problem.

Contemplating the quality of live rock: Fancy or just the base-ics

Live rock is sold in a few different forms based on its quality:

- **Fancy rock:** Decorative live rock is the expensive stuff. This is the live rock that has the most life (critters) on it. Depending on who is marketing it, higher quality live rock may be called *fancy rock, decorator rock, algae rock, premium rock, reef rock,* or just simply live rock.

- **Base rock:** Less expensive live rock is often referred to as *base rock* and as the name implies, it's used as the foundation or bottom layer of the mini-reef in your aquarium. Base rock looks pretty barren, but it's less expensive and has a lot of helpful bacteria.

Considering the two options: Cured and uncured

You can purchase live rock that's either *cured* or *uncured,* and the definition of this sometimes depends on the source. When live rock is harvested from the wild or from a cultivator, it's handled many times and in many ways before it gets to you. During this process, some of the life on the rock is going to die, and this simply can't be avoided. When a piece of live rock is cured, it's held in a facility at some point until dead and dying critters are cleared away by natural and man-made processes, and life on the rock has stabilized. Uncured live rock is harvested and shipped without this process.

Many live rock dealers sell both cured and uncured products, but the extent to which the live rock is cured differs among dealers. For example, some claim to cure the rock for six weeks in a holding pen, whereas others do so with salt spray. All claim to have the best method for removing dead or harmful critters.

TIP

My recommendations are as follows:

» Live rock that has been cured at your local trustworthy dealer for several weeks is best.

» If you're going to have cured live rock shipped to you directly by a dealer, don't add it to an established aquarium without curing it again in a separate tank (see the following section for details).

» If you just set up your aquarium for the first time, add cured live rock from the dealer and essentially cure it again in your aquarium.

» Live rock should only be added a little at a time, no more than 10 pounds at a time. The amount of live rock should not exceed 1 to 1.5 pounds per gallon, so that the aquarium isn't overwhelmed.

Curing the live rock yourself

If you didn't buy live rock from a local dealer that had time to cure it, you're going to have to cure it yourself. Some people call this *cycling* or *seeding* the live rock. I recommend that you do your curing in a tank separate from your main display aquarium. Many aquarists have another isolation or quarantine tank for dealing with isolating new fish and invertebrates, treating animals that are sick, and curing live rock. This process doesn't need to be a complicated setup, but the separate tank should have basic filtration, a protein skimmer, and some lighting. If you're establishing your main aquarium for the first time, new live rock can be cured right in the main aquarium before adding fish and other invertebrates. In this case, the curing process can actually jump-start the biological filtration in your tank.

As with most topics in the ever-changing aquarium hobby, how to cure your live rock is a matter of debate. The traditional method involves these steps:

1. **Remove dead critters with a small brush.**

2. **Isolate the rock for two to four weeks in a separate tank with no lighting.**

3. **Monitor the water chemistry.**

4. **Aerate the water.**

5. **Frequently clean the protein skimmer.**

This traditional method may allow dead organisms to cycle through the tank, but the conditions stress the living organisms.

Keeping Coral

By far, the most popular decoration for a tropical marine aquarium is coral and artificial coral replicas. These structures give the aquarium a natural look and provide excellent shelter for tank inhabitants and ideal substrate for algae (see Chapter 14). Real coral and other calcareous objects like shells also provide the added benefit of buffering the water for pH maintenance (see Chapter 13).

TECHNICAL STUFF

Coral is an animal with a calcium carbonate skeleton that lives in a colony of millions, forming large reefs. In a natural coral reef ecosystem, the outermost layer of the reef is the living coral colony. As the reef grows, layers are added extremely slowly, taking hundreds of years to establish. Because of this, efforts must be made to protect coral reef systems, and live reefs shouldn't be harvested without care and concern for nature.

Coral comes in a variety of forms, which are as follows:

Dead heads

The skeletal remains of coral are ideal for both fish-only and reef aquariums. They can be purchased at many aquarium dealers or collected at the shore of many tropical areas. Dead coral collected at the shore is perfectly suitable for the aquarium after it has been properly cleaned.

TIP

I recommend that you boil all dead coral regardless of where you get it before putting it in your aquarium. Doing so removes dead tissue, detritus, and organisms that might be harmful to your aquarium.

Most coral that you purchase will be bleached white. In a natural setting and in a well-balanced aquarium, this color won't last. Colonization by algae will add green and brown to the coral, diminishing its sterile look. Although some beginners find this "dirty" look unappealing, be assured that it's more natural looking (see Chapter 14 for more about algae). In fact, coral that's bleached white in the wild is unhealthy and should be avoided.

TIP

WARNING

I recommend boiling to remove the occasional algae if the algae's growth becomes excessive and unsightly.

Be sure to check with federal and state regulations regarding the collection of any kind of coral, whether live or dead.

Artificial

One of the alternatives to dead coral is artificial coral replicas. They're becoming increasingly popular and readily available as coral reef protection is increasing worldwide. These natural-looking synthetics are safe for the aquarium, come in a variety of colors, and provide the same benefits as real coral with the exception of water buffering.

Many large commercial aquariums utilize artificial corals to mimic the natural reef ecosystem. After the coral is overgrown with algae, the artificial coral is virtually indistinguishable from the real thing. Most importantly, fish can't tell the difference. The coral replica is clearly the best choice for the environment.

Some say that replica coral fixtures are expensive. When you compare them to both live and dead coral, you'll find that they actually cost less. Besides, coral replicas can't die.

Live coral

You've likely seen beautiful photos of saltwater aquariums teeming with life including live coral. These are reef tanks, and live corals are very common aquarium inhabitants that act as both pets and decorations. Because live coral is an invertebrate, I discuss it extensively in Chapter 4.

Adding Invertebrates

Many other invertebrate species act as natural decorations for a reef aquarium. Like coral, they're pets and furnishings at the same time. Clams, sponges, anemones, and sea cucumbers are just a few examples of invertebrates that add a lot of beauty to a reef aquarium. I talk more about these animals in Chapter 4 because they're more like pets than decorations.

Shells are popular natural additions to the saltwater aquarium. Be sure to boil shells before using them in your tank, however. Sea fans and sea whips provide plant-like decoration to the aquarium, but they must be soaked to expose the black skeleton before use.

Providing Plants

Although real plants are common in the freshwater aquarium, they're somewhat rare in saltwater tanks primarily because, with few exceptions, most of the ocean's plant life can be classified in the primitive group known as *algae*. The term *seaweed* actually refers to the many-celled forms of algae called *macroalgae*. Macroalgae are common in reef tanks and generally come with live rock. In a fish-only tank, macroalgae are consumed by the fish and may not last long. I discuss algae in more detail in Chapter 14.

Plastic and silk seaweed replicas are available, and some marine hobbyists like their plant-like appearance. Many of these fixtures are realistic and attractive. They have the added advantage of not being something that can die and cause water quality problems in the tank.

Offering Ornaments

Aquarium dealers sell a variety of tank decorations that can enhance your aquarium. Many come in the form of plastic, ceramic, or resin creations. By purchasing these tank decorations from the dealer, you're buying a product made for the aquarium, thereby avoiding the potential of adding toxic substances to your tank. Castles, mermaids, divers, and shipwrecks are common shapes that you or your child may want to add to the aquarium. Air can be pumped to some of these fixtures, producing interesting effects and providing aeration. My nephew Clayton has a sunken battleship in his aquarium. Not for me, but I'm not 4.

Making Sure You Add Saltwater

You can't do much with your aquarium if you don't have saltwater. I don't know about you, but if I turn on my faucet I get freshwater. And I don't need to remind you that this isn't a freshwater aquarium book. Hence, you need to get some saltwater, but what exactly is it? Can you grab a bucket of water and add table salt? No! You basically have the two following options when adding saltwater for your aquarium.

Natural seawater — Don't do it

The chemical composition of seawater is extremely consistent throughout the world. Although it's 96 percent pure water (one atom of oxygen bonded with two atoms of hydrogen: H_2O), it also contains many dissolved minerals and salts. These are mainly sodium and chlorine (85 percent of them), but magnesium, sulphate, calcium, and potassium make up another 13 percent, and bicarbonate and 68 other elements make up the remainder in *trace quantities* (really small amounts).

You need to mimic natural seawater in the aquarium as closely as possible. The best way to do this is to buy a synthetic salt mixture at your dealer.

WARNING

The natural inclination for any beginner is to try to obtain natural seawater from the local seashore. However, I strongly recommend that you don't do this unless you live very close to clean tropical seawater. I say this because:

» If you don't live in the tropics and intend to maintain a tropical aquarium, your local seawater will be colder. The colder water will contain species of plankton (small critters) that are adapted to these temperatures. Elevating the temperature to tropical levels will cause these organisms to die or rapidly proliferate, yielding polluted or poor quality water.

» The logistics of moving large quantities of seawater from the seashore is impractical and will probably break your back. Oh, you may say, "I won't have to do it often." Not true. Aquarium maintenance requires a steady supply of saltwater. It would probably be easier to run a pipe from the beach.

» You have no guarantee that your water source is free of pollutants. Seemingly clean seawater may contain high levels of toxic compounds and metals. Even if you live in a pristine coastal area, the quality of the water can change with the tide, and natural toxins can also be a problem. Why take any chances?

Artificial seawater — Your best bet

The science of marine chemistry has produced sea salt mixes that mimic the marine environment without the potential toxins. These mixes are dissolved in ordinary tap water when you set up the aquarium. Although most of these mixes are similar, you want to be sure that they are nitrate- and phosphate-free. Not all are created equal, so talk to your dealer. In addition, some manufacturers claim that their mixes will help detoxify tap water or add essential vitamins and minerals, which is always an added bonus.

TIP

You can purchase premixed aquarium saltwater online or from your dealer. Doing so is more expensive, but you'll have peace of mind because the water will be well-balanced and free of impurities.

Sea salt mixes are sold in a variety of sizes relative to the volume of saltwater that they can produce. Be aware that the actual volume of water in the tank will be less than the tank volume because of gravel, aquarium equipment, and ornamentation. So a 50-gallon mix will work for a 55-gallon aquarium because the actual volume of the tank is less. However, it doesn't hurt to have extra salt around for water changes.

Although the simplest technique is to add the salt directly to the aquarium after you fill it up, premixing your water in a separate container is better; most aquarists use 5-gallon bucket. Adding salt directly to a full aquarium makes it difficult to reach the correct salt-to-water ratio and can easily result in oversalting.

REMEMBER

When premixing your saltwater in a bucket, follow the instructions on the package. Although the most common mix is half a cup of salt to 1 gallon of freshwater, every brand isn't the same. I can't tell you how much salt to add per gallon — only the people who make it can. Read the package carefully.

Whether you add the correct quantity of salt to the freshwater or vice versa doesn't really matter as long as you mix it thoroughly. To make sure all the salt dissolves at the correct temperature, I like to add a submersible heater and a powerhead to the bucket while it sits overnight. Doing so may sound like overkill, but this technique results in water that is ready for your aquarium.

REMEMBER

Make sure you monitor the salinity during the entire process (see "Testing Your Water Chemistry" section later in this chapter). The ideal specific gravity for a reef aquarium is 1.025. You may need to tweak the mix by adding either saltwater or freshwater to the bucket to reach this value.

Always mix up additional, properly balanced saltwater for water changes and emergencies. Also, for smaller quantities of saltwater, many local dealers offer premixed saltwater, so you can save the hassle of mixing your own. Store additional batches of seawater in food-grade, nonmetallic containers in cool, dark places until needed.

Conditioning tap water

To make salt water, you're going to need freshwater. Now, I hate to tell you this, but the water out of your tap isn't pure water. In most places, the local water company chemically treats the water for health reasons. The typical treatment includes chlorine or chloramine, which can be toxic at levels much higher than found in natural seawater. In addition, tap water can contain nitrates, sulphates, phosphates, and heavy metals, which are also harmful to fish and invertebrates.

Call your local water company and ask how the water is treated and what the concentrations of these substances are because most companies routinely test their water.

In an ideal world, you'd start with purified freshwater for your aquarium. A number of water-purification units are available to the aquarist for the removal of impurities from tap water. These *reverse osmosis* (RO) and *deionization* (DO) units attach to your faucet and remove substances like nitrates, phosphates, toxins, heavy metals, and chlorine. They can be expensive, but if your water supply is known to have high levels of these toxins, you need to buy one. When you consider the total cost of your aquarium, including equipment and animals, why take chances? Even though you may be tempted to just use a smaller home-filter system, like a refrigerator or pitcher filter, those types of filters will only remove low levels of toxins from tap water and may not be as efficient as a good RO/DO unit.

Water straight from your tap can be fine for use with a fish-only saltwater aquarium, but you still need to *condition* your tap water. You can condition it in a couple of ways:

» One of the easiest methods for removing chlorine and chloramines is to let the water sit for 48 hours and let these chemicals percolate out. However, this won't do much to remove high levels of heavy metals or other compounds.

» The more efficient way to condition your tap water is to purchase a chemical water conditioner and dechlorinator. Your dealer will offer a variety of water conditioners and, if she is local, will probably know the best one for the water in your area. These conditioners can be added to your water to remove chlorine, chloramine, and heavy metals.

Adding reef supplements

While you're in the chemical section of your aquarium dealer, you'll probably want to pick up a couple of other supplements if you plan on having a reef tank. They're generally referred to as *reef supplements* and include important elements like iodine and calcium. These supplements are essential elements for your invertebrates that can be added to your aquarium water.

Also buy a solution of calcium hydroxide, commonly referred to as *kalkwasser*, which is German for *lime water*. This product helps maintain calcium levels in your reef tank. I discuss this in more detail in Chapter 13. Fish-only tanks don't require these kinds of supplements.

If you're really in the mood to spend money, you can also buy a dosing pump for dispensing reef supplements into the aquarium. This unit adds supplements accurately and automatically, without human error. These can be as simple as one that works with gravity like a hospital intravenous unit or one that has a built-in pump, which is much more expensive.

Testing Your Water Chemistry

As part of the proper care and maintenance of your aquarium, you have to routinely test the water chemistry. Believe me, this sounds a lot worse than it is. If your water passes the exams, your fish and invertebrates will be healthy. If not, you're going to have to make some corrections. If this a bit confusing, don't worry, because in Chapters 12 and 13 it all becomes much clearer. But because you're putting together the equipment for your aquarium, now is the time to buy all the essentials, which includes testing equipment.

Salt level

Have you ever been swimming in the ocean, tasted saltwater, and wondered how much salt is in the sea? Well, science has developed a couple of ways to measure the amount of dissolved salts in seawater. One measure is called *salinity* and another is called *specific gravity.* Although these measurements aren't the same, either can be used to determine the correct level of salt in your aquarium. In Chapter 13, I discuss these terms in greater detail.

For now, you need to make sure you have just the right amount of salt in your aquarium. To do this, you're going to measure the specific gravity with a *hydrometer* that measures specific gravity or a *refractometer*, which measures salinity.

Hydrometer

There are basically two kinds of inexpensive hydrometers on the market: floater and swinger.

» **Floater:** The traditional floating hydrometer looks like a large floating thermometer and sometimes may actually have one inside it. It consists of a long-necked tube with a scale inside. The level at which the tube floats depends on how much salt is in the water. You read the scale at the point where the water's surface meets the hydrometer and, bingo, the specific gravity. However, water movement makes the floating hydrometer difficult to read accurately.

» **Swinger:** The swing-needle hydrometer is easier to read (see Figure 9-1). This is basically a small plastic box with a needle in it that pivots when the box is filled with aquarium water. When the needle settles, it points to a scale that tells you the specific gravity and salinity. This hydrometer is also known as a pointer hydrometer or floating-needle hydrometer.

FIGURE 9-1: A swing-needle hydrometer is the most commonly used model.

© *John Wiley & Sons, Inc.*

Refractometer

Once considered too expensive for the average aquarist, a refractometer is now a reasonably priced instrument that measures salt level with greater accuracy than a hydrometer. The heart of the refractometer is a prism, which bends light based on the amount salt in your water. You simply place a few drops of your aquarium water on the prism, look through it, and read the salinity and specific gravity.

Specific gravity should be in the range of 1.021–1.025 and salinity in the range of 33–35 ppt. More importantly, salt levels should be maintained as constant as possible within this range. Even minor fluctuations can cause problems for your tank inhabitants.

REMEMBER

Water chemistry test kits

You're going to have to closely monitor the water chemistry of your aquarium in order to maintain a healthy home for your pets. Sorry, there is no way around it. The number of tests you conduct depends on whether you have a reef tank or a fish-only tank (see Chapter 1). The latter isn't as complicated, and its inhabitants really don't care about the levels of certain elements.

Throughout the rest of this section, I give you a simple shopping list of the test kits I think you should buy, depending on the kind of aquarium you set up. You may see some terms that don't make a lot of sense to you, but don't worry about that. Chapters 12 and 13 go into great detail about water chemistry, and you'll be brought right up to speed in no time.

The following test kits are the ones you need to set up and maintain your aquarium:

>> pH

>> Ammonia

>> Nitrite

>> Nitrate

These four tests will tell you how well your biological filtration is working. Other tests include alkalinity, calcium, copper, phosphate, dissolved oxygen, iodine, and a number of others that are now common in this hobby.

Use Table 9-1 as a general guide for purchasing test kits. As your tank becomes more complicated, you can always add to your test kit collection.

TIP

TABLE 9-1

Test Kits for Your New Aquarium

Test Kit	Fish-Only Tank	Reef Tank
pH	Yes	Yes
Ammonia	Yes	Yes
Nitrite	Yes	Yes
Nitrate	Yes	Yes
Alkalinity	Yes	Yes
Dissolved oxygen	Optional	Optional
Copper	Optional	No
Phosphate	Optional	Yes
Calcium	No	Yes

Because test kits are used to tell you the quantities of various substances in your aquarium, how much testing you do depends on how much you need to know. The more you test, the more you know — and the more you can monitor the quality of your aquarium environment and make corrections. Newer aquarists have a tendency to test the water more frequently than seasoned veterans, and there's nothing wrong with that.

Test kits are made so that you don't have to be a chemist to use them. Although a couple of methods have been developed, the most common involves adding drops of a test chemical to an aquarium sample that changes the color of the water. You then match the water color with that on a color chart, which tells you the correct level of what you're testing.

REMEMBER

Be sure to follow the instructions that come with the test kit so that you get accurate results.

Test probes

As the world becomes more and more electronically oriented, aquarium-testing monitors become more widespread and less expensive. In addition to the salinity and specific gravity meters, there are also pH and dissolved oxygen probes available. These provide fast, reliable, and accurate measurements without test chemicals, but they're much more expensive than the average test kit.

Understanding the Purpose of a Quarantine Tank

The *quarantine tank* is really just another small aquarium that you use to isolate a fish or an invertebrate. That's why it's also called an *isolation tank,* but I think that sounds too lonely.

A quarantine tank is a piece of equipment that you use to isolate new fish and new invertebrates to make sure that they're healthy before putting them into your well-established aquarium (see Chapter 5). More importantly, a quarantine tank can also be used to isolate diseased fish for treatment (see Chapter 18). This is particularly true for reef tanks because you can't treat fish with invertebrates.

A quarantine tank is a straightforward setup that includes a small tank with simple filtration, a heater, and minimal ornamentation. So, a 10- to 20-gallon tank with a sponge or box filter, a clamp-on heater, and a couple of ornaments plastic plants will do the trick.

TIP

Frankly, the quarantine tank is a nice idea, but if your budget is limited, you can delay the purchase of this setup until your main aquarium is fully established. You can also purchase fish from some suppliers that have already gone through quarantine.

Handling Your Wet Pets with Nets

All aquariums should be well-equipped to handle fish and other tank occupants, which means that you definitely need a fishnet or two — see Figure 9-2. You'll likely use a net more than you think. A net comes in handy when you need to remove a fish that is ill or dead, one that's too aggressive, or one that you simply want to get rid of.

Aquarium nets come in a variety of shapes and sizes. Here is what you need to know:

Size

Nets for the aquarium come in variety of sizes, from a couple of inches across to 10 inches wide. Too small a net will be difficult to use to corner a fish, and too large a net will be difficult to maneuver in the tank. Match the size of the net with the size of the fish and the size of the tank. Trying to catch a 6-inch fish in a 55-gallon tank with a 4-inch net is pretty entertaining to watch.

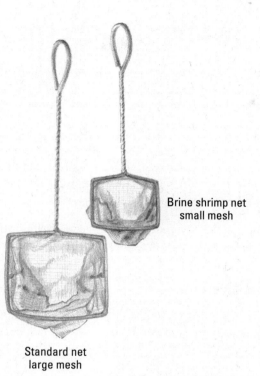

FIGURE 9-2:
Nets for the
aquarium are a
must.

Brine shrimp net
small mesh

Standard net
large mesh

Meshing around

The netting itself is called the *mesh*, and it can be either fine or coarse. Fine mesh tends to be softer and less abrasive to the fish, but it moves slower in the water. On the other hand, coarse mesh may scrape the fish, but you'll probably catch it faster. You have to strike the right balance. The more you chase your fish around the tank, the more stressed it becomes, and the more you disrupt the aquarium and its other inhabitants. So, I tend to buy a larger net with mesh that allows me to move the net quickly and effectively through the water to bag the fish.

REMEMBER

Consider keeping a couple of sizes handy. For example, a fish that's ill probably isn't moving much and needs to be handled with care, so a fine-meshed soft net is best for this critter. But that irascible wrasse that has been terrorizing the tank needs to be removed quickly, and a coarse-meshed fast net will do it with minimal disturbance. Face it, a healthy fish doesn't want to be caught. Just ask my brother Paul, the fisherman.

Identifying the Cleaning Tools You Need

As you develop your talents as an aquarist, you're going to accumulate many accessories for your tank that make your job easier and help you to maintain a well-balanced aquarium. This section shares a few items that will give you a head start.

WARNING

When I talk about cleaning your aquarium, it doesn't in any way, shape, or form mean that you use any kind of soap. Household detergents leave residues that are toxic to your pets. Glass cleaners are fine for the outside of the tank, but make sure that you apply them to a cloth without spraying the tank. Spray goes everywhere, including inside the tank, which means bye-bye fishy.

You can purchase special nontoxic chemical cleaners for your aquarium. These include disinfectants, fungicides, and sanitizers that leave no residue.

A good bucket

You may laugh at this, but I think one of the most important pieces of standard aquarium equipment is the common bucket. I really don't need to fully explain why because you're going to find out soon enough.

Right from the get-go, you should have at least one (or many) bucket(s) committed to your aquarium, and only to your aquarium. Going into the cabinet under the sink or into the broom closet for a bucket isn't a good idea because you know what those buckets are used for: cleaning the house. And what did I just say about soaps and detergents?

You use a bucket to fill your tank, hold tank inhabitants, empty your tank, hold aquarium fixtures and decorations, mix new water, transport new water, transport old water, hold aquarium equipment, sit on, store conditioned water, and on and on. Go for a bucket that is considered food safe and holds at least 5 gallons.

TIP

Write in big letters on the side: FOR AQUARIUM USE ONLY or MY AQUARIUM or whatever, but mark it in some way to keep your brother Bernie from changing his car's oil with it.

Substrate sucking

Part of your maintenance routine includes cleaning the gravel, particularly if it's coarse. This doesn't mean scooping it out of the tank and washing it — no way. In the old days, I used to use just a short piece of hose to suck the debris off the surface of the gravel. Now, the much simpler way involves the use of a gravel vacuum (shown in Figure 9-3), which lets you get into the gravel to clean it.

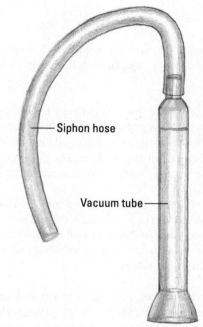

Siphon hose

Vacuum tube

FIGURE 9-3:
A typical gravel
vacuum is
required to keep
the gravel free of
debris.

© John Wiley & Sons, Inc.

Gravel vacuums remove the debris that accumulates in the gravel, clogs your undergravel filter (if you have one), and causes water-chemistry problems. Most gravel cleaning is done during water changes, which is a great time because gravel vacuums are designed to remove water and debris at the same time. A number of models are available, from pump-, siphon-, or battery-powered to those that connect directly to the faucet for bucket-free cleaning.

REMEMBER

Be aware that topping off evaporated water is different from changing the water. Adding freshwater when topping the tank off is okay, but you don't want to add freshwater to an established aquarium during partial water changes; doing so messes up your salinity. Instead, add premixed saltwater of the same salinity. So, gravel vacuums that remove water, clean the gravel, and refill the aquarium are fine as long as they don't add water directly from the faucet.

TIP

In addition to your gravel vacuum, keep a short piece of hose available. It will come in handy for the occasional siphon job.

Algae scrubber

Algae will grow in your aquarium and on your aquarium. If it gets out of hand, you won't be able to see your fish. Hence, the algae scrubber is an essential piece of equipment.

A variety of algae styles are available, but the concept is pretty straightforward: Rub the algae off the glass. Aquarium pads, scrapers, scrubbers, and mitts are all available to do the job. I tend to favor the scrubbing pad on a stick with a head that angles so you can apply pressure to stubborn areas. The pads are usually made for acrylic or glass tanks because you don't want one that will scratch.

Some folks prefer to place their hands in the tank and use scrubbing pads or mitts. This is fine as long as you don't disturb your tank inhabitants too much. Every time you go into the tank, your pets are going to be disturbed, and any way you can minimize that, the better. A big hand with a scrubbing mitt in a small aquarium may drive the fish into hiding for days.

TIP

If you want to be completely hands-off, use one of those magnet setups that has a scrubbing pad on a magnet inside the tank held by a magnet outside the tank. Moving the magnet on the outside moves the magnet on the inside and cleans the glass. However, they don't clean stubborn and tight areas very well.

Odds and ends

Tongs and grabbers let you work in your aquarium without having to place your whole hand and arm in the tank. Using one minimizes disturbances to your fish and invertebrates. Suppose you want to adjust the placement of a fixture or your nephew Gregory dropped your car keys in the tank. Grab the tongs and take care of it without having to go swimming.

Another handy item is a tube brush. It keeps aquarium intake and output tubing clear and free of algae. The brush is round in diameter and flexible so it inserts into the tube. Standard scrubbers and brushes simply don't do the job. You do, however, have to size the brush to the tube, but that's no big deal.

Chapter **10**

Partial to Salt — The Brackish Aquarium

Many folks think that there are only two options when it comes to aquariums — saltwater or freshwater — but this isn't the case. Another option you have is the *brackish* water aquarium, which is really just a freshwater aquarium with some salt or, if you prefer, a saltwater aquarium with less salt. It's somewhere in between the two — a gray area, if you will.

The brackish water aquarium is a unique environment that tends to be more like a freshwater aquarium than a saltwater aquarium. The critters that thrive in a brackish water aquarium are equally unique, as are the special kinds of live plants that thrive in this ecosystem. If you like the saltwater aquarium look, yet want the hardiness and feel of the freshwater world, then the brackish water aquarium may be the right choice for you. The purpose of this chapter is to introduce you to the brackish water aquarium and its unique characteristics. Perhaps the color gray is right for you.

Taking a Closer Look at the Brackish Water Environment

Ponds and rivers are typically what come to mind when you think of freshwater environments and the fishes that live in them. On the other hand, typical saltwater habitats include the Atlantic, Pacific, and Indian Oceans and unique ecosystems like coral reefs. Because all freshwater rivers ultimately flow into the saltwater ocean, there are places where these two worlds collide. Freshwater mixes with saltwater to form brackish water, and these areas create special habitats for all kinds of animals. Typical brackish water environments include river mouths, such as where the Mississippi meets the Gulf of Mexico, and bays, like where the Potomac River meets Chesapeake Bay.

REMEMBER

An area where saltwater and freshwater collide is typically called an *estuary*. Delaware Bay is a good example of a large estuary. These areas are among the most productive in the world. Some species of fish spend their entire lives in *estuarine* areas, and a remarkable number of fishes spend at least some part of their lives in an estuary.

Brackish water environments tend to be dynamic areas that are not only influenced by freshwater flow, but also by rising and falling tides. Hence, the mix of saltwater and freshwater is always changing. The fishes and invertebrates that live in brackish water are well adapted to rapid changes in salinity and tend to be hardier than fish that live exclusively in saltwater.

Identifying the Equipment You Need (or Don't Need)

The ever-changing environment of the estuary need not be re-created in your aquarium if you choose to set up a brackish water environment. However, you do want to mimic the basic conditions of an estuary and may even want to keep brackish water plants.

In Chapters 6 through 9, I discuss the equipment that you need to set up a healthy marine aquarium. Because the brackish water aquarium is more similar to a freshwater aquarium, your equipment is going to more closely mimic that of a freshwater setup. For more information that I provide here, you can check out the newest edition of *Freshwater Aquariums For Dummies* by Madaleine Francis Heleine (John Wiley & Sons, Inc.).

Tank

Although I recommend that the minimum size of a saltwater aquarium is 30 gallons (see Chapter 6), this isn't the case for the brackish water aquarium, which can be as small as 10 gallons. However, many of the brackish water fishes are highly active, schooling critters that need a lot of space — keep this in mind when choosing a tank. Other than this, the brackish water aquarium differs little from the saltwater setup in terms of tank type (either glass or acrylic), tank stand, and canopy.

Filter

Although biological filtration is important for any kind of aquarium setup, advanced filtration, such as a trickle filter, isn't needed for the brackish water aquarium. Live rock won't survive in the fresh-ish water of the aquarium, and the undergravel filter won't work with the sandy substrate. Instead, the best filter systems for the brackish water aquarium include power filters that hang on the side of the tank and canister filters. Both these filter types provide adequate mechanical, chemical, and biological filtration. I suggest you read Chapter 7 for specific information on these filters.

REMEMBER

Although a protein skimmer is essential for the average saltwater aquarium, it isn't required for the brackish water setup. However, it certainly doesn't hurt.

Light and heat

Lighting and heating is standard for the brackish water aquarium (see Chapter 8). However, the shorelines of many brackish water areas are shaded by plant life like mangrove trees. Therefore, many brackish water aquarists prefer to have low to medium lighting or a shaded area of the aquarium. This shouldn't be the case if you plan to keep brackish water plants, because they need adequate lighting for optimal growth. In this case, the plants will provide shaded areas for your fishes.

Other ingredients

Most of the items that an average saltwater aquarium needs, such as a hydrometer to measure salt levels, water test kits, nets, and cleaning tools, are equally as handy for the brackish water aquarium. (Refer to Chapter 9.) However, there are few exceptions, which the following sections discuss.

Substrate

Although I thoroughly recommend calcium-based gravels for the saltwater aquarium, sand is the most natural substrate for the brackish aquarium. That's because most brackish environments have bottoms composed of mud and sand, which is ideal for plants. If you plan on keeping plants, I recommend a sand layer of about 1 inch with soil mixed into the lower layer. Otherwise, keep your substrate layer very thin so as to avoid the development of *anoxic* zones, that is, areas without oxygen.

Salt

The brackish water habitat is largely freshwater mixed with some saltwater. So, you'll need to have some salt on hand to make your aquarium a wee bit salty. Although I've seen some folks use table salt to do this, I strongly recommend the use of an artificial seawater salt mixture that is available at all saltwater aquarium dealers (see Chapter 9).

WARNING

If you're setting up a saltwater aquarium, you follow the directions on the package and the steps in Chapter 11 to properly balance the correct salt level (specific gravity or salinity) in your aquarium. However, the brackish water aquarium doesn't contain full-strength seawater. So, (I don't write this too often) don't follow the directions on the package when you add salt to your brackish water aquarium.

For this discussion, the level of salt in your aquarium is called its *specific gravity*, which is the ratio of densities of seawater to pure water at various temperatures. You use a hydrometer to measure specific gravity in your aquarium (see Chapter 9).

In the standard saltwater aquarium, specific gravity should be established in the range of 1.021 to 1.025. However, the level of salt in the brackish water aquarium should be much lower and largely depends on the salt preferences of your brackish water fish. In general, most of the brackish water fishes highlighted later in this chapter prefer brackish water with a specific gravity of 1.005 to 1.010.

TIP

When setting up your brackish water aquarium, follow the steps in Chapter 11, but reduce the amount of salt that you add to the tank to establish the correct salt level. A good estimate to begin with is 1 to 2 tablespoons of marine salt per gallon. Allow the salt to fully dissolve over 24 hours, and then fine-tune the specific gravity as needed.

Going Fishing for the Brackish Water Aquarium

The critters that inhabit the brackish water environment tend to be hardier and easier to keep because they're well-adapted to an ever-changing, dynamic world. For this reason, you don't have to be an aquarium expert or a seasoned veteran to house many of the common brackish water fishes. In addition, many of the fishes from brackish water readily live happily in full marine or full freshwater aquariums, should you decide to go in either of these directions.

In the following sections, I list the most common of the brackish water fishes available if you have a brackish water interest. This is by no means the most comprehensive list of all the species available, but includes those you're most likely to encounter at your local dealer.

Mollies (Poeciliidae)

Anyone who has kept a freshwater aquarium is well aware of mollies because they're the most common live-bearing fish sold in the aquarium trade. However, few folks know that mollies are also ideal brackish water fishes. This family includes more than 340 species.

The sailfin molly (*Poecilia latipinna*) is available in many varieties and color patterns, but the most common are silver green. Mollies spawn readily in captivity, and the conscientious aquarist can raise high-quality fry by paying attention to water quality. Mollies eat a variety of aquarium foods, but take care to include vegetable matter. These smaller fish only get to be about 5 inches and ideal for smaller brackish water aquariums.

Monos (Monodactylidae)

Sometimes called *mooneyfishes* or *fingerfishes,* the monos look very similar to and are often confused with common freshwater angelfishes. In the wild, these fish form large schools at the mouths of rivers, so you should consider keeping more than one in your aquarium.

The Mono or Malayan angel (*Monodactylus argenteus*) has a silver body with black and yellow fins. Juveniles are found in fresh and brackish water, but they move into saltwater as they get older. For this reason, large monos (longer than 3 inches) need an aquarium with more salt in the water and are best kept in a marine aquarium. Monos readily accept all kinds of aquarium foods, including fresh seafood and flakes. A similar species is the sebae mono (*Monodactylus sebae*). These fish are omnivorous and grow to about 10 inches.

Scats (Scatophagidae)

Members of the scat family only comprise four species from the Indo-Pacific. In the wild, these fishes inhabit harbors, bays, estuaries, the lower reaches of fresh-water streams, and mangroves.

The scat (*Scatophagus argus*) is a good species for the community brackish water aquarium. They're available in a large number of varieties with differing colors and patterns, ranging from brown to green and from spots to vertical stripes. Scats are best kept in schools of several fish. They're hardy fish that will readily accept a diverse array of aquarium foods and particularly like plant material. This latter attribute makes them poor additions to heavily planted brackish water aquariums. They grow to about 12 inches and require a large tank of at least 100 gallons.

Archerfishes (Toxotidae)

The archerfishes are so named because they spit a stream of water to knock down insects, which are their preferred food. Archers can be trained to spit in captivity by leaving a large space of 4 to 6 inches above the waterline and placing food items on the glass in this space.

The common or banded archerfish (*Toxotes jaculatrix*) is a deep-bodied fish with vertical black bands that needs a larger tank because of its large size. This fish is best kept singly because it can be aggressive to its own kind. Although archerfish are carnivorous and prefer live foods like insects, they'll accept fresh seafood, such as shrimp. They grow to about 10 inches.

Puffers (Tetraodontidae)

In Chapter 3, I discuss some of the pufferfishes available to the marine aquarist, but this diverse family also contains members that live in fresh and brackish water habitats.

Like most puffers, the green spotted puffer (*Dichotomyctere nigroviridis*) should be kept singly because it's aggressive to other puffers. In the wild and in captivity, pufferfish prefer to eat shellfish, such as snails, which they crush with their heavy teeth. This species has been known to adapt to processed food pellets as well. It only grows to about 4 inches.

Recognizing Plants That Are Partial to Salt

In the typical marine aquarium, algae will be your only plant–like inhabitant. However, brackish water habitats throughout the world almost always contain a broad array of true plants ranging from small marine grasses to large mangroves trees. Adding plants to your brackish water aquarium is a great idea because they help to stabilize water quality, produce oxygen, provide food and habitat, and add aesthetically pleasing natural fixtures to your tank. These sections identify which plants are best, depending on the fish you choose for your brackish aquarium.

Providing for grazers

Many brackish water fish species consume plant material and will actively graze on your plants. Although providing natural food for your pets is great, too much grazing will prune your plants to the roots, thereby wrecking your garden, so to speak, and disrupting water quality. Therefore, if you're a beginner, avoid softer and tastier plant varieties that tend to be more palatable to your fishes.

The following plants are attractive, easy to keep, and stand up well to grazers:

» **Java fern (*Microsorum pteropus*):** This is a popular and commonly sold plant ideally suited for the brackish water aquarium. The plant doesn't need to be buried in the gravel, and it attaches to rocks and other fixtures. Java fern thrives in low lighting and isn't disturbed by burrowing and plant-eating fishes. In addition, the Java fern with its broad green leaves readily propagates in your aquarium.

» **Water sprite (*Ceratopteris* species):** Considered by some to be the best aquarium plants, water sprites are beautiful, thick- or thin-leaved plants that float or root in your aquarium. Though water sprites derive their nutrients with their leaves, some soil in their substrate is beneficial. Medium lighting is sufficient for these plants, which readily cast shadows throughout your tank.

» *Swamp weed (**Hygrophila** species):* Often called *hygros*, these plants, which vary considerably in leaf shape and color, thrive under a variety of aquarium conditions. Hence, they're ideal for the beginner. Moreover, many brackish fishes generally don't consider them palatable.

» **Tape grass (*Vallisneria* species):** For those looking for tall, grass-like plants, the tape grasses are nice additions to the brackish water aquarium.

» **Pygmy chain sword (*Helanthium tenellum*):** As the name implies, this is a smaller plant that is perfectly suited to the foreground part of the aquarium. This plant needs a rich substrate and medium to high levels of lighting. It propagates rapidly by running roots under the gravel.

Planting and tending your garden

As is the case with the purchase of all your aquarium pets, be they animal or plant, always shop at a reputable dealer and choose healthy-looking plants from clean aquariums. Also, be just as careful when adding new plants to your brackish water ecosystem. Just because they seem hardier than fish, they aren't necessarily (although, you really don't need to talk to them). Make sure that the water chemistry is similar between the tank from which the plants are coming and the tank to which the plants are going. That is, check specific gravity, pH, water hardness, and temperature. Radical differences between the two tanks will shock and kill your new plants.

REMEMBER

After your plants are established in your aquarium, your work isn't done. Like algae, some plants can overrun a tank, so they need to be pruned. Also, remove any and all dead and dying plant leaves, roots, or stems so the rotting plant material doesn't impact the water quality. Finally, just as you routinely fertilize your vegetable garden, you may need to enrich the substrate of your aquarium. That doesn't mean you can dump a bag of fertilizer in the tank! Instead, routinely (about once a month) mix soil with clay into the lower levels of your substrate.

Chapter **11**

Getting Your Aquarium Up and Running

Perhaps, if I were a fly on the wall, I'd see you scratching your head standing next to an empty aquarium (on a stand with a hood or glass canopy) with some lighting fixtures, a heater or two, one or two filters, filter media, a protein skimmer, a thermometer, a hydrometer, a bucket full of rinsed gravel, some aquarium decorations and fixtures, fishnets, water conditioners, a bag of artificial salts, a spare bucket or two, an aquarium background, test kits, and some algae scrubbers.

If that doesn't sound like the components you've put together, read the chapters in Part 1 and then come back.

Here I help you put them all together. In this chapter, I walk you step-by-step through the process of setting up your new saltwater aquarium. The aquarium components may differ from system to system, but the same general steps apply. For best results, follow this chapter in the order presented here.

Placing Your Stand and Aquarium

Putting the aquarium stand in the appropriate location and taking into account floor stability, access to water and electricity, aesthetic value, visibility, and adequate distance from doors and windows is important. Make sure the stand is level, stable, and doesn't rock. Leave enough room for air-line tubing, electrical cords, and any equipment that hangs on the back of the tank (filter, protein skimmer, and heater).

Giving your aquarium a rinse

Before you place the aquarium where it will sit for a long time (I hope), move it to a place where you can rinse it. In the summer, you can do this outside with a garden hose, but in the winter you may not want to go outside, especially if you live where water freezes. In this case, rinse the tank in a bathroom tub or in the kitchen. This doesn't require thorough washing, just a simple rinse with fresh water and a clean sponge to remove dust and dirt. If the aquarium is too large to move about, simply wipe out the tank with a clean sponge dampened with fresh water.

WARNING

Remember, though, don't use any soap or detergent, which can leave toxic residue. Just rinse with water.

Putting your aquarium on the stand

Make sure you place the aquarium on the stand so that it sits properly. That means there is no overhang, and the tank sits perfectly flat on the stand. Double-check to make sure you left enough room behind the aquarium for equipment.

Applying the background

If you have background, now is a good time to put it on the back of the tank. (Refer to Chapter 9 where I discuss the background in greater detail.) Otherwise, applying it later may be tough to do so after the filters and tubing are in place. Most backgrounds are affixed with regular tape.

Adding Your Filter

With the exception of the live rock, now is the time to set up your filter system. But I mean only *set it up,* not *turn it on,* so don't plug it in or fill it with water.

In Chapter 7, I discuss filters in great detail. In this section, I walk you through how to set up the most common varieties. If you have a fish-only aquarium, you may have chosen one of the simpler, traditional aquarium filters, like undergravel or canister. If you're planning a reef tank, then live rock and a sump system is your likely choice. If so, find the filtration system that applies to your aquarium in the following list and always read the instructions that come with the filter from beginning to end:

>> **Undergravel:** Place the undergravel filter into the aquarium and make sure it sits flat inside the tank and the lift tubes are at the back of the tank. Put the powerheads in place, clipping them to the back of the aquarium. If your undergravel filter is powered by air, attach the airstones to the rigid tubing, place them in the lift tubes, and put the exhaust caps on the tubes. Attach the air-lines to the tubes and run them to an air pump. Angle the powerheads or the exhaust ports toward the front center of the tank.

>> **External power filter:** Rinse the filter media and put it in the filter as recommended by the manufacturer. Hang the external power filter on the back of the tank, but don't fill the filter with water yet. Trim the filter so it hangs straight up and down on the back of the tank.

>> **Canister filter:** Follow the manufacturer's instructions and fill the canister with rinsed filter media. Snap the top into place, paying particular attention to the O-ring, making sure it's sealed correctly. Check with the written directions to see whether the canister should be filled with water before closing it up. Place the canister in the desired position and run the intake and output lines to the aquarium, attaching them with suction cups, if supplied.

>> **Trickle filter and/or sump:** Place the trickle filter and/or sump into the appropriate position under the tank. Follow the instructions provided by the manufacturer to install the overflow system on the back of the tank, add the filter media, and set up the lines to and from the aquarium with appropriate valves as needed.

>> **Fluidized bed filter:** Most fluidized bed filters hang on the back of the tank and receive water from a powerhead or a separate pump. Follow the instructions supplied by the manufacturer to set up the plumbing to and from this unit.

>> **Protein skimmer:** With so many designs available in today's market, I can't tell you how to set up your particular brand. Most protein skimmers require a break-in period, which needs to be taken into consideration. My best advice is to follow the instructions closely and seek assistance from your local dealer. If you have a sump, place the protein skimmer in the appropriate compartment.

WARNING

At this point, don't even think about adding live rock or you might as well change the name of it to dead rock. If live rock is a main source of filtration for you, don't worry about setting it up until a few steps down the list. I discuss doing so in the "Adding Live Sand and Rocks" section later in this chapter.

Adding the Substrate

After rinsing your gravel or sand (see Chapter 9), add this substrate to the tank. Feel free to provide a little depth to the aquarium by sloping it downward gently toward the front of the tank. Follow my guidelines also in Chapter 9 regarding the maximum depth of your gravel.

WARNING

Don't place live sand in the tank at this time because it too requires water to stay alive, and you haven't gotten that far yet.

Including Ornamentation

Add the decorations in the pattern you've planned. Now's the time to pull out that piece of paper with your design on it and see how it looks. (Chapter 9 discusses tips and tricks to decorating your tank.)

TIP

Start by placing large and heavy rocks down through the gravel and close to the bottom of the tank for stability. If your aquascape includes plastic plants, add them at this point, even though you may want to adjust them later.

WARNING

Don't put live rocks or live coral in at this time because they really need water!

Focusing on Circulation

Mount powerheads in the appropriate positions, typically the corners, to maximize circulation — you can adjust them later. If you're using airstones, place them or run air-lines to aerating ornaments in the aquarium. Make sure you put the airstones near the substrate. Run air-lines to the air valves or directly to the air pump.

Attaching the Heater

Clip the hanging heater on the back of your aquarium or place the submersible heater in the tank or sump. Always place the submersible heater near the bottom of the aquarium at the back and use suction cups if you have them. Make sure you position it so you can see the indicator light. See Chapter 8 for more on heaters.

WARNING

Don't plug the heater in because it will overheat and break if not submersed in water.

Filling Your Aquarium with Water

Place a large saucer or bowl on the substrate in your aquarium. Doing so buffers the force of water and keeps it from upsetting your gravel and decorations.

Using a bucket, fill your aquarium by pouring the premixed saltwater into the bowl or saucer so that the overfill spills gently over the sides uniformly.

Use your thermometer to make sure that the temperature of the water you're adding is between 76 and 80 degrees F. After the tank is filled to within an inch of the top, remove the saucer or bowl.

TIP

At this point, make sure that your tank has no leaks. Dry the entire outside of the tank with paper towels and closely inspect the seams for drops of water. If you see a leak, empty the tank and return it to the dealer.

Placing the Hood

Now that all the equipment is in place, but not started, place the hood or glass canopy on the tank to fit it properly.

You may have to adjust not only the hood, but also other aquarium equipment such as the heater or protein skimmer, to make the hood sits correctly. Now is the time to move equipment, before it's up and running. Some hoods need to be fitted by adjusting and trimming, so follow the instructions that came with your hood to make sure you do it right. You may need to remove the hood to complete the aquarium setup, but now you know that components are where they should be and replacing the hood is easy.

Getting the Right Temperature with a Thermometer and Heater

Place your thermometer in or on the aquarium, depending on the model that you purchased. Check your temperature and make sure the temperature is between 76 and 80 degrees F. Plug your heater in and adjust it accordingly to set the temperature in this range. If you need to calibrate your heater, flip to Chapter 8 and review how.

Starting Your Filters

After your aquarium is full of water, fire up your filter systems to get the ball rolling. How you do this depends heavily on the type of filter you have. The following list helps:

>> **Undergravel filter:** This is pretty simple. Start the powerheads or plug in the air pump if you have an air-driven system. You should see bubbles pouring out of the exhaust ports.

>> **External power filter:** Fill the filter box with water from the tank and plug it in. Make sure that water is flowing out of the filter. It will expel bubbles at first, but the bubbles will end shortly, and the filter should run smoothly.

>> **Canister filter:** Follow the manufacturer's instructions to start the canister filter. Some need to be primed with water before being plugged in.

  This filter will also spit bubbles until the air is driven out of the system. You may need to fill the intake hose with water to get it going. If you have an undergravel filter with a powerhead, use it to fill the intake line. Otherwise, you can draw water into the output line from the tank end.

>> **Trickle filter and/or sump:** My best recommendation for firing up the trickle filter or sump is to closely follow the manufacturer instructions. That's because with so many models out there, what works for one doesn't apply to another. These filters provide excellent filtration, but they can be a bit complicated to get going properly. Don't be afraid to go to the source and talk to the dealer who sold it to you.

>> **Fluidized bed filter:** This simply involves plugging in the pump or powerhead that drives the water into the filter. Make sure all connections are tight.

>> **Protein skimmer:** Follow the instructions that came with your protein skimmer to get it going. You'll need to adjust the airflow to make sure that the unit is working properly.

WARNING

You're almost there, but not quite yet. Keep the live rock out of the aquarium until the temperature and salinity have stabilized. Your best bet is not to pick up your live rock from the dealer until your aquarium is ready.

Turning on the Powerheads or Air Pump

Start your powerheads or air pump and check your air-lines and connections for air leaks. Make sure the airstones are positioned properly. If you have a wave-maker, get it going.

Considering Lighting

After your filters are running and the hood or glass canopy is in place, you can set up the lighting fixtures. Strip lights are placed on top of the tank, while hanging lamps and pendants need to be suspended from the ceiling attached to a ceiling hook. After all the lighting is in place, plug everything in and turn your lights on. Chapter 8 examines the different lighting options for your aquarium.

Making Any 24-Hour Adjustments

Your filters are running, the heater is working, and the lights are on. What do you see? Foggy water. Don't worry, the fogginess will clear up pretty rapidly, usually overnight. Over the next 24 hours, carefully monitor water temperature and salinity (specific gravity) and adjust your heater and add salt as needed. If your specific gravity is too high, you may need to take water out and add fresh water. Refer to Chapter 9 for the specific levels your aquarium needs.

Adding Live Sand and Rocks

If your first 24 hours went smoothly, the aquarium is now well balanced with salt and heat, your filters are running smoothly, and the water has cleared.

Now you can add some live sand to introduce bacteria into the tank and start to build the biological filtration. You can add live rock now as well. This, too, will start the tank-maturation process and get your aquarium into the nitrogen cycle, which I talk about in Chapter 12.

TIP

Make sure you don't add too much live rock at this point, particularly if it's not properly cured. (*Cured* refers to live rock that has been properly prepared for the aquarium — see Chapter 9.) Also, be sure to remove some water before adding the rock so the tank doesn't overflow.

Ensuring Your Tank Is Mature

Your aquarium needs to mature before you add fish and invertebrates. What do I mean by *mature*? Well, in Chapter 12, I discuss this thoroughly, but it means that a healthy bacterial colony needs to be established, and the tank needs to be *cycled*. So don't run out and buy fish and invertebrates until you read that chapter.

At this point, though, you can run some water chemistry tests for pH and ammonia. Start a chemistry log and write down the results you get, because they're going to change, and you want to follow these changes. Chapter 13 explains pH tests in greater detail.

Adding Fish

When your aquarium has matured, you can add fish slowly. Which fish you add is a big decision, and I discuss that in Part 1.

3

Taking Proper Care of Your Aquarium

Understand the nitrogen cycle, know the importance of bacteria for proper water maturation, and recognize the need for water quality testing.

Measure how much salt is in your aquarium water and explore other water quality parameters, including pH, alkalinity, water gases, and calcium.

Enter the fascinating world of algae, which can be both a helper and a nuisance in your aquarium, and understand how and when you need to remove them.

Keep your aquarium clean with preventative maintenance by developing daily, weekly, and monthly duties and know how to respond to emergencies.

Chapter **12**

Tackling the Nitrogen Cycle

This chapter gets into the nuts and bolts of water chemistry. You're probably thinking, "Chemistry . . . ugh!" Don't worry, I stick to the basics and limit my discussion to what you really need to know to maintain a healthy saltwater aquarium. Though some of the concepts may seem complex at first, they really aren't too bad.

When I established my first aquarium more than 40 years ago, I was excited and antsy to have a fully stocked, beautiful aquarium. And my family knew it. So, just a week after setting it up, my brothers, sisters, and parents loaded me up with some nice tropical fishes, including angels, butterflies, triggers, and even a lionfish. Well, you guessed it, within days, my fish started dying and, by the end of a week, I had literally flushed hundreds of dollars down the drain. Why? Overstocking too fast without a well-established nitrogen cycle! That was a tough lesson to learn, but this chapter helps you avoid a similar experience.

Understanding the Nitrogen Cycle — In and Out

Fish and invertebrates are living creatures that require food for energy, burning it with the help of oxygen that they respire (breathe from the water). These processes produce waste products that are returned to the environment through the gills and in the urine and feces. These wastes are primarily carbon dioxide and nitrogenous compounds (like ammonia), which are extremely toxic to fish.

In the aquarium, these wastes must be removed. Carbon dioxide (CO_2) generally leaves the water through water circulation and aeration at the surface or through photosynthesis by aquarium algae. Ammonia, on the other hand, must be converted to nitrite, which is then converted to nitrate, a less toxic compound. This conversion of harmful ammonia into nitrite and then nitrate is called the *nitrogen cycle* (see Figure 12-1).

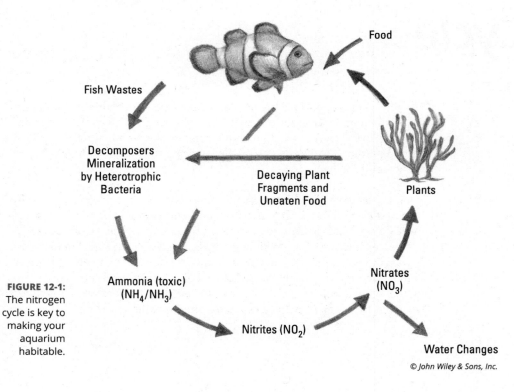

Food

Fish Wastes

Decomposers
Mineralization
by Heterotrophic
Bacteria

Decaying Plant
Fragments and
Uneaten Food

Plants

FIGURE 12-1:
The nitrogen cycle is key to making your aquarium habitable.

Ammonia (toxic)
(NH_4/NH_3)

Nitrites (NO_2)

Nitrates
(NO_3)

Water Changes

© *John Wiley & Sons, Inc.*

Why do you need to know about the nitrogen cycle? Because it's the basis of biological filtration, and your filters use biological filtration to keep your aquarium clean. As I discuss in Chapter 7, without biological filtration, your aquarium won't survive!

REMEMBER

Your marine animals aren't the only source of nitrogenous wastes. Every time you feed your pets, excess food will decompose into harmful compounds, including ammonia. That is why you need to make every effort to feed your fish carefully so as not to leave excess food in the aquarium.

Before you can fully stock an aquarium, you need to establish the nitrogen cycle. The following sections help you do so.

Grasping the role of bacteria

A healthy aquarium depends greatly on the nitrogen cycle to reduce toxic ammonia into less-toxic nitrogen compounds. In your aquarium, ammonia builds slowly but decreases as it's converted to nitrite. Then as the nitrite is converted to nitrate, nitrite decreases, and nitrate slowly accumulates. Ultimately, your healthy aquarium will have consistently low levels of ammonia and nitrite, while nitrate slowly builds.

TECHNICAL STUFF

Biological filtration is actually *bacteriological* filtration. Believe it or not, the nitrogen cycle is driven by bacteria. Bacteria that convert ammonia (NH_4) into nitrite (NO_2) belong to the genus *Nitrosomonas*. Nitrite, in turn, is converted into nitrate (NO_3) by bacteria of the genus *Nitrobacter*. These processes together are called *nitrification*.

You may be wondering what happens to the nitrate. Well, nitrate will be assimilated by algae, and it will be converted to nitrogen gas by denitrifying bacteria. In most aquarium systems, however, nitrate slowly accumulates in the water because these two processes generally can't keep up with nitrate production.

Although nitrate is relatively harmless to fish, it must eventually be removed or diluted before toxic levels are reached. You do this with frequent water changes (removing a portion of the aquarium water and replacing it with fresh batches of premixed saltwater, as I discuss in Chapter 15).

Testing the cycle

The nitrogen cycle needs to be established in a biological filter, which is a requirement for all marine aquariums. Even with a properly functioning biological filter, however, you want to frequently monitor the levels of ammonia, nitrite, and nitrate. You do this with commercial test kits that are available at your fish dealer.

With the test kits that I outline in Chapter 9, you can watch the cycle as it develops in your aquarium, and you'll see your aquarium mature. I discuss what a mature aquarium looks like in the next section.

TIP

Keep in mind that most serious fish dealers provide free water testing. Take full advantage of this service, because it allows you to compare the dealer's results with those that you're getting at home.

TIP

Write down and date the results of your water testing so that you can follow the nitrogen cycle. Figure 12-2 shows an example of what my records look like. Feel free to model yours after mine. By keeping these records, you'll know when the cycle is firmly established in your aquarium. I even plot my results in a spreadsheet program, so I can see the rise and fall of ammonia and nitrite — I guess that makes me officially a fish geek. Some websites and apps are available where you can post your test parameters; they even make the charts for you.

Date	Water Change %	Temp °F	Specific Gravity/Salinity	pH	Alk dKH	NH₃ Ammonia	NO₂ Nitrite	NO₃ Nitrate	PO₄ Phosphate	I Iodine	Ca Calcium	Mg Magnesium	Sr Strontium	Livestock Added/Notes

FIGURE 12-2:
An example of recordkeeping.

© John Wiley & Sons, Inc.

Waiting for Your Aquarium to Mature

When you complete the setup steps in Chapter 11, you have a tank filled with salt-water, but you don't have the working, well-balanced habitat for fish that I call an aquarium. To get to this, you need to let the tank *mature*. And I'm sorry to say, you have to be a little patient: It's going to take a few weeks. Read on for tips on making it happen as fast as possible.

The maturation process means simply that you're establishing a biological filter and, therefore, allowing the nitrogen cycle to get going. Nitrogen will often cycle more than once, and you may see multiple cycles as the *bioload* in your aquarium is increased. That is, as you increase the number of animals, they produce more ammonia, which needs to be converted to nitrite, and then converted to nitrate. So, your aquarium will cycle again. The key is to stimulate bacterial growth without overwhelming the system.

You don't want to add more than a couple of fish to your tank without a working nitrogen cycle.

Taking the Next Step: Just Add Bacteria

Water circulation, temperature regulation, and filtration help your water to mature, but establishing bacterial colonies sufficient to drive the nitrogen cycle can take as long as six weeks.

After your aquarium is set up and the components are turned on, the water maturation process begins. There are a few proven methods for accelerating this process so that your aquarium doesn't remain empty for long. Which method you use depends on how fast ammonia and nitrite levels peak and then drop. Basically, to move the maturation process along and turn your infant aquarium into a teenager as fast as possible, you need to add bacteria, as I discuss in the following sections. These methods aren't mutually exclusive and can be done in conjunction with each other.

When I was a little younger, the most common maturation process involved the introduction of a few hard fish, typically damsels (see Chapter 3), which would produce ammonia and jump-start the process. However, this is not only inhumane, but damsels are highly territorial and the survivors will likely have to be removed, which will be disruptive to the aquarium. Nowadays, more humane and far better fishless ways are available to mature your aquarium.

Regardless of which method you use to mature your water and establish the nitrogen cycle, plan on the process taking a minimum of two to six weeks.

Add the rock

The most effective way to speed up water maturation involves the use of live rock and live sand to seed a new aquarium. As I discuss in Chapters 7 and 9, live rock and live sand are loaded with helpful bacteria that are already nitrifying the ammonia being produced by the many critters living on the rock. You can add live sand and live rock after your tank has been running for about 24 hours, providing your salinity and temperature have stabilized.

REMEMBER

The use of live rock to condition and to filter your aquarium can mature your aquarium in as little as two weeks.

TIP

Make sure you use only *cured* live rock in your new aquarium. See Chapter 9 for details on cured rock.

Seed it

If you're not going to use live rock or live sand in your aquarium, the next most effective (and inexpensive) method to establish your nitrogen cycle is to "seed" the aquarium with bacteria from an already established aquarium. After your aquarium is set up and filled with water, go to your local pet store or a fellow hobbyist and ask for a handful of gravel from one of their systems that has been well established. Mix that gravel in with your gravel. Doing so accelerates water conditioning by seeding the new system with the right bacteria.

REMEMBER

Of course, make sure that the source of your bacteria-rich gravel has healthy fish and well-maintained aquaria. If it doesn't, don't use it.

You can also seed your filters by adding material from the filter of an established aquarium. In fact, you'll find that when you clean your filters during routine maintenance, you'll want to keep some filter media in the filter to maintain the nitrogen cycle and biological filtration.

Accelerators

A number of products on the market today are available to accelerate the maturation process in your aquarium. These contain helpful nitrifying bacteria that are used to seed your aquarium. Some of these products can be quite effective.

Taking the Final Steps to Maturity

Test your water daily to monitor the nitrogen cycle and other water chemistry parameters that I discuss in Chapter 13. In general, after you've seeded the tank with bacteria, the sequence of events will proceed as follows:

1. **After seeding and waiting a couple of days, low values of ammonia begin to increase, peaking in about seven days.**

2. **As ammonia builds and the bacterial colony grows, the ammonia is converted to nitrite, and for about a week, the level of ammonia falls as nitrite increases.**

3. **As the bacterial population proliferates, ammonia drops out, and nitrite decreases as nitrification continues.**

   Nitrate slowly builds and stabilizes.

TIP

During the cycling process your tank may experience a *brownout,* which is a fine brown dusting on the gravel and decorations caused by single-celled algae called *diatoms* (see Chapter 14). This is a normal occurrence during the cycling process and will disappear as quickly as it appeared.

The filter bed won't be completely established for several weeks, so be conservative when you add your first fish. Start with a low number (two to four) of peaceful, inexpensive fish. The introduction of territorial fish (see Chapter 2) may make adding more fish difficult because these fish establish territories and can be aggressive toward new fishes.

TIP

In a healthy, mature, well-established marine aquarium, ammonia and nitrite levels in your water should be close to zero, and nitrate levels should be kept less than 20 mg/L.

Handling Problems When They Occur with the Nitrogen Cycle

If something goes wrong, and ammonia doesn't decrease within two weeks, don't panic. Your bioload might be too large, and the bacteria in your tank are overwhelmed. The best thing is to just let the tank continue to mature. Eventually, the bacteria will catch up, and your tank will cycle.

However, if your fish are stressed or dying, you probably need to do one of the following:

» Physically get rid of the ammonia by conducting a partial water change (see Chapter 15).

» Use a commercial ammonia neutralizer available at your dealer.

Chapter **13**

Considering Chemistry: Salt, Acidity, and Gases

Consider this chapter to be the second major part of your chemistry education. In Chapter 12, I discuss the nitrogen cycle thoroughly. In this chapter, I address some of the other water chemistry parameters that you need to measure to monitor the quality of the water in your tank.

Grasping the Importance of Water Quality

The quality of the water in your aquarium is the most important part of a healthy marine environment. That's why I emphasize proper filtration in Chapter 7. Fish can live for days without food, but they'll certainly perish in minutes without high water quality.

But how do you determine whether the water in your aquarium is healthy? Cloudy or discolored water is a dead giveaway, but in most cases you simply can't *see* whether your water is polluted. That's why you want to examine certain chemical aspects of the water.

Think of test kits as the only way your aquarium water can communicate with you if something is wrong. When you test the water, you're the doctor, and the tests tell you whether your patient is healthy.

In Chapter 9, you find out that test kits are important accessories to add to your equipment list, and I give you the lowdown on the kits you need. In this chapter, I explain what each of these kits actually does.

I try to keep the information in this chapter simple, so that you're not turned off by the water chemistry aspects of the hobby. Just the basics here, my friend — you don't need to be a chemist to be an aquarist.

My friend Rick has the right idea: He set up his aquarium several years ago. Allowing for water maturation, he stocked his tank slowly with the right number of compatible aquarium inhabitants. During this process, he religiously monitored his water quality on a weekly basis, all the while not allowing himself to be obsessed by the chemistry. Rick and his family enjoy their aquarium, which is well balanced and a picture of beauty. You want to be cognizant of the chemical processes and use them to your advantage. They are a means of keeping your pets alive.

Checking Your Salt Level

The chemical composition of seawater is extremely consistent throughout the world. Although it's 96 percent pure water (one atom of oxygen bonded with two atoms of hydrogen: H_2O), it also contains many dissolved minerals and salts. These minerals and salts are mainly sodium and chlorine (85 percent), but magnesium, sulphate, calcium, and potassium make up another 13 percent, and bicarbonate and 68 other elements make up the remainder in small quantities.

You need to mimic natural seawater as closely as possible in your aquarium, which means that you need to make sure the amount of salt in your water is correct. Science has developed a couple of ways to measure the amount of dissolved salts in seawater. One measure is called salinity and another is called specific gravity. Although these measurements aren't the same, either can be used to determine the correct level of salt in your aquarium.

An affinity for salinity

Salinity refers to the actual concentration of major dissolved ions in the water, and it isn't influenced by temperature. It's expressed as a ratio of parts-per-thousand (ppt). To directly measure salinity, you need a *refractometer*, which used to be quite expensive but is now quite affordable for the average aquarist. If you choose to measure salinity, a value of 34 to 35 ppt is optimal for invertebrates, though fishes can tolerate lower salinities.

Specific gravity

Another common way to monitor the salt level in your aquarium is to measure specific gravity (see Chapter 9). *Specific gravity* refers to the ratio of densities of seawater to pure water at various temperatures. For example, a specific gravity of 1.025 means that a liquid is 1.025 times denser than freshwater. However, because the specific gravity of a liquid is directly related to its temperature, your *hydrometer* (an instrument used to measure specific gravity) may not be calibrated to the temperature in your aquarium. Most hydrometers are calibrated at 60 degrees F (don't ask me why), so you need to use a conversion factor to adjust your hydrometer reading to true specific gravity. The conversion table should be included with the instructions that come with your hydrometer.

REMEMBER

Under standard aquarium temperatures (75 to 79 degrees F), the conversion usually results in the addition of 0.002 to the hydrometer reading. For example, if your hydrometer reading is 1.023 and your water temperature is 77 degrees, the actual specific gravity of your aquarium is 1.025. Specific gravity should be established in the range of 1.021 to 1.025, but more importantly, it should be *maintained* at a specific level within this range. Even minor fluctuations can cause problems for your tank inhabitants.

Fluctuating salt

The greatest cause of salt level change is evaporation of freshwater from the tank. When water evaporates in a marine aquarium, the salts don't. They remain in solution, and therefore the water becomes more concentrated over time, thereby increasing the salinity and specific gravity. You must monitor water levels in the aquarium to head off these fluctuations. Evaporation is easily remedied by adding freshwater, not additional saltwater, to the tank.

TIP

Don't wait until water levels have dropped significantly before you top off the tank with freshwater; instead, do so regularly with small quantities.

Although water evaporation is the major source of fluctuating salt levels, you can also *lose* salt from the tank from the protein skimmer (see Chapter 7) and from crystallization on the hood and other fixtures. Keep an eye on the hydrometer.

Knowing What Acid and pH Are

Although you don't need to become a chemist, it's really important that you have a basic understanding of how your marine pets alter the basic chemistry of their surrounding water. These alterations pollute the water, and the first thing to change is the amount of acid in your aquarium. Your job is to remove that pollution with filtration. You can monitor the success of your efforts by measuring the water's pH, which is a good indication of the acidity.

TECHNICAL STUFF

When I write about acid, I'm referring to levels of hydrogen ions in solution. *Ions* are simply atoms with an electrical charge. These hydrogen ions are also called *hydrogen protons* because they have a positive charge. They're written like this: H^+.

You can measure the number of hydrogen atoms on a scale called pH. You may have heard of pH in reference to a number of solutions, ranging from blood to shampoo.

Scaling pH

The pH scale, shown in Figure 13-1, tells you how many hydrogen atoms are in a solution and, therefore, how acidic it is. It ranges from 0 to 14, with a pH of 7 being neutral, a pH of 1 being very acidic, and a pH of 14 being very alkaline, which is the opposite of acidic. The lower the number on the scale, the more hydrogen atoms are present, and the more acidic the solution is.

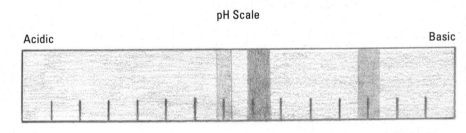

pH Scale

Acidic   Basic

REMEMBER

The pH scale is *logarithmic*, which means that each number is ten times stronger than the preceding number. For example, a pH of 2 is ten times more acidic than a pH of 3 and 100 times more acidic than a pH of 4. Therefore, a single incremental change represents a huge change in the number of hydrogen protons in your water.

Saltwater is more alkaline than freshwater. If you had a freshwater aquarium, you probably maintained the pH within the range of 6.5 to 7.5. On the other hand, the pH of seawater is about 8.2 and should be maintained in the aquarium between 8.1 and 8.4.

REMEMBER

Although maintaining the correct pH is important, it's even more critical that you avoid large changes in pH. This is because, with few exceptions, pH is very stable in the oceans so most saltwater fishes aren't well adapted to big changes in pH. When this happens, they suffer immediately.

Recognizing pH fluctuations

A number of factors influence the pH in your aquarium water. These include the amount of carbon dioxide and fish wastes in the water. The accumulation of either or both of these will cause the water to acidify and the pH to drop. In fact, the nitrogen cycle itself will often produce acids that will alter the pH of your aquarium.

TIP

Add a pH test kit to your repertoire of commercial test kits. The kit is simple to use and is an important step when monitoring the quality of your aquarium water. Monitor this water parameter every week to detect any changes. An abrupt drop in pH may be indicative of an increase of carbon dioxide or nitrogenous fish wastes. An increase in water circulation and a partial water change (refer to Chapter 15) are necessary to alleviate the problem before the lives of tank inhabitants are compromised.

The ability of a solution to resist changes in pH is called its *buffering capacity*. Most commercial salt mixes contain buffers that keep pH from falling dramatically. However, over time, the buffering capacity of your water will diminish, and carbon dioxide or waste buildup causes pH to drop.

Adding pH solutions

Regular 10-percent water changes (see Chapter 15) will maintain your pH at correct levels by replenishing your aquarium's buffering capacity. However, if your pH falls rapidly out of the acceptable range, you can restore it by adding one of the following:

>> **A commercially manufactured aquarium buffer:** Available at most aquarium dealers, these chemicals buffer your aquarium when used properly. Be sure to follow the manufacturer's instructions carefully and use the buffers in conjunction with a waste-removing partial water change.

>> **A solution of calcium hydroxide:** Commonly referred to as *kalkwasser* or *limewater*, this helps boost calcium levels, thereby increasing pH.

Comprehending Hardness and Alkalinity

The amount of dissolved minerals, namely calcium and magnesium, in the water is called its *hardness.* Water with high concentrations of minerals is said to be *hard,* whereas low levels are indicative of *soft water.* Measuring water hardness in your aquarium is important, and the following sections tell you how.

Hardness is easy

Though general hardness is important for the typical freshwater aquarium, the salt in your marine aquarium dictates the water hardness. So, you really don't need to pay much attention to general hardness. However, you don't get off the hardness hook that easily. There is a specific kind of hardness called carbonate hardness that you *do* need to measure.

Carbonate hardness

In the "Knowing What Acid and pH Are" section earlier, I mention buffering capacity with regard to the ability of your aquarium water to resist changes in pH. pH is really just a measurement of the amount of positively charged hydrogen atoms in your water. The more positive charges, the more acidic the water, and the lower the pH.

All these hydrogen protons create a lot of positive charges in the water. The best way to counteract a positive charge is with a negative charge. So the water contains molecules and atoms that are negatively charged to buffer the positive charges. The amount of negative charges and, therefore, the ability of the water to resist the positive charges make up the buffering capacity.

The negative molecules that are typically found in seawater and that act as buffers are called *carbonates* and *bicarbonates.* Therefore, if you measure the amount of carbonates in your water, you're measuring the buffering capacity, and this is important. If buffering capacity diminishes, your pH will fall, and problems can occur.

Checking carbonate hardness (alkalinity)

When you measure the amount of carbonates in your aquarium, you're measuring the carbonate hardness. This is often referred to as measuring the *alkalinity,* but don't get this confused with a pH measurement that is alkaline. Carbonate hardness does affect pH, but you're not measuring pH.

TIP

You can measure carbonate hardness with a standard kit that's available from your dealer. Keep in mind that it may be called an *alkalinity test kit*. Carbonate hardness is usually reported in dKH, which means degrees Karbonathärte (German for carbonate), and the level in your aquarium should be in the range of 8 to 12 kDH.

Adjusting carbonate hardness

If the carbonate hardness (and, therefore, the buffering capacity of your aquarium water) is below the recommended level, you need to make some adjustments. In all likelihood, your pH will probably be decreasing, as well. In fact, the methods you use to adjust your pH are used to increase your carbonate hardness:

>> **Conduct a partial water change.** Doing so increases the buffering capacity of your water by removing old stale water with fresh buffered saltwater (not freshwater!). This should be your first step. (See Chapter 15 for more on conducting a water change.) Wait a day and then test the water again. If carbonate hardness is still low, try the next two tips.

>> **Use a commercially manufactured aquarium buffer.** Available at most aquarium dealers, these chemicals when used properly buffer your aquarium. Be sure to carefully follow the manufacturer's instructions and use these in conjunction with a waste-removing partial water change.

>> **Add a solution of calcium hydroxide or kalkwasser.** This increases the buffering capacity (alkalinity) of your water.

TIP

Use calcareous calcium–based substrates (gravels; see Chapter 9) in your saltwater aquarium because they interact with the carbon dioxide excreted by your pets, increasing the buffering capacity of the water.

Monitoring How Well Your Pets Can Breathe — Water Gases

Through the process of *respiration*, humans use oxygen and produce carbon dioxide when they breathe. These molecules are well known by most people simply because without them, you (and every other human) would certainly perish. Well, your marine friends are just like you in this respect. Without oxygen, they would die, and with every breath, they excrete carbon dioxide. The following sections explain how you can measure these important gases to make sure your pets can breathe.

Oxygen (O$_2$)

Like most living creatures, marine fish and invertebrates need oxygen to live. Whereas humans can breathe oxygen from the air, marine critters must extract it from the water. Therefore, they need oxygen that's dissolved in water, called *dissolved oxygen.*

Most oxygen exchange occurs at your aquarium's surface where the water meets the air. You can increase the amount of dissolved oxygen in your aquarium by agitating the surface area of the tank through increased circulation. This process is called *aeration.* As I discuss in Chapter 7, aeration and circulation go hand in hand. To maintain high levels of dissolved oxygen in your aquarium, you need to aerate the water.

Despite what most people think, air delivered by airstones and diffusers help to increase circulation to enhance oxygen exchange at the surface, but they don't contribute much oxygen directly to the water.

REMEMBER

Test kits and electronic probes are available to measure the amount of dissolved oxygen in your aquarium, but only reef tank enthusiasts should consider buying one. If you use a test kit, make sure that dissolved oxygen levels are maintained above 7.0 mg/L.

Carbon dioxide (CO$_2$)

Oxygen in, carbon dioxide out. That is how a living, respiring system works. For every molecule of dissolved oxygen that you want in your tank, carbon dioxide will be produced when your critters utilize it.

In your aquarium, carbon dioxide combines with water molecules and calcium in a dynamic equilibrium that produces hydrogen protons, bicarbonate ions, and calcium carbonate. Without going into great detail using chemical equations and lots of capital letters, realize that the levels of these compounds are influenced by the amount of carbon dioxide production (respiration) in your aquarium.

Carbon dioxide can profoundly affect your water quality. Excessive amounts lower your pH; however, it also impacts the buffering capacity of your water and lowers your carbonate hardness (alkalinity). Moreover, carbon dioxide affects calcium levels in your water, and as discussed in the "Calcium (Ca)" section, later in this chapter, you need high calcium levels for your invertebrates.

REMEMBER

The bottom line: Carbon dioxide is a product of metabolism that needs to be removed from your aquarium. However, test kits for carbon dioxide aren't common, and the best ways to keep carbon dioxide levels low are as follows:

>> Maintain high levels of aeration and circulation so that carbon dioxide is removed from the water.

>> Conduct regular partial water changes to physically remove carbon dioxide (see Chapter 15).

>> To limit carbon dioxide production, don't overstock your aquarium with inhabitants.

>> Maintain proper pH levels.

>> Allow some growth of algae, which remove some of the carbon dioxide (see Chapter 14).

>> Don't overfeed your pets.

Considering Other Chemical Factors

A number of water tests are available to the average aquarist, so you may be a bit confused in the beginning. In Chapter 9, I list those tests that may be useful to you, depending on whether you have a fish-only or a reef tank. I discuss a few of these parameters throughout this chapter, and I cover a few more here.

Calcium (Ca)

Many invertebrate species, such as corals and snails, possess calcium carbonate skeletons and shells (see Chapter 4). Therefore, for these animals to thrive and grow, they need to extract calcium from the water. As you can probably guess, the level of calcium in the water is important to monitor if you keep a reef tank. If you have a fish-only aquarium, the calcium levels in your water are adequately maintained by your partial water changes.

REMEMBER

Calcium test kits are available, and levels should be maintained at 375 to 475 ppm (parts per million) in the reef aquarium. If testing indicates that you don't have enough calcium in the water, add calcium supplements, such as limewater, to the aquarium. These supplements are commercially available and should be administered slowly.

Phosphate (PO_4)

Dissolved inorganic phosphorous, also called *phosphate,* enters your aquarium primarily through excretion by fishes, the breakdown of uneaten food, and tap water. These phosphates are readily absorbed by growing algae. In most cases, phosphate isn't a problem until excessive algal growth occurs on the live corals of a reef aquarium.

Therefore, make efforts to monitor levels of phosphate with a test kit. A phosphate level in excess of 0.10 ppm causes an algal bloom, so reduce phosphate levels by increasing aeration and using a protein skimmer (see Chapter 7). Maintain a phosphate level less than 0.10 ppm.

TECHNICAL
STUFF

Phosphate becomes bound to organic matter that binds to rising air bubbles. When the bubbles burst at the surface, the phosphates are lost to the atmosphere.

Copper (Cu)

Even though you make every effort to maintain a healthy aquarium, eventually one of your fish will need to be treated for disease (as I discuss in Chapter 18). The most effective treatment for many parasitic infestations is copper. I prefer to treat diseased fish in a separate hospital aquarium, but some fishkeepers add copper directly to their display tanks.

In the aquarium, copper readily binds to calcium carbonates and becomes ineffective, so copper levels need to be maintained continuously. At the same time, excessive copper is toxic to fish. Hence, test copper levels in your aquarium during the treatment period to maintain adequate levels while avoiding excessive treatment.

WARNING

Copper is toxic to invertebrates, so if you keep invertebrates, don't use copper. Many houses, particularly older ones, have copper pipes that can, on occasion, leach out enough copper to be toxic to many invertebrates. If your home has copper pipes, it's worthwhile to have a copper test kit to make sure your tap water is safe.

Chapter **14**

The Lowdown on Algae

P lants are an integral part of the freshwater aquarium but are somewhat rare in the saltwater tank. This is because, with few exceptions, all the ocean's plant life is classified in the primitive group known as *algae*. The term *seaweed* actually refers to the many-celled forms of algae.

Algae can be either good or bad for the marine aquarist, depending on whether or not they get out of control. In moderation, algae assimilate nitrates and other excess nutrients from the water and provide food for herbivorous fishes and invertebrates. This chapter explains the pros and cons of the algae in your aquarium. The latter part of the chapter reviews the types of algae, including those that you want to keep.

Knowing What Algae Are

Algae are photosynthetic organisms that occur throughout the world in many habitats ranging from freshwater to saltwater and from the poles to the equator. For many years, algae were grouped with the fungi into the class of plants known as *Thallophyta*. Later, some scientists classified these plant-like organisms into their own kingdom, called the *Protoctista,* and the fungi into their own kingdom called *Fungi.*

Most recently, however, the term *algae* describes an extremely diverse assemblage of photosynthetic organisms that doesn't include land plants. This is a pretty broad definition, but the rest of this chapter gives you a sense of just how different the various kinds of algae actually are.

Algae are relatively simple organisms that range in size from the one-celled microscopic types to large seaweeds that grow to more than 230 feet. Algae are also hardy organisms that have a tremendous reproductive capacity. They can enter your aquarium as algal spores borne by the air or carried by tank furnishings from another aquarium.

The term *alga* is singular, and more than one alga is called algae.

All aquarium algae have one thing in common: They need light and nutrients to propagate. The following sections explain what algae do, how algae grow, and why you need some in your aquarium.

Understanding the ins and outs of algae

Algae have adapted to all kinds of water conditions. They're important as primary producers at the base of the food chain. Although they provide oxygen and food for aquatic life, some forms of algae can contribute to the mass mortality of other organisms. In tropical regions, coralline algae can be as dominant as corals in the formation of reefs.

Algae can be *planktonic,* meaning they float freely in the ocean, and when they do they're called *microalgae.* The term *seaweed* refers to larger species of algae, called *macroalgae,* that live in the marine environment attached to the bottom. Despite their size, which can exceed 230 feet, seaweeds are simple organisms that aren't well understood. They don't have roots and shoots the way that plants do, but they do have root-like attachment structures and leaf-like fronds.

In your aquarium, algae can be found on the water's surface, suspended in the water, or on the surfaces of the aquarium glass, rocks, gravel, coral, and tank decorations. Many species are introduced on live rock or coral, but some enter your aquarium with water from other aquariums and as spores. You can also purchase seaweeds from your dealer to add plant-like decor to your aquarium.

Needing light and nutrients to thrive

Whether or not algae are plants, they act like them. They need light to grow and prosper just like your favorite backyard tree. And like that same tree, nutrients like nitrates and phosphates are the fertilizers that form the building blocks of algae. In your aquarium, these natural ingredients are well-represented. Strong lighting and nitrate from the nitrogen cycle fuel the propagation of algae.

In addition, algae are photosynthetic, so they utilize carbon dioxide and convert it into oxygen. (Chapter 13 tells you that the reduction of carbon dioxide in your aquarium is a good thing.) However, this characteristic is a double-edged sword because algae need light to photosynthesize, and at night they respire, producing carbon dioxide.

REMEMBER

Algae act as convenient repositories that can be used to remove excess nutrients from your aquarium. By routinely scraping some (not all!) of your algae from the tank, you're physically getting nitrates, phosphates, and other nutrients out of your tank. Another great place to grow algae is in the refugium of your sump, where nitrates from the display tank provide fertilizer and the algae can be easily harvested.

Avoiding the sterility syndrome

The primary reason that people find algae to be a problem is associated with what I call the *sterility syndrome.* Many new aquarists think that a sterile-looking aquarium is a clean and healthy aquarium, so they remove as much of the algae as they can at all times to keep the tank clean-looking. Well, this belief couldn't be further from the truth. Next time you go snorkeling or diving in the ocean, look closely at the rocks, coral, and sand: You'll see algae literally covering all the exposed surfaces.

Algae are an integral part of the natural coral reef ecosystem. Many species of fish and invertebrates feed exclusively on algae, and some important species of algae actually live inside some invertebrates, providing them food (see Chapter 4). Unfortunately, even in the wild, excess algal growth can smother a coral reef ecosystem. Rising water temperatures associated with global changes in climate have promoted the suffocating effects of algae and resulted in the loss of coral reefs worldwide.

TIP

Don't succumb to the sterility syndrome. Get used to seeing algae and promoting algal growth in your aquarium, yet routinely remove *some* of it to maintain a clear view of your pets and to get rid of excess nutrients.

Algae Are Out of Control

As in the wild, at some point your aquarium algae may get out of control. Excessive algae literally choke an aquarium by consuming oxygen during the night and covering live corals and live rock. They clog your filter system and obscure your vision by covering the walls of your tank. You can physically remove the excess algae, but doing so may only remove the symptom and not solve the problem. You need to take the following steps if you have too much algae.

Go to the source

When the algae in your aquarium become a nuisance, consider this a sign that something is wrong in your aquarium. Algae need light and nutrients to propagate in your aquarium, so when algae become a nuisance, check these factors.

TIP

First, check your light levels: Is your aquarium too close to a window, allowing for excess sunlight? Is your light being kept on too long? Are you using the correct kind of lighting? How old is your light source? The quality of a light will degrade as it ages, and this may contribute to your algae problem.

REMEMBER

In most cases, excess algal growth is caused by a problem with nutrient levels. In other words, your tank has too much fertilizer in it. Now is the time to check your water chemistry, looking at the factors that I outline in Chapters 12 and 13. Start with the nitrate and then check pH, carbonate hardness, and phosphate. Have you conducted routine water changes (see Chapter 15)? Is your circulation and aeration adequate (see Chapter 9)? Check your filtration, as well.

If you find that one or more of these parameters is out of balance, take steps to remedy them. Flip to Chapters 12 and 13 to determine how to solve your water problems.

Feed some fish

One of the best and most enjoyable ways to control algae is to stock your aquarium with algae-eating critters. Chapters 2 and 3 introduce a number of species of fish and invertebrates that eat algae. Among those species that readily consume algae are the following:

>> Blennies

>> Hermit crabs

>> Rabbitfish

- » Sea urchins
- » Snails
- » Tangs

Harvest time

At some point, removing algae will become a part of your routine maintenance. Even if it's not out of control, algae will cover your glass and obstruct the view of your pets. You can purchase algae scrubbers and tube brushes to remove algae, as I discuss in Chapter 9.

TIP

If beneficial *green* algae are excessive, simply remove them from the aquarium fixtures by rinsing. A vacuum will help remove algae from the gravel. If the excessive algae are the *blue-green slime* algae, make every effort to remove *all* the algae and the causes of it. Poor water quality must be improved. Test the water, conduct a partial water change (see Chapter 15), and check the operation of your filters. The next section of this chapter helps you discriminate among different types of algae.

REMEMBER

Removing algae is a great way to remove excess nutrients from your aquarium, but if the algae are the beneficial variety, *don't* fall into the sterility syndrome and remove them all.

Identifying Your Algae

One thing is certain, not all algae are alike. Although a number of formal classifications have been set up for algae, and scientists recognize at least eight major divisions, not all occur in the typical aquarium. Some kinds are desirable, and others are not. Some are typically referred to as seaweeds, others are planktonic, and some are both.

There is really no point in reviewing all the various kinds of algae, so the following sections concentrate only on those that you're most likely to encounter or purchase for your marine aquarium.

Green algae

Traditionally called the *Chlorophyta*, green algae have now been technically separated into several taxonomic groups, but green algae is a much easier term to remember. With more than 7,000 species, this group of algae is the most diverse, but only about 10 percent of the green algae are marine forms. These are typically the most beneficial of the algae, although some species are less desirable. They're green in color because their chlorophyll pigments are identical to those of higher plants.

Although many green algae are seaweeds, the planktonic spores of some species aren't visible to the naked eye but appear as a green cloudiness in the water. These algae sometimes form a green film on the aquarium glass. Larger green algae species may come in desirable plantlike shapes or less desirable hair and mat-like forms. The most attractive species of green algae are cultivated and sold as attractive additions to your aquarium.

The following types of green algae are popular:

>> **Caulerpa**: This is the most popular and common genus of green algae in the aquarium (see Figure 14-1). Members of this group come in a variety of colors ranging from lime green to bluish brown. They typically have a single stalk with blade-like leaves. These prolific algae are cultivated and offered by many marine aquarium dealers.

>> **Chaetomorpha**: Typically referred to as *Chaeto, spaghetti algae,* or *green hair algae,* these hair-like algae remove phosphates and nitrates from the water. This algae are an excellent macroalgae for the refugium, but don't introduce them into the main aquarium.

>> **Halimeda**: Unlike the *Caulerpa,* members of this genus are *calcareous,* meaning they contain calcium. They resemble underwater cacti growing as a series of circular flat plates. After death, the white calcium from these algae contributes to the sparkling white sand that you see on Caribbean beaches. In the aquarium, they're indicative of a healthy environment.

>> **Ulva**: Commonly referred to as sea lettuce, this group contains excellent algae for the refugium where they consume nitrates and phosphate. These leafy green algae are nutritious and readily accepted by herbivorous fish as well as invertebrates.

>> **Valonia**: These species of algae are called *bubble algae* because they form clusters of spherical bubbles. Although they have an attractive silver appearance, bubble algae can overgrow an aquarium and should be watched closely and regularly cropped.

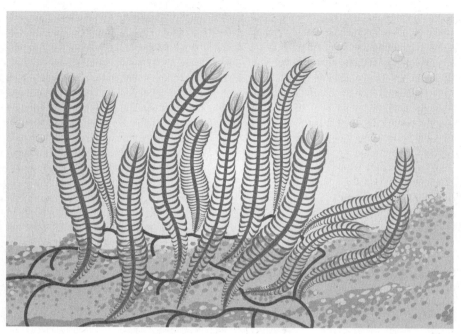

FIGURE 14-1:
An example of
Caulerpa, the
most common
type of green
algae.

WARNING

Hair algae are less desirable. These algae form thick, hair-like mats that can carpet your aquarium. For a fish-only tank, this matting will be simply ugly, but in the reef tank, it can smother and kill live corals. Make efforts to control hair algae in the main aquarium.

Red algae

This group of algae, called the *Rhodophyta*, contains more than 7,000 species, and many are marine seaweeds. Although most red algae are multicellular and grow attached to rocks and other algae (see Figure 14-2), some are single-celled forms.

TECHNICAL
STUFF

Red algae are red because of the pigment called *phycoerythin*, which absorbs blue light and reflects red light. Their coloration, which depends on how much of this pigment they have, ranges from reddish yellow to bright red to greenish blue and brown. Because blue light penetrates much deeper than red light, these algae typically live at deeper depths and are well adapted to low lighting conditions.

© John Wiley & Sons, Inc.

FIGURE 14-2:
An example of
red algae.

A lot of red algae are introduced into the aquarium on live rocks. The most common are called *coralline red algae,* which secrete a hard calcareous shell the way corals do. These algae are considered important in the formation of tropical reefs and, in some areas, may contribute more to reef structure than corals. They're beneficial to an aquarium, encrusting rocks and even spreading to the fixtures and glass.

Brown algae

Belonging to the class *Phaeophyceae,* the brown algae comprise about 2,000 species that are predominantly marine seaweeds. There are no single-celled forms of brown algae (the simplest is a branched filamentous organism, which is technical information that you don't need to remember).

Their brown coloration results from the dominance of a *xanthophyll* pigment, which masks other pigments including chlorophyll. Colors of brown algae range from pale beige to yellow-brown to almost black.

TECHNICAL
STUFF

The most common brown algae, called *kelp,* are the largest algae, the ones that attain lengths greater than 200 feet. The giant kelp forms expansive seaweed forests off the coast of North America and provides habitat and shelter for many organisms. Tropical waters have fewer species of brown algae.

Some forms of brown algae come attached to live rock when you purchase it. Like the red algae, small amounts of brown algae are generally beneficial for a saltwater aquarium.

Diatoms

Sometimes referred to as brown algae because of their coloration, *diatoms* are microscopic cells composed of overlapping half shells of silica. The diatoms are planktonic and *benthic* (live on the bottom) algae that spend their lives floating in the ocean or in the sediments. Their silica shells, called *frustules,* are remarkably geometric in shape, but their microscopic size makes them difficult for the average aquarist to see.

In the ocean, diatoms form a major part of the plant-plankton called *phytoplankton,* providing important food for the animal-plankton called *zooplankton.* Chapter 7 discusses how the frustules of diatoms are used in diatom filters as filter media.

These algae proliferate in aquariums with high nitrate levels. They're usually the first algae to establish themselves. Diatoms form a brown slime on the gravel, rocks, decorations, and aquarium glass (see Figure 14-3). Heavy concentrations of diatoms discolor the water. As the aquarium matures, these algae should disappear. Until they do, you can scrape them away to keep a clear view of your aquarium pets.

FIGURE 14-3: Diatoms form a brown slime on rocks and other tank decorations.

© John Wiley & Sons, Inc.

Dinoflagellates

Members of this group are single-celled organisms that have the characteristics of both plants and animals (refer to Figure 14-4), but they're still considered algae. Although it sounds like a prehistoric reptile, the name *dinoflagellate* actually refers to their forward swimming motion created by their tails, which are called *flagella.*

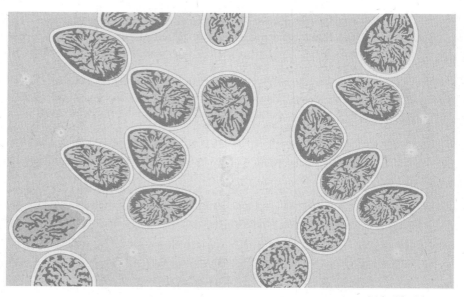

FIGURE 14-4: Dinoflagellates can be both good and bad for your aquarium.

TECHNICAL STUFF

Not all species of dinoflagellates are photosynthetic, and some species are planktonic, while others are *benthic*; that is, they live on the bottom. Some species of dinoflagellates are harmful to sea life and those that eat it. Dinoflagellate blooms, called *red-tide*, turn coastal waters reddish-brown, producing serious toxins that can affect human health.

Dinoflagellates can be both dangerous and healthy for your aquarium. Some kinds actually thrive when you have very low nutrient levels — little to no nitrates and phosphates — in your aquarium. These dinoflagellates are able to harness light and photosynthesize their own food, allowing them to overrun your aquarium and create a brown slime. If this happens, you can use commercial remedies, physically remove the algae, reduce flow in your aquarium, introduce competitive organisms like live rock, and turn off the skimmer. Those dinoflagellates that utilize aquarium nutrients are good for your aquarium, as long as they aren't allowed to proliferate out of control. In some instances, excessive nutrient levels cause dinoflagellate blooms in your aquarium. If this happens, the algae must be physically removed with a siphon.

The best defense against dinoflagellates is to maintain a proper biological balance in the aquarium and avoid situations of extreme cleanliness.

The dinoflagellates that are of greatest interest to aquarists are those that live in live corals, sponges, clams, and anemones. These are called *zooxanthellae,* and I discuss them in Chapter 4. These algae form a *symbiotic relationship* with their hosts, providing beneficial organic carbon that they produce by photosynthesis.

If you're an invertebrate enthusiast, make sure you have sufficient lighting to keep zooxanthellae dinoflagellates alive. If they die, in all likelihood, their host will die.

Blue-green algae

The blue-green algae are technically not algae at all: They are bacteria. For years, they were considered algae because they're aquatic and make their own food. This group of bacteria is called the *Cyanobacteria,* and it has the distinction of being the oldest known group of organisms at more than 3.5 billion years old. Because they're bacteria, blue-green algae are small and single-celled, but they grow in large enough colonies that you can see them. Although called blue-green algae, they can have colors ranging from black to red to purple.

They may be earth's bacterial heroes, but when these algae are in your aquarium they can be both good and bad. Like a lot of bacteria, blue-green algae in your substrate are beneficial to the health of your aquarium, feasting on *detritus* (organic wastes). However, in cases of poor water quality, high nutrients, and poor circulation, they form a dark brownish-red gelatinous mat, called *red slime,* on rocks, gravel, and plants in your tank. They're also capable of producing toxins that poison aquarium fish. If allowed to proliferate, they smother the tank. Unfortunately, few critters feed on blue-green algae, so they must be physically removed with a siphon during a partial water change.

Several products on the market help eliminate slime algae, but the key is to stay on top of your water chemistry, water changes, and water circulation.

Chapter **15**

Keeping Your Aquarium Clean and Handling Issues

A fish living in the open ocean isn't generally too concerned about water quality. Waste products and detritus are, after all, diluted by massive amounts of water. In the closed aquarium system, however, this isn't the case. *You* must keep the aquarium clean.

My friend, keeping an aquarium is all about preventative maintenance. You know that your house, your car, and even your body benefit from routine care and maintenance. Everything lasts a lot longer with fewer problems. Your marine aquarium is no exception.

Ben Franklin said, "An ounce of prevention is worth a pound of cure." Aquariums are a testament to Franklin's quote. This chapter tells you how a little work every day will keep your aquarium healthy in the long run.

Performing the Basics

Cleaning an aquarium involves a conscientious effort on your part. In fact, maintaining a fish tank isn't for the lazy at heart. Don't set up a saltwater aquarium if you don't intend to follow through and keep it clean and healthy. All too often, an aquarist's interest wanes after the first couple of months of ownership, and the aquarium occupants ultimately suffer the consequences.

REMEMBER

Realize that going into this hobby requires a real commitment on your part. You need to show concern at every step and on every level. Your fishes' lives depend on your attention to detail.

TIP

If you're a parent, and your children have an aquarium, it's your responsibility to help them maintain the aquarium. You probably experienced the empty promises made by children who want a new pet. Make a game out of it and try to keep it fun. As soon as it starts to feel like work, you're on your own.

Basic tasks need tended to on a regular basis. They're listed as follows, and I cover them in detail in the following sections:

>> Vacuum the gravel.

>> Clean and maintain the filters.

>> Test your water quality.

>> Conduct partial water changes.

In the "Sticking to Your Maintenance Schedule" section later in the chapter, I give you a schedule for some of these tasks, but this isn't set in stone, and you should customize the schedule as you see fit. The frequency with which you clean your aquarium depends on how dirty it gets, and that depends on the number of occupants, the quality of your filtration, and the amount of food that is left to foul your tank.

Sucking it up

Vacuuming is one of the most important parts of maintaining your tank. You must reduce the accumulation of detritus in the gravel so that your biological filters aren't overwhelmed.

Detritus is the combination of fish wastes and uneaten food that sinks to and decays on the bottom of the aquarium. If not removed, this organic waste breaks down into ammonia and overwhelms the nitrogen cycle (refer to Chapter 12 for more about this cycle). This will, in turn, disturb your water chemistry, snowballing into a series of problems that will ultimately harm your fish and invertebrates.

Detritus can be particularly damaging to an undergravel filter. Too much clogs the undergravel filter, preventing water flow through the gravel and reducing the filter's ability to do its job.

Although an aquarium vacuum is a nice piece of equipment, the old-fashioned garden hose also works to siphon wastes (see the section "Siphoning water" later in this chapter). If you choose to purchase an *aquarium vacuum*, sometimes called a *substrate cleaner*, more than likely you can find them at your aquarium dealer. Chapter 9 addresses the kinds of gravel vacuums available to you.

The most efficient way to vacuum your aquarium is while conducting a water change, because water is removed in the process anyway. This accomplishes two goals at once:

>> Vacuuming detritus

>> Removing water from the tank for replacement

See the "Changing the water" section later in this chapter to figure out how to vacuum your aquarium while changing your water.

When you vacuum, make sure you gently rake the gravel. If you have an under-gravel filter, don't mix it up too aggressively or you will disrupt the filter bed.

Cleaning your filters

Many filters have their own maintenance schedule. The level to which you clean your filter depends on the kind of filtration that it provides. A filter that's strictly mechanical can be cleaned thoroughly to remove debris, whereas a biological filter shouldn't be touched except to remove large detritus. Somewhere in the middle is the chemical filter, which should be recharged every month.

Filters remove wastes from the aquarium and either retain them (mechanical and chemical filtration) or convert them to less harmful compounds (biological filtration). With the exception of the natural biological filtration of live rock, wastes accumulate in most filters until you remove them by cleaning.

In the following sections, I touch briefly on each filter that I describe in Chapter 7, giving you a maintenance routine.

Inside box filter

Although you may not be using inside box filters except in a quarantine tank (see Chapter 5), you can easily maintain them. Simply replace the activated carbon and the filter floss every month, retaining about half of the latter for the bacteria that they harbor.

Sponge filter

Because the sponge in this type of filter provides the filter medium for mechanical and biological filtration, there are no other media to change. Sponge filters are easy to maintain by rinsing them in water every two weeks to a month, but be careful not to wash them out too thoroughly (keep those bacteria!).

Undergravel filter

After a healthy undergravel filtration system is established, this filter can be used indefinitely without being disassembled and cleaned. There is no filter floss or carbon to change, and the only medium is the gravel itself. Nonetheless, debris does accumulate in the gravel, so the gravel needs to be vacuumed to keep the filter from clogging. Vacuum during routine partial water changes every two weeks (more on this in the "Changing the water" section, later in this chapter).

TIP

Every month, make sure that you check the airstones that power your undergravel filter and replace them if they're clogged or crumbling. If you have powerheads, make sure the intakes are clear and the impeller inside is clean. I like to take them apart every month and clean the moving non-electrical parts under running tap water. If they have excessive buildup of coralline algae, soak them and other fixtures in white vinegar for a couple of hours; doing so will dissolve the calcium.

Power filters

Power filters are easy to maintain. Most have cartridges that can be replaced every two to four weeks, depending on bioload (see Chapter 12) and waste accumulation. However, make every effort to retain 50 percent of the used filter media or use a sponge type medium so helpful bacteria aren't lost. If your filter has two cartridges, alternate their replacement so bacteria are always present. Activated carbon should be replaced every month, as well.

If your filter is equipped with a biowheel, you can retain bacteria even though you have to replace the internal filter media. Biowheels don't need to be cleaned.

Filter impellers should be cleaned every month under running tap water so that they continue to run efficiently.

Canister filters

The canister filter contains compartments with various kinds of filter media, like activated carbon, filter sponges, filter floss, and ceramic bodies. The use of multiple filter media allows valuable bacteria to be retained when the filter is cleaned every month, depending on waste accumulation and bioload.

When the canister filter is cleaned, the activated carbon is replaced, the ceramic bodies and filter sponges are rinsed and retained, and 50 percent of the filter floss is replaced.

The number of filter components depends on the brand of canister filter — many are available. Read the manufacturer's instructions and follow its recommended maintenance schedule.

Don't forget to check those impellers and clean them, as well.

Trickle filters and sumps

Trickle filters offer great advantages over other filter systems relative to filtration efficiency and effectiveness. In addition, they require little maintenance. Like the canister filters, you can find many brands, and the level to which you clean them depends on their components. Every month, replace the carbon and rinse the sponges and filter pads that are providing mechanical filtration. Bioballs and ceramic bodies can be rinsed every six months to a year.

Live rock

The natural biological filtration of live rock needs little to no maintenance. As long as the aquarium remains healthy and circulation is maintained, live rock is self-cleaning and self-perpetuating. That's why this natural choice of filtration is becoming so popular.

Protein skimmers

Daily checks are required for the protein skimmer to make sure that it's working properly and to empty the collection cup if needed. Airflow components, like airstones, air ports, and tubing, should be checked regularly and then cleaned and replaced as needed. Every month, clean the powerhead or water pump impellers, as well.

Follow your manufacturer's maintenance schedule so that your protein skimmer is kept running efficiently.

Testing, testing, testing (your water)

When you first set up your aquarium, testing the water every day is critical to monitoring the water-maturation process. As you begin to add fish, water chemistry will change radically, and water-quality monitoring remains essential for the survival of your fish. After this sensitive period, which can last several weeks, it's still important to test your water. I recommend that you do so at least once every week. Doing so gives you a good understanding of the mechanics of the nitrogen cycle and tells you when the nitrates, carbonate hardness, pH, and other parameters are to the point at which a water change is needed. As for temperature and specific gravity/salinity, you should keep an eye on those parameters every day.

Look out for sudden behavioral changes in your fish, fish disease, fish mortality, excessive algal growth, smelly water, and cloudy water. All these warrant an immediate water-quality test and possible water change.

Keep track of the results of your water testing in a journal so you can compare them to previous test results. If you notice a dramatic change since the last test in any water parameter, you may need to do the following:

>> If the pH is too low, conduct a water change, and see Chapter 13 for more information on how to raise it.

>> If the ammonia, nitrite, or nitrate levels are too high, conduct a water change and see Chapter 12 for more information.

>> If carbonate hardness is too low, conduct a water change and see Chapter 13 for more information.

>> If your salinity or specific gravity is too high or too low, see Chapter 13 for information on how to adjust it.

Changing the water

Water changes are one of the most important aspects of cleaning and maintaining your aquarium. Waste products build slowly in your aquarium and the resilience of your water is slowly depleted (as I discuss more in Chapters 12 and 13). The only way to solve both of these problems is to physically change your water, removing the wastes and replenishing valuable trace elements.

Deciding how much and how often

The typical preventative water change usually involves 10 to 20 percent of the tank's volume being replaced with properly balanced premixed seawater. The added water, which should be the correct specific gravity and temperature, will also replace exhausted trace elements and nutrients. The amount you change varies with the quality of your water, the aquarium's bioload (number of critters), and the frequency of water changes.

REMEMBER

Most experts recommend a 10 percent water change every week or a 20 percent change every two weeks. If your aquarium is crowded, your son Wilson has a tendency to overfeed the fishes, or you're unable to change your water frequently, you may need to change a greater volume. However, if your aquarium isn't heavily stocked, you're careful when you feed, and you're religious about water changes, you can get away with less.

I recommend that you start with a water change of 20 percent every two weeks and modify it either up or down depending on the type of filtration and water quality. For example, a 55-gallon saltwater aquarium with live rock or a trickle filter (wet/dry filter) and a protein skimmer can probably go longer between water changes.

TIP

Keep an eye on nitrate levels because they tell you if you need to increase or decrease the frequency and volume of water changes. Chapter 12 explains how to test your nitrates.

Siphoning water

The best way to conduct a water change is to use an aquarium vacuum and a large plastic bucket. The vacuum has a large diameter tube attached to a siphon. The siphon is used to draw water from the aquarium, while the vacuum is thrust into the substrate, stirring the gravel and allowing detritus to flow out with the water into the bucket.

The surface gravel should be stirred during every partial water change for two reasons.

>> If you have an undergravel filter, stirring breaks up impacted areas in the filter bed where water flow has become restricted.

>> Stirring puts detritus into suspension where it can be siphoned out with the old water.

TIP

When you change the water, make every effort to efficiently cover as much of the substrate as possible, but don't rush over spots. If you can't cover it all, make a mental note where you left off and start at that spot with the next water change.

REMEMBER

If your substrate is sand, only move the vacuum over the top of the sand and be careful not to suck it right out of the tank. These steps explain how to siphon:

1. **Fill the tube completely with water, making sure no air is trapped in the tube.**

   Ensure the siphon and your hands are clean. You can fill the hose by submerging it in the aquarium, but do this only if your aquarium is large enough to accommodate the hose without spooking the fish. Otherwise, place one end of the tube in the tank, put your mouth on the other, and draw the aquarium water that way to start the flow.

2. **Make sure the bucket end is lower than the aquarium, or siphoning won't work.**

   If you filled your siphon in the aquarium, plug one end of the hose tightly with your thumb, lift it from the aquarium, and bring it lower than the tank to the bucket.

3. **Release your thumb, and the water will begin to flow rapidly from the aquarium into the bucket.**

   You can control the water flow by pinching the hose.

4. **Discard the water in the bucket.**

Figure 15-1 illustrates both siphoning water to and from the tank.

Adding water

When you need to add water, make sure you use premixed and conditioned saltwater that you store in a cool, dark place. Heat your replacement water to the same temperature as your aquarium and aerate it for about 15 minutes before conducting the water change (see Chapter 7).

To add water, pour the premixed saltwater slowly into your tank, making sure not to disrupt the aquarium or its inhabitants.

REMEMBER

Verify the water you add is the same temperature and specific gravity as the water in your aquarium.

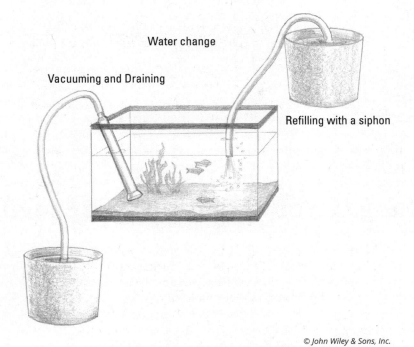

Water change

Vacuuming and Draining

Refilling with a siphon

FIGURE 15-1:
Use a siphon and vacuum to clean your gravel and change your water.

WARNING

Water out of your tap may be loaded with chlorine, chloramine, heavy metals, phosphates, and other ions. Many of these compounds are harmful to fish, so they need to be removed. This process is called *water conditioning*. It doesn't hurt to read the water-mixing sections in Chapter 9 to review how to premix and condition saltwater.

REMEMBER

Your local water company routinely checks the water supply for these compounds. Check with them to find out what's in your tap water.

Topping off

Don't confuse water changes with adding water that has evaporated from the aquarium. Depending on the amount of aeration and circulation that you have (see Chapter 7), you may have more or less water evaporation. When water evaporates, dissolved salts are left behind, and the specific gravity of the water increases.

WARNING

Pay attention to this process, because changes in specific gravity cause severe problems for your tank's inhabitants.

Water evaporation is readily solved by adding *freshwater*, not premixed conditioned saltwater, to your aquarium. The water you add should be conditioned tap water. If you don't have a lot of evaporation, the use of store-bought distilled water relieves you of the need to condition the water.

TECHNICAL STUFF

Distilled water is pure water, that is, pure H_2O without additives and toxic compounds.

REMEMBER

Many aquarium shops sell filtered water specifically for saltwater aquariums.

Sticking to Your Maintenance Schedule

The list in this section gives you a rough guideline for keeping up with preventative maintenance. Use this as a starting point and fine-tune it to fit your needs and those of your new pets. Most of these steps are self-explanatory, requiring just a few minutes of your time.

Every day

Every day, do the following:

>> **Turn the aquarium lights on and off.** Most aquarists prefer to use an automatic timer and/or dimmer. If you choose not to, try to turn the lights on and off in a consistent pattern. Marine animals are accustomed to consistent light patterns.

>> **Observe your fish and invertebrates carefully for signs of stress, disease, or death.** Be prepared to remove or treat fish that aren't well.

>> **Feed the fishes and invertebrates twice a day, removing any uneaten food.** Some fishes may require more frequent feeding, while others not so much. Make every effort to cater to the needs of each species.

>> **Conduct water tests until the water matures and the nitrogen cycle is established.** Routine tests include ammonia, nitrite, nitrate, and pH. Record the test results.

>> **Check the water temperature and specific gravity or salinity.** Adjust the heater as needed.

>> **Empty the protein skimmer collection cup as needed.** Follow the manufacturer's instructions to do it properly.

>> **Check the water levels of tank and/or sump and top off as needed.** Be sure to add freshwater due to evaporation.

>> **Check all aquarium systems: heater, filters, aerators, protein skimmer.** Make sure they're running properly and smoothly and pay special attention to intakes and siphon tubes. Ensure nothing is leaking.

Every week

Once a week, complete the following tasks:

>> **Remove excess algae.** Doing so keeps beneficial algae at acceptable levels and gets rid of nuisance algae (see Chapter 14).

>> **Clean the glass, both inside and out.** Don't use glass cleaner; vinegar works well. Remove salt-creep deposits.

>> **Conduct all water tests weekly after the water matures and the nitrogen cycle is established.** Include alkalinity, calcium, and phosphate. Record all test results and add trace elements and buffers, as needed.

Every two weeks

Every two weeks, do the following:

>> **Clean filters as needed.** Partially change or rinse the filter media on some filters if the bioload is high, the media is dirty, or the flow is restricted.

>> **Change 20 percent of the tank water while vacuuming the gravel.** Use the siphoning steps in the "Siphoning water" section in this chapter.

Monthly

Every month, be sure you complete these tasks:

>> **Conduct thorough filter checks.** Replace the filter carbon and rinse the filter media and components as needed and depending on bioload.

>> **Clean the protein skimmer.** Follow the manufacturer's instructions.

>> **Clean the outside of aquarium, removing salt and calcium deposits, dust, and dirt.** Scrape away the deposits and use a nontoxic substance, like vinegar, for the glass.

>> **Rinse any tank decorations that suffer from excess algae.** Remember not to use any soaps or solvents, just a thorough rinse.

Quarterly (every three months)

Every three months, conduct a thorough examination of all aquarium systems, including lighting, heating, filtration, aeration pumps, and tubing. Replace or clean parts as needed.

In the long run

If you maintain a freshwater aquarium, you're encouraged to break down your aquarium completely every year, essentially starting from scratch. This isn't the case in the marine aquarium. The effectiveness of a well-established biological filter will last for years.

REMEMBER

However, if you're using an undergravel filter, it may become heavily clogged over a long period. In addition, the substrate itself may begin to break down in about two years. However, you can slowly replace the gravel over several months by removing a thin strip of gravel and replacing it with new gravel. The following week, repeat the procedure and continue to do so until the entire substrate has been replaced without disrupting the aquarium. Under no circumstances should you break down a healthy aquarium and replace the gravel in one step.

Taking Care of Emergencies

This section makes me cringe as I write it. Nobody likes to think of extreme situations when something goes terribly wrong with an aquarium or the systems that keep it going. But, like all preventative maintenance, contingency plans must be in place, and you need to know how to keep your pets alive.

What do I mean by emergencies? The most common are power failure, water leaks, overheating, and pollution, and I discuss each in the following sections.

By definition, you never really know when an emergency is going to strike. If you did, it wouldn't be an emergency. One thing I've done is establish an arrangement with my dealer, Condo. He temporarily houses my fish and invertebrates during extreme emergencies.

Pay particular attention to your fish and invertebrates after any kind of emergency. These kinds of events cause extreme stress, which can, in turn, lead to disease that will become apparent over the following two weeks.

When a power outage strikes

Power failure is a pretty common emergency, but you can't do a lot to prevent it. Because most power outages are temporary and last less than 24 hours, your fish and invertebrates will be fine if you aerate the water while the power is down. For these situations, it's a good idea to own a battery-powered air pump, which helps you circulate the water and maintain dissolved oxygen levels. To keep heat in the tank, wrap a thick blanket or sleeping bag around the tank. Don't feed your fish while the power is down, because your filters aren't working.

Unfortunately, you may live in an area that's prone to frequent power failures, lengthy power failures, or hurricanes, which can knock out power for days. If so, make the investment and buy a portable generator for your aquarium or a battery back-up system. It can be an expensive option, but I look at it this way: You've already invested hundreds of dollars in your aquarium and its inhabitants. Why take the chance of losing everything in one power failure? In the long run, you'll save both time and money with a generator.

When your aquarium leaks

Another major emergency occurs is when your aquarium springs a leak. I know that the likelihood of your tank leaking is pretty low, but the chance of little Eve hurling a baseball through it isn't beyond the realm of reality.

If this happens, collect as much of the water as possible into buckets and place your aquarium inhabitants into them. Make sure you aerate the water, and then rush out and replace the tank as soon as possible. Transfer your filtration and all other equipment, including your gravel, to the new tank. Then add your water and fish.

If you try to repair the tank, the process may take too long. And your fish shouldn't live in buckets for more than 24 hours. It's better to buy a new tank.

When your heater malfunctions

A malfunction of your heater can lead to aquarium overheating. Most tropical fish and invertebrates can handle water temperatures as high as 86 degrees F, but they don't necessarily like it. If the heat keeps cranking, you're going to literally boil them alive.

REMEMBER

The best way to deal with overheating is to avoid it. One way to do this is to use two smaller, less powerful heaters instead of one large one. That way, if the heater malfunctions, you can detect it during a daily check and before the water temperature is driven to lethal levels.

TIP

If you find your aquarium overheated, immediately turn the heater down, remove 20 to 50 percent of the water, and place floating ice bags in the aquarium. Save the water that you removed in buckets and let it cool. Monitor the water temperature closely and return the water when temperatures in the aquarium and in the buckets are similar.

When the water is polluted

If your aquarium is well balanced, and your filtration is working properly, it's unlikely that you will sustain a major pollution event. However, suppose right after you walk out the door one morning, one of your fish dies. Suppose that fish sits in your aquarium for a day or two because you're traveling. See where I am going? Ammonia will skyrocket, pH will drop, and dissolved oxygen will plummet. Pollution city!

REMEMBER

When you walk through that door and discover a pollution event because the water is cloudy and not smelling very good, you need to mobilize emergency procedures immediately. I recommend a 40 to 50 percent water change. Change the carbon in your filters and conduct water tests. Conduct another 20 percent water change if conditions don't improve. Don't feed your fish until conditions have stabilized and returned to normal. After aquarium conditions return to normal, change or rinse the filter media and replace the filter carbon.

4

Caring for Your Fish

Understand that good nutrition is the key to keeping your aquarium pets healthy, discover the kinds of foods available, and know how to properly feed your fish and invertebrates.

Get a grip on stress in your aquarium and understand how it affects your pets, identify those conditions that are stressful to you and your fish, and take steps to prevent and cope with stress.

Know how to identify common aquarium diseases and take the steps necessary to properly treat your fish when they aren't feeling well.

Keep a watchful eye on your aquarium pets, monitor their behavior while maintaining a good aquarium log, and take photos when you're inspired to show off.

Chapter **16**

Feeding Your Fish

F ish and invertebrates are alive, just as people are alive. And people need fuel for energy and growth, and that comes in the form of food. In their natural environment, fish and invertebrates have to find their own food. They hunt, they scavenge, and they graze. In your aquarium, your pets are spoiled. They don't have to work too hard to feed. However, this puts the responsibility on you to provide them with a well-balanced diet that keeps them alive and healthy.

One of the most enjoyable parts of owning an aquarium is feeding its occupants. The tank seems to come alive at feeding time, and your children, grandchildren, and friends will get a big kick out of it. This chapter helps you provide your fish and invertebrates with the right food. When considering nutrition, living marine animals are no different from your other pets: They need a well-balanced diet.

Giving Them Their Meat and Veggies

The raw materials needed for life and growth are called *nutrients*. Fish, like all other animals, need these nutrients for sustenance, growth, and reproduction. They can get these nutrients only from organic matter that has, at one time or another, been alive.

Keep several considerations in mind when providing food for your fish. In their natural habitat, fish have evolved various feeding strategies to optimize their ability to obtain nutrients. With all the different kinds of fish and habitats, you can imagine the many feeding strategies that exist.

In general, fish can be divided into three general groups based on feeding strategy: carnivores, herbivores, and omnivores.

Before you buy a fish or invertebrate, find out its feeding preferences.

Meat eaters (carnivores)

Fishes and invertebrates that are predators or scavengers are called *carnivores.* In their natural habitat, they feed on fishes or invertebrates that they bite, engulf, or crush. These are flesh-eaters. The predators are active hunters of live animals whereas the scavengers feed on the carcasses of dead critters. If these creatures were human, they would prefer steak, chicken, fish, or any other meat. Carnivores eat a variety of animals, ranging from tiny plankton to large species of fish. Invertebrates, such as corals, that filter-feed on small plankton from the water are actually carnivorous.

In the aquarium, many tropical marine fishes and invertebrates have been successfully fed dead food, commercially prepared pellets and flakes, or live critters. Most carnivores take pieces of fish, shrimp, and other meats, but some species simply won't accept anything but live food to start. In these cases, you can offer live shrimp or black worms until the picky eater can be weaned off live food.

Although live freshwater fishes, like guppies and goldfish, were once commonly offered to carnivorous predators, I don't recommend it. Marine fishes didn't evolve eating freshwater fishes, so this could result in serious health issues.

Grazers (herbivores)

Critters that prefer to eat vegetative matter, which is mainly algae, are called *herbivores.* If these animals were people, they would be vegetarians — the salad or tofu eaters. Some tropical marine species of fish, such as tangs, are exclusively herbivorous, deriving all their nutrients from plants and algae. However, from a practical standpoint, there are few strictly herbivorous fishes in captivity, and most can be conditioned to eat other foods.

Studies have shown that all marine aquarium fishes known to feed exclusively on plants in the wild will accept animal tissue in captivity. Regardless, having a lush growth of algae in your aquarium is important if you intend to house fish or invertebrates that are herbivorous by nature. Many options are available on the market for herbivorous fishes, including prepared flakes and dry marine algae sheets. You can also augment their diet with household vegetables, like blanched lettuce and spinach.

Meat and potatoes (omnivores)

If a species of fish isn't selective relative to whether it eats meat or vegetables, it's called *omnivorous*. These fish and invertebrates feed on a variety of foods and have no specific dietary preferences. (Most humans are omnivorous by nature, mixing meats, fruits, and vegetables in their diet.)

TIP

Many of the recommended species I outline in Chapter 10 are considered omnivorous. As a new hobbyist, you don't want to worry about special feeding strategies when setting up a saltwater aquarium for the first time. Although these fish will accept commercially prepared flake and pellet foods, providing a good variety of foods is necessary to meet all their dietary requirements. Many invertebrate species are omnivorous as well, scavenging organic matter and algae from the substrate.

Knowing the Building Blocks of Fish Nutrition

Like all living animals, fish have dietary requirements for proteins, fats, carbohydrates, vitamins, and minerals. In their natural environment, fish meet their own needs by foraging and hunting. In the aquarium, fish rely entirely on you to meet their dietary needs.

Unfortunately, the nutritional needs of tropical marine organisms are poorly understood. These requirements can differ by species, age, water temperature, and many other factors. The best that any aquarist, including the professionals, can do is to feed the fish a variety of foods and thereby approximate their requirements.

REMEMBER

By consuming different types of food, the fish is more likely to obtain all its nutritional requirements.

>> **Proteins:** *Proteins* are major constituents of all animal tissue, and they're essential in the diet to maintain normal growth. Younger fish, in particular, require more protein in their diets than do larger, older fish.

>> **Lipids (fats):** *Lipids,* commonly called *fats,* are critical components of cell membranes. They also provide an immediate supply of chemical energy and stored energy. Most people probably have a little too much stored energy, if you know what I mean.

>> **Carbohydrates:** *Carbohydrates* are broken down into units of glucose, which is a major source of energy. They can also be converted to lipids for energy storage.

>> **Vitamins and minerals:** These important compounds play the same important roles in fish as they do in mammals. They provide the necessary ingredients for proper metabolism and skeletal stability.

Identifying the Types of Food

You can find many different types of food for your tropical marine fish. Carnivores eat flake food, brine shrimp, and almost any kind of seafood — crab, lobster, oysters, mussels, squid, clams, and fish. Herbivores adapt to an omnivorous diet, taking flake and frozen foods and vegetables while grazing on aquarium algae. Omnivores eat all these foods.

Aquarium foods can be grouped into a variety of categories, and experts do it differently. I prefer to classify aquarium foods into three general categories: natural foods, prepared foods, and live foods.

Natural foods

This group of foods includes items that are obtained fresh, frozen, or freeze-dried. They aren't heavily processed. They can be fed to the fish fresh, cooked, or dried. Foods under this category are leafy-green vegetables, fish and invertebrate flesh, and frozen or freeze-dried seaweed and invertebrates.

Leafy greens

Providing vegetative matter in the diet is essential because some of the marine species are naturally herbivorous. Although the algae in your aquarium may be enough for some grazing fishes and invertebrates, you can also feed vegetables that are fresh, blanched, or thawed after freezing. Common vegetables include lettuce, spinach, cabbage, parsley, kale, and watercress, to name a few.

Some aquarists prefer to *blanch* the vegetables to aid in their digestion. This means that vegetables are boiled for just a few minutes to soften them up and break down cell membranes.

You can also feed them *nori*, which is dried sheets of red algae. Nori, which means *edible seaweed* in Japanese, is sold for human consumption as sushi wrap, but it's also ideal for saltwater fish. Just be sure not to buy nori that is seasoned in any way.

In general, vegetables are composed mostly of water and are low in energy, protein, and lipid but contain high concentrations of carbohydrate, fiber, and certain vitamins. You don't want to feed only vegetables to your omnivorous fish; be prepared to provide them to your herbivorous fish.

Meaty foods of the sea

If you live in the sea, it only makes sense that you eat seafood, which includes a variety of foods comprising fish and invertebrate meats served fresh, thawed, or cooked. Cooking these foods doesn't lower their nutritional value. Some experts prefer to cook raw seafood because some species can carry infectious diseases that can be transmitted to the aquarium fish. Cooking can involve boiling, steaming, or using foods that are canned in water, which are already boiled.

Only feed your marine animals flesh from other sea animals because you want to serve them foods that have a similar composition to themselves. In other words, don't scrape your Thanksgiving turkey leftovers into the aquarium.

The variety of meats available is vast. This category includes fishes like herring, anchovy, smelt, mackerel, silversides, and tuna, as well as shellfish like clams, shrimp, mussels, scallops, oysters, crabs, and squid. In general, meaty foods contain less water and carbohydrate and substantially more protein and lipid than vegetative matter.

You must include meaty food for carnivorous fishes.

Frozen and dried

These foods often provide the greatest portion of your fish's diet, because many are specifically produced for aquarium use and are widely available. The dietary value of this food is similar to that of meaty foods. Some of the most common commercially available frozen foods in this category include mysis shrimp, brine shrimp, plankton, krill, and other shrimps. Also, many of the seafoods such as fish, squid, scallops, shrimp, and clams are offered frozen.

Frozen food is one of the best options for saltwater fish because of its nutritional value, which is much higher than in pellet and flake foods. Also, most commercial processors treat frozen foods with gamma rays to ensure that they are free of disease.

REMEMBER

Frozen foods are generally packaged in such a way that you can break off a chunk and put it in the aquarium. I prefer to thaw the food first in a small cup of water from the tank and then pour the mixture into the aquarium.

Freeze-drying has made it possible to preserve a variety of natural foods for aquarium fish. For the marine aquarium, the process has most often been applied to marine algae, brine shrimp, and other small invertebrates such as krill, tubifex worms, and bloodworms. These foods aren't processed, and what you see is what you get, simply the whole animal or algae without water.

WARNING

Dried and frozen foods help increase the variety of the foods that you're feeding your fish, but they shouldn't be the only food offered to them.

Prepared foods

This category of food not only contains the flake and dry foods that are commercially processed for aquarium fish, but also includes frozen processed foods that contain a number of healthy ingredients. Prepared foods try to approximate the basic requirements of proteins, fats, and carbohydrates. They're also supplemented with vitamins and minerals.

These foods come in many varieties, depending on the type of fish (carnivore, herbivore, or omnivore), and new formulations are being added every year to better estimate the dietary needs of specific species.

WARNING

Don't feed foods that are processed for freshwater fish to saltwater fish.

Prepared foods came in many forms, depending on the size and the feeding behavior of the fish. Flakes, tablets, pellets, and crumb forms are available. For example, larger predatory fishes should be fed pellets as opposed to flakes, because they prefer to consume a large quantity. In addition, fish that feed on the bottom may not venture to the surface for flakes, so they must be fed pellets or tablets that sink to the bottom. You can also stick pellets to the aquarium glass for the grazing species in your tank.

REMEMBER

You can feed prepared foods to many of the fish I review in this book. However, if you want active, colorful, and healthy fish, you must vary their diet. Flake is good as a staple food, but you need to make every effort to substitute other foods (every day) that enrich your fish.

Live foods

Live food is an excellent source of nutrition for the tropical marine aquarium. Fishes and invertebrates that are fed live foods ordinarily grow fast, have vibrant colors, and maintain high survival rates. This is because live foods retain active enzymes that make digestion more efficient. Also, because few fish species refuse live foods, offering live foods is the best way to get the picky eaters to eat.

Live foods are an essential requirement of captive fishes, and they must be included as a dietary supplement. The type of live food you give your pets depends on the size of the fish or invertebrate you're feeding. The following sections discuss some common live foods you can feed your fish.

REMEMBER

Some local dealers carry live foods, and you can also order them online.

Brine shrimp

The most popular live food for tropical marine fish is brine shrimp (*Artemia* species), a primitive crustacean inhabiting shallow salt ponds in more than 160 locations around the world. Those in your local pet store probably originated in San Francisco Bay or Great Salt Bay in Utah. They're one of the best sources of nutrition available for marine aquarium organisms of any type. Tiny hatchlings, called *nauplii,* are ideal for filter-feeding organisms, as well.

Brine shrimp are an excellent source of lipids and protein. Of all the live food available, they're the safest because they don't carry disease.

TIP

You can buy live brine shrimp at a local dealer or online. When you feed them to your fish, don't dump the water into your aquarium because it contains lots of impurities. Instead, net the shrimp from the container and rinse them with some of your aquarium water before feeding.

An added advantage to brine shrimp is that you can raise them yourself because many dealers sell brine shrimp eggs.

To raise brine shrimp, follow the instructions accompanying the eggs. However, I have found that the following simple steps work well:

1. **In a plastic or glass container, make a solution of seawater with a standard specific gravity of 1.021–1.025.**

2. **Bring the water temperature of the hatch solution up to about 75 to 80 degrees F.**

   Use an immersion heater if you must.

3. **Place an aerator in the solution and adjust the air to produce a slow stream of bubbles.**

   Too much air causes the eggs to collect along the edges of the container.

4. **Add the brine shrimp eggs, called *cysts,* at a concentration of about one teaspoon of eggs per gallon of hatch solution.**

   Handle them with care because they're small and delicate.

WARNING

5. **After 10 minutes, illuminate the container with a 40-watt light about 8 inches from the container for about 10 minutes.**

   Doing so initiates hatching.

6. **After 24 hours, shut off the aerator and allow the empty shells and unhatched eggs to separate from the *nauplii* (hatchlings).**

7. **After 15 minutes, attract the nauplii to a corner of the container using a small flashlight.**

   The young brine shrimp are attracted to light. This takes about 15 minutes, depending on how far they have to swim.

8. **When they're concentrated, drain or siphon them into a fine mesh net and rinse them well with artificial seawater.**

REMEMBER

You can also find containers at your dealer that fit in your aquarium for hatching brine shrimp eggs.

Brine shrimp can be fed to your fish or placed in a container of seawater for growing to larger sizes. If you choose to keep the young shrimp, bring the water temperature to about 86 degrees F and provide low aeration. The nauplii can be fed brewer's yeast or powdered rice bran dissolved in water for several days. Aquarists who want to raise the brine shrimp for longer periods should try to obtain one of the encapsulated feeds devised for crustacean larvae that are available commercially.

Other live foods

Other common live foods that may be available at your dealer include the following:

» **Blackworms and tubifex worms:** Many dealers carry these freshwater worms that are readily consumed by aquarium fishes. Although they're only worms, be aware that they won't live long in saltwater, so feed them sparingly. California blackworms are considered one of the best foods for picky saltwater fishes.

>> **Copepods:** These tiny crustaceans sometimes hitchhike into your tank on live rock or live sand, can be added intentionally, and/or can be cultured in your aquarium or refugium. Many species of fish will feast on copepods, which are rich in nutritional value.

>> **Glass shrimp:** Although these little decapods aren't easy to find, they make excellent live food for both fish and invertebrates in your aquarium. Their name comes from the fact that you can see right through them.

>> **Rotifers:** These tiny, planktonic animals are ideal for filter-feeding invertebrates. At one time, rotifers were difficult to obtain, but now they are readily cultivated by breeders and online distributors. You can also culture them at home.

Putting Food in Their Mouths

The biggest questions when it comes to feeding your critters are how much and how often to feed them. Some fish are gluttons, whereas others stop when they're full. You probably know people from both ends of this spectrum.

TIP

Have the same person or people feed the aquarium. This ensures that the feeding is done consistently and with an eye for the right quantities. Letting Uncle Bill feed the fish when he visits may result in a lot of waste and water pollution. Also, keep a tight lid on the tank during a party. Inevitably, everybody wants to feed the fish.

REMEMBER

Feeding them too little is better than too much. Use the following guidelines (and see Figure 16-1) when feeding and you'll develop a working sense of how much and how often to feed them.

>> **Offer as much food as your fish will eat in 5 minutes.** Flakes should sink no deeper than one-third the height of the tank. Provide tablets, pellets, or sinking food for bottom fish and invertebrates.

>> **Feed your fish in very small portions over the 5-minute period.** If any food is left over after this time, you're an overfeeder. Bear in mind, however, that some foods, such lettuce or spinach, are nibbled over time, so the 5-minute rule doesn't apply to leafy vegetables. Some foods can be attached to the side of the tank with a food clip, as Figure 16-1 shows.

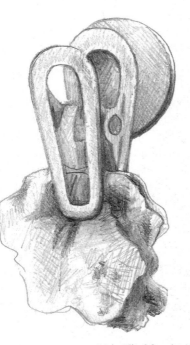

FIGURE 16-1: Nibblers appreciate food being clipped to the side.

>> **If you're home during the daytime, feed your fish and invertebrates very small portions over the course of the day.** In this case, reduce feeding time to about a minute or two per session. If you're not home, feed them twice a day at the same times every day: once in the morning, once in the evening.

>> **Always feed your fish at the same spot in the tank.** Doing so lets you sneak food down to bottom-dwellers while the surface fish are distracted.

>> **Rehydrate or thaw food beforehand.** Use a separate container, such as a glass (refer to Figure 16-2).

>> **Don't overfeed the fish, no matter how much you think they need more food.** Overeating stresses your fish and causes detritus to accumulate in the tank, degrading water quality.

Dealing with the oddballs

You'll find a lot of exceptions when feeding your wet pets. For example, some invertebrates, such as sea anemones and corals, house photosynthetic bacteria that provide them with nutrients, so you don't need to feed them every day. Their diet, however, should be augmented once or twice a week with fresh, frozen, or live foods.

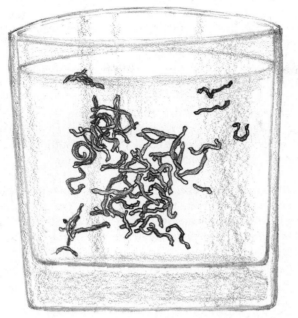

FIGURE 16-2:
Thaw frozen food before adding it to your tank.

Also, large carnivorous fish typically consume one large meal at a time, so you don't need to feed them more than once every day or two.

REMEMBER

It's better to underfeed than to overfeed your fishes and invertebrates.

Keeping a watchful eye

Watch all your fishes during feeding. During this time you can also assess your fishes' health and take a head count. Try to make sure that each gets its share of food, but that's not always possible. In the ocean world, it's eat or go hungry, so don't expect a lot of goodwill.

Remember that fish have different mouth shapes, which allow them to feed at different levels in the tank. Some species don't move to the surface to eat; they wait for food to disperse throughout the tank. Don't rely on surface feedings and the leftovers of others to feed bottom fish. Pellets or other foods that sink to the bottom should be provided to these fish. You may have to offer food through a turkey baster or distribute food via a feeding stick.

REMEMBER

Refusal to eat is one of the first signs of illness, so keep an eye out for fish that seem to have no interest in food.

TIP

Always remove food from the tank that hasn't been consumed. Allow nibblers time to eat — an hour or two — before removing leftovers.

Offering a variety

Freshwater fish and saltwater fish aren't the same — you know that. If you've ever had a freshwater aquarium, more than likely you sprinkled just dry flake food in your tank every day. You need to break that habit. Although you can offer a daily staple, variety is the spice of life for marine organisms.

You can try flake food and frozen brine shrimp as your staples, but mix in different foods as your fish acclimate to your aquarium. Try not to feed your fish right after turning on the light, because they won't be fully alert until about 30 minutes later. In addition, make sure you match the size of the food with the size of the fishes' mouths. You may need to crush or mulch the food for fish with small mouths. But don't grind the food too small. Doing so adds fine particles to the water that aren't ingested and that degrade water quality.

Going away

If you're going to be away from your aquarium for one or two days, the fish will be fine without food. In the wild, most fish feed sporadically and can go days without food, so a little fasting doesn't hurt them. When you return, don't feel that you have to feed your fish twice as much because they missed a meal. If you do, much will go uneaten.

If you plan to travel for longer periods, you have a couple of options:

>> **You can arrange for someone to feed your fish.** Prepare portions ahead of time and give detailed instructions on how to properly feed your animals. Don't let her do so at her own discretion unless she's an experienced aquarist.

>> **You can purchase an automatic feeder.** This specialized piece of equipment dispenses dry food for you while you're away. You wouldn't want to load it with fresh seafood, but many processed foods work well.

WARNING

Test your automated feeder before going away. A feeder that is set up improperly or malfunctions can be deadly to your aquarium. Nobody wants to come home to dead pets.

Feeding Your Invertebrates

While discussing feeding in this chapter, I make every effort to reference invertebrates as well as fishes. Nonetheless, I think it's important to touch on a few extra points about feeding invertebrates because they're such a diverse group.

REMEMBER

The key to invertebrate feeding is to do so *sparingly*. They don't need as much food as their fishy counterparts.

In general, invertebrates can be divided into three kinds of feeders: carnivorous predators and scavengers, herbivorous grazers, and filter feeders.

Hunting and gathering (carnivorous)

Many invertebrate species, such as lobsters, squids, conchs, and large crabs, are predators or scavengers of meat. If you choose to keep any of these critters, you can provide them with many meaty foods, like seafoods, including clams, mussels, squid, and shrimps. Feed these invertebrates once a day — quantities depend on the size of the animal. Be sure to remove uneaten food after about an hour, because these invertebrates tend to eat slowly.

Scraping (herbivorous)

Herbivorous invertebrates, like small snails and crabs, prefer to graze algae from the walls, gravel, and decorations in the aquarium. They can typically subsist on this while scavenging minute organic matter, as well.

Sifting (filter feeders)

Strict filter feeders, like featherduster worms and soft corals, generally aren't recommended for the aquarium of a beginner. However, if you simply can't resist the beauty of these critters in your reef tank, you have to feed them liquidized seafoods, newly hatched brine shrimp nauplii, live rotifers, or commercial liquid feeds. Feed filter feeders once per day: The general quantity is about one drop of liquid food per animal. Note, though, that the food requirements of suspension feeding creatures are quite specific, so make sure you're providing the right food for the species you're keeping.

Several species of filter feeders, such as anemones and hard corals, contain photosynthetic algae that provide them with a lot of their nutritional needs. However, don't assume that all their nutritional requirements are met by these algae. In nature, these animals still filter feed, so they must be fed in captivity, as well. Any of the filter-feeder foods listed here will work. Anemones can be fed small bits of seafood, as well, but do so sparingly, only once every week or two. A number of commercial foods for filter feeders are also now on the market, and most contain marine phytoplankton. You can buy phytoplankton or cultivate it at home.

Chapter **17**

Preventing Stress

I f you intend to be a tropical fish hobbyist for a long time, inevitably one of your fish will become infected with some kind of disease. Marine tropical fishes are subject to all kind of maladies. Pathogenic organisms that cause disease include parasites, bacteria, viruses, and fungi. They're present in the ocean and in the aquarium, and it's difficult to eliminate them. Many are introduced with new fish, and many are highly contagious.

However, whether or not disease actually breaks out depends on the resistance of your fish. A healthy fish has a strong resistance and an immune system that keeps pathogens in check. A fish or invertebrate with stress is a fish that's vulnerable to disease. This chapter focuses on what stress is in your aquarium, what causes an animal to be become vulnerable, and how to prevent it.

Stopping the Stressin'

Everyone knows what stress is, but I'm sure that everybody's definition isn't the same. What one person considers stressful may be a routine day at the office for another. When I use the term *stress*, I'm referring to the biological interpretation: any condition in which the normal biological functioning of an animal is disrupted.

TECHNICAL STUFF

In biological terms, the normal, healthy condition of an animal is called its *homeostasis.* Anything that disrupts the animal's homeostasis is a *stressor,* and the animal is said to be *stressed.*

Stressors can be physical, biological, or psychological. Here is a quick overview of these three:

>> **Physical:** A *physical* stressor causes mechanical stress on the body. Typical examples include injuries or external temperature changes. In the aquarium, a broken heater will cause a dramatic drop in temperature, which quickly becomes a physical stressor on your fish.

>> **Biological:** Any pathogen that causes infection or disease is a *biological* stressor. When your fish are sick, they're dealing with biological stress.

>> **Psychological:** A *psychological* stressor causes emotional or mental disruption. Although it's easy to measure in humans, it's a bit tougher in your aquarium pets. A good example is when one of your fish is aggressive or territorial — it causes psychological stress to others.

These kinds of stressors can impact any animal, including your aquarium pets. When an animal's homeostasis is disrupted, its immune system is often compromised, which means that its resistance to harmful pathogens is reduced.

Two forms of stress can affect your pets:

>> **Chronic:** If the conditions that produced the stress persist, the situation is called *chronic stress,* and the animal can succumb to disease. Poor living conditions weaken your fish, cause chronic stress, and ultimately lower the fish's resistance. That's when your fish is most vulnerable to disease, and those pathogens living in your aquarium make their move.

>> **Acute:** On the other hand, short-term stress is called *acute.* Acute stress can be as lethal as chronic stress. The physical consequences of acute stress can lead to death from respiratory failure, infections from physical damage, and immune-system failure and disease. Fish and many invertebrates have a protective mucous layer that acts as a first line of defense against infection and disease. When this layer is removed or damaged, one of their defenses is compromised, and an avenue for pathogens is opened.

The best way to deal with stress is to avoid it.

Identifying Stressful Conditions

In the closed system of an aquarium, fish and invertebrates are exposed to stressors that their wild counterparts can typically avoid. Your pets depend on you to make sure stressful conditions are avoided.

Table 17-1 lists stressful conditions and the corresponding chapter numbers in this book where you can find solutions to these problems. After the table, I discuss each stressor individually.

TABLE 17-1

Causes of Stress and Problem-Solving Chapters

Stressful Condition	Chapter(s)
Poor water quality	7, 12, 13, 15
Handling	5
Injury	17
Lack of nutrition	16
Overcrowding	3
Aggressive behavior	2, 3
Temperature changes	8
Salinity changes	9, 13
Disturbances	1, 8

Poor water quality

First and foremost on the list of stressors is poor water quality. For your pets, the water in your aquarium is like air to humans and other land animals. Humans can live for days without food, but without clean, breathable air, humans will die quickly. Similarly, fish and invertebrates in your aquarium won't live long without clean water. They also literally need water like you and I need water because they drink it, as well.

Fish excrete wastes into the very water that they use to stay alive. In the open ocean, this isn't a problem, but in the closed system of an aquarium, it can be dangerous. That's why I emphasize filtration in Chapter 7 and maintenance in Chapter 15. Clean water means healthy water, which means healthy fish and invertebrates.

When the water is polluted with wastes, the pH drops, ammonia and other nitrogenous compounds increase, the buffering capacity diminishes rapidly, carbon dioxide builds, and dissolved oxygen plummets. When these conditions develop, the water then acts as a stressor, and your marine animals become stressed.

Under the stressful conditions associated with poor water quality, fish and invertebrates have to work harder to breathe, their heart rates increase, internal ion balance is disrupted, and internal pH drops. In addition, their bodies react by producing a number of hormones that compromise the immune system. If the level of pollution is extreme, the inability of the fish to offload carbon dioxide in exchange for oxygen will kill it immediately. The animal will literally drown, which is something people generally don't consider when it comes to organisms that live in the ocean.

However, if water quality degrades slowly, the stress becomes chronic, and the animal becomes increasingly susceptible to the harmful pathogens that live around and inside its body. The fish will become sick and could die.

REMEMBER

To avoid poor water quality, make sure you have adequate filtration for the size of your aquarium, don't overcrowd your aquarium, and properly maintain your aquarium and its filtration. Use water parameter tests to look for and diagnose signs of water degradation.

Handling

Every time you chase your fish with a net, catch them, spook them, bag them, move them, or remove them from the water, you're stressing your pets — *you* are the stressor. This kind of stress is typically known as *capture stress* or *handling stress.* It's an acute form of stress.

Unfortunately, you can't avoid handling stress. In fact, when you buy your fish, they've already been subjected to a lot of handling stress from, in most cases, capture in the wild, transport to your dealer, removal from his tank, and transport to your home. There is no way around it. The only way to deal with handling stress is to minimize it, keeping the following principles in mind:

>> **Select species that have been bred or cultivated in captivity.** These critters are hardy and well adapted to captivity. They have no history of capture stress and are generally less susceptible to stress associated with life in an aquarium.

>> **For animals harvested from the wild, make sure you buy fish and invertebrates that have had a chance to recover from the handling stress associated with capture and transport to your dealer.** They should have been in your dealer's possession for at least a week. Feeding is a good sign that they have recovered.

>> **Minimize handling stress by reducing the amount of chase time and net time when you're moving a fish.** I know this is easier said than done, but don't chase a fish around the aquarium in an effort to tire it out. This will exhaust the fish, and the consequences may be lethal. Instead, try to coax the fish with food to an area when it can be snatched with the net or cornered quickly. After the fish is in the net, move it to the container or bag as quickly as possible, keeping it out of the water for only seconds. Keep the travel container as close as possible.

>> **Keep travel time short.** The more time in the container or bag, the more stress. Keep in mind that water quality in the container degrades quickly. Fish bought at your local fish dealer will experience less travel stress than those purchased online and exposed to overnight shipping.

>> **Use a net that's not only soft on the fish but also large enough to accommodate the whole fish.** Doing so will minimize damage to the protective mucous layer on their skin. If an animal doesn't fit into the net properly, it may flip out during transfer, and physical damage will surely occur.

Injury

Anything that causes injury to your fish and invertebrates applies physical stress that can lead to immediate death or delayed mortality due to infection or disease. An injured fish, like any injured animal, bleeds when its tissues are damaged. Veins and arteries carrying blood throughout the body of the fish can be damaged when the fish is bitten, dropped, or physically abused in some way. The bleeding may be external or internal depending on the nature and the extent of the damage. Other fish in the tank can also, in some cases, sense an injured fish, which also can cause stress.

If a physical injury doesn't cause immediate death from blood loss, at the very least it will compromise the protective mucous layer of the skin, which can lead to infection. In addition, an injured fish isn't a healthy fish. It may stop feeding, and its immune system may become compromised, leading to more serious ailments.

Whereas handling stress can obviously cause physical damage, there are a number of injurious aquarium conditions to watch out for, as well. Overcrowding, incompatibility, territoriality, and certain social behaviors can also cause injuries to a fish or invertebrate.

Lack of nutrition

If an animal isn't eating right, it won't be healthy and strong. An unhealthy fish will be stressed. It won't be able to power its immune system, and the door to disease will be wide open. Poor nutrition can manifest in a couple different ways:

>> Your fish or invertebrate may not be eating right for a couple of reasons. You may not be feeding it the right kinds of food or meeting its nutritional needs. Read Chapter 16 to make sure you're feeding your wet pets the kind of food they need. Make every effort to offer the right foods in terms of content, size, and placement.

> >> Another cause of poor nutrition can be associated with the inability of the fish or invertebrate to physically get to the food. Perhaps aggressive tank mates eat everything, or maybe the fish prefers to feed low in the tank and food is not getting to it. You may have to take extra steps to feed those fish or invertebrates that are having this problem.

REMEMBER

Don't forget that invertebrates with photosynthetic algae, such as corals and anemones, need adequate amounts of light to feed. Poor lighting stresses these animals.

Overcrowding

Having too many occupants in your aquarium can have several stressful effects, both acute and chronic. The immediate physical effect of overcrowding is associated with lack of personal space. Not having enough room leads to territorial disputes, fighting, and injuries. Injuries lead to infection, disease, and death.

Overcrowded conditions inevitably lead to poor water quality. Too many animals produce too much waste, which leads to pollution. Pollution, of course, leads to stress, and so on.

Aggressive behavior

Some species of animals simply don't get along with their own kind, let alone with other species. When placed in the same tank, these fish can get aggressive. Chapter 3 gives the lowdown on fish compatibility.

Aggressive behavior can be exhibited because of territoriality, competition for food, or sexual behavior. It usually results in fighting and injury. Injury, of course, can cause immediate death or lead to secondary infection and disease. Moreover, a fish that's constantly harassed by another fish is prone to jumping from the aquarium, has a general lack of appetite, and lives under chronic stress.

TIP

When choosing fish and invertebrates for your aquarium, make sure to choose animals that get along. A single bad seed can cause severe problems for your aquarium and may ultimately live alone. When stocking your aquarium, add the most aggressive species last instead of first.

Temperature changes

If your heater malfunctions, you have a serious problem. If it fails to work, the temperature of the aquarium plummets, and your fish will stress. If it fails to turn off, the temperature soars, and your fish will stress. If temperature rises or falls to levels outside the thermal tolerance of your pets, the acute stress will kill them immediately. If not, the acute stress may cause secondary physical effects associated with temperature fluctuations that weaken the animal, compromise the immune system, and lead to disease.

However, water temperature doesn't have to rise or fall to levels that the critters can't tolerate in order for them to be stressed. The rate of temperature change can be just as detrimental. If your aquarium temperature rises or falls rapidly but stays within the tolerance of your pets, the sudden change can still kill or cause problems. The same thing happens if you move your animal from the transport bag to an aquarium full of much cooler or warmer water.

TIP

You can readily avoid extreme temperature changes if you frequently check your heater and water temperature. Also make sure that water temperatures are the same between two containers when fish and invertebrates are being transferred.

Salinity changes

While you must maintain salt levels within a specific range, you must also avoid sudden changes within that range. Any changes in salinity stress your aquarium pets. In Chapters 9 and 13, I discuss the level of salt in your aquarium, which is measured as *salinity* or *specific gravity.*

TECHNICAL
STUFF

Stress from changes in salinity is called *osmotic stress* because it disrupts osmotic balance. Osmotic stress disrupts the animal's normal function because it creates an osmotic imbalance that needs to be corrected, and this requires energy. Ultimately, other bodily functions, like the immune system, may fail as energy is redirected to corrective osmoregulation, and disease can result. You can review osmoregulation in Chapter 2.

WARNING

Sudden dramatic changes in salt levels cause acute osmotic stress that can be lethal if salinity rises or falls outside the osmotic range of the animal. More gradual changes in salinity may not be lethal, but they can still cause chronic stress.

TIP

Avoid sudden and dramatic changes in salinity by closely monitoring salt levels in your aquarium and conducting regular water-level maintenance (top off the tank — see Chapter 15).

Disturbances

Any sudden change in light or sound can stress your fish. This includes that annoying habit some people have of tapping on the glass of your aquarium, thinking that they're going to attract the fish. These disturbances cause acute stress that may not be detrimental if they occur only once in a while, but they can be a problem if they're repeated often.

TIP

Try to avoid switching the light on while the fish are resting during late-night hours. Avoid sudden changes in noise level and keep people from tapping on the glass.

Recognizing Stress

The first step to dealing with stress and disease in your aquarium is to recognize and identify the problem. You should be able to determine whether an animal is healthy by checking its appearance and its behavior. This isn't complicated and doesn't take long. Because you're feeding your aquarium inhabitants every day, feeding times are the best times to give them an examination.

TIP

With any kind of stress symptoms, determine whether the problem is affecting only one critter or the whole aquarium. If more than one fish is displaying symptoms of stress, your problem may be systemic. Conduct water tests, check your notes, and run down the list of stressful conditions listed earlier in this chapter to isolate the cause. If only one fish is affected, you probably need to isolate it for treatment to keep any malady from spreading.

So, what exactly are you looking for? Chapter 5 shares telltale signs of unhealthy fish that you want to look for when you purchased them. Those same signs manifest themselves in your aquarium if your fish or invertebrates are stressed or suffering from some ailment.

The following sections include some of the most common signs to watch for in your aquarium pets. Basically, look for something unusual or weird.

Acting weird

How an animal acts betrays the way that it feels. Unlike my daughter who simply doesn't want to go to school, fish and invertebrates don't fake their behavior. If they don't feel right, you know it fairly quickly. The following sections discuss a couple of behavioral signs.

Not being hungry

One of the first signs of stress or illness is the loss of appetite. Think about it. How hungry are you when you're sick? The fact that the animal was eating but suddenly has no interest tells you that something is wrong. If you suspect that one of your pets isn't interested in food, try offering something that it normally can't refuse, like live food.

Laziness

Another symptom of stress is a general laziness. If one of your pets loses its pep and becomes more sedentary, something is wrong. If it feeds only half-heartedly or avoids other fish, it's clearly fighting some kind of ailment. Other symptoms include hiding and keeping to itself. Lethargic fish typically keep their fins folded close to their body.

TIP

Keep in mind that everything is relative when diagnosing your fish. It's the *change* in behavior that counts. Some species are naturally lethargic or prefer the safety of hiding places. This doesn't mean they're sick.

Gasping

If your fish is spending an inordinate amount of time hyperventilating or gasping at the surface, you have a clear sign of stress. This behavior isn't necessarily a sign of disease, but it's probably indicative of poor water quality and low dissolved oxygen. By the way, your fish isn't breathing oxygen from the air at the surface but trying to pull oxygen from the richer surface layers. Fish with gill parasites have increased respiration as well and appear to cough; they may position themselves in front of powerheads or areas of high water motion.

Rubbing

Any fish that displays rubbing or twitching behavior is stressed by some kind of problem. It's not unusual for an animal that's infested with parasites to rub itself against the substrate and aquarium decorations.

Looking weird

By far, the best way to determine whether your fish and invertebrates aren't well is to check their physical appearance. Anything out of the ordinary should be considered a sign of stress or disease, and you must take appropriate steps. Many of these signs apply to fish and invertebrates alike. Physical characteristics that are indicative of stress or disease include the following:

>> **Discoloration:** Faded colors and discoloration are classic signs of stress. Strange white, red, or black spots or blotches may be infectious pathogens or parasites. Cuts and scrapes in the skin are signs of injury.

>> **Clouded eyes:** Glazed or cloudy eyes are indicative of stress and disease. The eyes of fish and invertebrates (if they have any) are normally clear and alert.

>> **Frayed fins:** Fins that are shredded or frayed are indicative of fighting or disease. Also, fins that are kept folded or close to the body for extended periods may betray a problem.

>> **Abnormal stomach:** When your fish has a *pinched stomach,* it usually means that the fish isn't feeding. When the stomach is *distended* (pooched out), the fish is probably feeding too much.

>> **Strange feces:** The color of your fish's poop can tell you if it has a parasite. Poop that is stringy, white, or glaze colored could be indicative of an infection.

Making a Diagnosis

Suppose one of your fish or invertebrates is showing one of the signs that the preceding sections outline. Now what? At this point, you suspect that your pet is suffering from stress and may very well have a disease. You need to conduct more investigative work to determine the cause of the problem.

Find out whether just one fish is exhibiting the symptom or if more than one critter is. If more than one is showing symptoms, your problem may be systemic — the problem has spread throughout the aquarium. In these situations, consider the list of stressful conditions that pertain to the whole system, such as water quality, and evaluate each one.

If, however, only one animal is showing signs of stress, check for the stressful conditions that may be specific to a single animal, such as injury, bullying from a tankmate, or lack of nutrition.

After you isolate a stressful condition, make every effort to stop it. Use Table 17-1 (earlier in this chapter), which gives you the chapter numbers in this book in which you can find solutions to your problem. If poor water quality is a problem, read Part 3. If your fish have nutritional problems, read Chapter 16. Whatever the problem, make sure the stressor doesn't persist.

REMEMBER

It's one thing to treat the symptom, it's another to stop the cause. You need to stop the cause. However, in some cases, isolating and stopping the stressor simply isn't possible. At times, everything checks out and you can't find a stressful condition. All you can do at this point is treat the ailment (see Chapter 18).

» Knowing what to do with sick fish

» Understanding common aquarium diseases

Chapter **18**

Playing Fish Doctor — Diseases and Treatments

N asty pathogens that cause disease are in and around your fish in their natural setting and in your aquarium. These pathogens may be bacterial, viral, fungal, or parasitic. Fortunately, many of the diseases caused by these agents manifest themselves with identifiable symptoms. Unfortunately, not many treatments are available for the home aquarist, and you have no guarantee that your pet will be saved.

The most effective way to deal with disease is to prevent it by minimizing stress. Unfortunately, even the most effective stress management can't keep disease from striking one or more of your marine pets.

Some of the symptoms of stress may disappear when you isolate the stressful condition and stop it. For example, a gasping fish may stop gasping when you increase aeration and improve water quality.

In some cases, though, the stressor takes its toll, the fish's resilience is diminished, and the fish contracts a disease. Right from the beginning of your diagnosis, the telltale symptoms of some ailments tell you that there's a problem. If that's the case, you have to treat the animal and, if the problem is systemic, you have to treat the entire aquarium. This chapter helps you recognize and treat those diseases that are most common in the home aquarium.

Identifying the Treatment Methods

The best remedy for disease in the marine aquarium is prevention. Nonetheless, if disease does strike one of your animals, you have a few methods for treating it. These include direct aquarium treatment with therapeutic agents, the hospital tank, the dip method, and internal medication, all of which I discuss in the following sections.

REMEMBER

Always use commercially available treatments instead of homemade remedies. Some experts recommend chemicals, like malachite green or potassium permanganate. These chemicals must be handled in exact dosages, which can be tough for you to do. If a fish is overdosed with one of them, it will kill the fish faster than the disease would have. Discuss all the possible remedies with your local dealer and let that person advise you on the best commercial remedies. When you apply the remedy, follow the directions exactly.

Don't be afraid to call your veterinarian and ask a few questions. If your veterinarian doesn't handle fish, she can usually recommend somebody who does. You can find a lot of information online in chat groups or through fish clubs. Just carefully vet that information.

TIP

Remove activated carbon from your filters when you medicate your aquarium. Carbon neutralizes many medications.

Direct aquarium treatment

Direct aquarium treatment involves the application of therapeutic agents directly into the aquarium containing the diseased fish. This method is sometimes called the *long bath.* It can be effective against some diseases, but not always. In some cases, the aquarium decorations or filter trade may absorb the medications, or the meds may be toxic to filter bacteria. Moreover, fish medications are toxic to invertebrates. You're better off isolating the infected fish in a hospital tank.

The hospital tank

Some aquarists isolate new fish in a *quarantine tank.* This small aquarium is also called an *isolation tank.* In this simple setup, the fish or invertebrate can be evaluated for signs of disease before it's introduced into the main aquarium. (Refer to Chapter 5 for more information.)

You may choose not to set up a quarantine tank to isolate new fish, but I do recommend that you set up a hospital tank to isolate your wet pets that are suffering from disease. A hospital tank reduces the likelihood of the disease spreading to others in the aquarium. It also provides refuge for a fish that may ordinarily be harassed by healthy fish. The hospital tank helps you to treat the fish without subjecting other fish to the treatment. And it helps you observe and diagnose the ailing fish.

The hospital tank need not be large: A 10-gallon tank will do. It does need adequate filtration and aeration, but elaborate decorations and gravel should be left out. Try to provide some kind of cover for the fish, in the form of rocks, flowerpots, or short lengths of PVC, as a source of security. An external power filter, sponge filter, or internal box filter is sufficient for the hospital tank.

As your expertise in this hobby increases, you'll accumulate expensive fish that you simply don't want to expose to disease. At that point, a hospital tank will be mandatory. It will also act as a quarantine tank as long as it hasn't recently housed a diseased fish.

The dip method

The *dip method* involves removing the infected fish from the aquarium and dipping it into a bath containing freshwater or a therapeutic agent. The dip is brief enough not to injure the fish, but long enough to kill the pathogen. Unfortunately, this method doesn't treat the main aquarium, just the fish.

The *freshwater dip* has become as useful to the marine aquarist as the *saltwater dip* is to the freshwater aquarist. This method involves dipping a saltwater fish infested with parasites into a freshwater bath for 3 to 5 minutes. The difference in salt concentration between the aquarium and the treatment bath is enough to rapidly kill the pathogen without harming the fish. This is best for external parasites like flukes and marine velvet.

The bath is prepared as follows:

1. **Fill a 1- to 2-gallon container full of conditioned freshwater, matching the temperature and pH of the main aquarium.**

   The pH can be elevated by adding sodium bicarbonate to the container.

2. **Add a quart of saltwater to the bath to reduce the osmotic shock to the fish.**

3. **Net the fish and place it in the container for 3 to 5 minutes.**

   It may show signs of disorientation for a moment, but it should recover.

Internal medication

Some remedies need to be administered internally. This is usually accomplished with injection or by feeding the remedy to the fish. I don't recommend injecting fish until you're extremely experienced. Feeding the fish food that has been medicated can be difficult, as well. In many cases, the dosage is difficult to estimate, the fish isn't feeding normally anyway, and you can't guarantee that the fish being treated is getting the proper amount of food.

Internal medication can be effective to treat internal parasites, but you might need to use supplements to entice your fish to eat it.

Getting to Know Common Medications

The treatments available to the home aquarist — copper and antibiotics — are somewhat limited for marine fish diseases. The fact of the matter is that they are successful only some of the time. The following sections explain a bit more.

Copper

Copper is a pollutant and toxic in the marine environment. Many experts think that copper is beneficial for killing parasites. However, copper can have adverse effects on fishes, it isn't very stable in saltwater systems, and its fate in the aquarium isn't fully understood. Some experts feel that copper should be eliminated as a treatment of aquarium fish diseases. Nonetheless, copper-based medications are still widely used in the aquarium trade. However, avoid the use of copper unless you have absolutely no alternatives. If you do use it, isolate the fish in a hospital aquarium (see the preceding section) for treatment. Also use a copper test kit to monitor water levels.

Two types copper are available on the market for treating aquarum fish: ionic and chelated copper. In general, ionic copper is less stable and has a lower therapeutic level, whereas chelated copper can be used on more fish species.

Copper is toxic to invertebrates, so don't administer copper in an aquarium with any kind of invertebrate.

Antibiotics

Antibiotics are chemotherapeutic agents that seem to be the most effective way of treating some of the common aquarium diseases. When possible, treat fish in a hospital tank to avoid the effects of these compounds on a mature, established aquarium. Don't, however, expect miracle cures from these compounds, because many haven't been found to be fully effective against disease.

REMEMBER

With so many tradenames on the market, be sure to check the label for the active ingredients in your fish medication.

Recognizing and Treating the Bad Guys

Hundreds of possible maladies can afflict fish. Some are specific to certain species, and some can easily be transferred between species. The causes of common aquarium ailments include bacteria, viruses, fungi, or parasites. Not all are common in the average home aquarium. Here I discuss them and offer some possible treatment options.

Bacterial infections

You can find good bacteria and bad bacteria. Regardless, all bacteria are microscopic one-celled organisms capable of rapid reproduction. Thousands of species of bacteria inhabit many different habitats. Some are beneficial to the aquarium in the nitrogen cycle, but some can cause infection.

Fin rot

>> **Causes:** *Aeromonas, Pseudomonas, Vibrio* bacteria

>> **Symptoms:** This external bacterial infection causes erosion or rotting of the fins and the fin rays. The base of the fins usually reddens, as well. In advanced stages, the disease spreads to the skin, causing bleeding and ulceration, and to the gills.

>> **Treatment:** The occurrence of this disease is thought to reflect deteriorating water quality, and immediate steps should be taken to improve conditions. Remove uneaten food, do a partial water change, and change the activated carbon in your filter. The antibiotics erythromycin, neomycin, and nitrofurazone can be effective.

Fish tuberculosis, wasting disease

>> **Causes:** *Mycobacterium* bacteria

>> **Symptoms:** External signs of this disease are often lacking. A fish that seems outwardly healthy may be internally infected. Fish that are infected may live a year or more before succumbing. Skin lesions, emaciation, labored breathing, scale loss, frayed fins, and loss of appetite are all clinical signs of this infection. Unfortunately, by the time these symptoms are manifested, it's probably too late to save the fish.

>> **Treatment:** These bacteria are transmitted orally through raw infected fish flesh, detritus, and feces of infected fish. They can also infect skin wounds and lesions. The best treatment is prevention by not feeding raw fish and shellfish to your aquarium occupants. Antibiotics, including kanamycin, erythromycin, and streptomycin, have shown some promise against these bacteria if the disease is diagnosed. If the aquarium is heavily infected with this disease, it must be sterilized and the water discarded.

Vibriosis, ulcer disease

>> **Cause:** *Vibrio* bacteria

>> **Symptoms:** A variety of symptoms are associated with this disease, but they depend on the species of *Vibrio* and the species of fish. They can include lethargy; darkening of color; anemia; ulcers on the skin and lower jaw; bleeding of the gills, skin, and intestinal tract; clouded eyes; loose scales; pale gills; and sudden death.

>> **Treatment:** These bacteria commonly inhabit the intestinal tracts of healthy fish. They become dangerous only when stress allows infection. Poor water quality, crowding, excessive handling, and copper treatments are common causes of stress in aquarium fish. Vaccination against infection is possible but not feasible for aquarium fish. Immersion treatments with antibiotic compounds, including erythromycin and nitrofurazone, have met with some success.

Viral disease

Viruses, simple microscopic organisms, thrive by invading the cells of their hosts. In most cases, there are no treatments for the few viral diseases of the marine aquarium.

The most common viral disease is called cauliflower disease or *lymphocystis:*

>> **Causes:** *Lymphocystis* virus

>> **Symptoms:** Fin and body lesions that are raised, whitish, warty, and have a lumpy texture, like cauliflower. These lesions may take three to four weeks to reach their full size. Diseased fishes typically show few signs of distress and continue to feed and behave normally. The infection generally isn't fatal, but it can be transmitted to other fish in the tank. It is sometimes confused with marine ich and very common in butterflyfish and angelfish.

>> **Treatment:** There is no effective treatment for this viral infection other than to isolate the fish immediately and let the fish's natural immune system deal with it. This may take as long as several months. Some aquarists scrape the lesions off the animal.

Fungal disease

Fungi are plant-like organisms, some of which are parasitic on fishes.

One of the most common fungal diseases is *exophiala* disease.

>> **Causes:** *Exophiala* fungus

>> **Symptoms:** Lethargy, disorientation, and abnormal swimming are signs of this fungal infection.

>> **Treatment:** This is a poorly understood fungus, and no treatment is known. Isolate the fish to prevent other aquarium fishes from contracting the fungus.

Parasitic infestations

Parasites exist in a variety of forms, including tiny one-celled organisms called *protozoa,* as well as larger invertebrates, like crustaceans and worms. A parasite doesn't usually kill its host, but it can cause lesions that become secondarily infected by bacteria. Parasites can be internally or externally located on their hosts; the latter are more readily identified.

The following provides a general overview of those parasitic diseases you're most likely to encounter in your aquarium.

Clownfish disease, Brooklynella disease

>> **Causes:** The ciliate protozoan *Brooklynella hostilis*

>> **Symptoms:** Pale skin, cloudy eyes, skin flaking, excess mucus, and troubled swimming and breathing. This parasite feeds on gill tissue and skin cells, causing irritation. It's commonly associated with damselfishes and clown-fishes, but it also infects a variety of other species.

>> **Treatment:** Unlike other infestations, this parasite has no encysted stages, but other fish in the aquarium can become quickly infected. A 5-minute freshwater dip will provide temporary relief, but a lengthy formalin bath appears to be the most effective treatment.

Crustacean infestations

>> **Causes:** Copepod, isopod, and argulid crustaceans

>> **Symptoms:** Most of these tiny, crab-like organisms are visible to the naked eye. Copepods remain fixed in the same position, while isopods and argulids move over the surface of the fish. These groups feed by piercing the fish, causing tissue damage. Fishes with heavy infestations swim erratically, rub against objects, and jump. Bacteria infect lesions.

>> **Treatment:** Remove fish that are infested immediately. Also remove aquar-ium decorations and either dry them to kill egg masses or immerse them in 2 percent bleach solution for 2 hours. Treat infested fishes by immersing them in freshwater, trichlorfon, or malathion baths.

Ichthyophonus disease, whirling disease

>> **Causes:** The protozoan *Ichthyophonus*

>> **Symptoms:** Once considered a fungus, this single-celled parasite invades the internal organs of the fish, infecting the kidney, heart, spleen, and liver. Clinical signs include emaciation, spinal curvature, darkening or paling of the skin, roughening of the skin, fin erosion, and skin ulcers. Erratic swimming behavior also can be a symptom of the disease. Internal examination after death reveals white nodules on the organs.

>> **Treatment:** This parasitic organism has a complex life cycle. Fish usually ingest the cysts, where they burst and enter the bloodstream, infecting

internal organs. Typically, fish with this disease die up to two months after infestation. Treatment is difficult due to the internal nature of this disease. The infected fish should be immediately removed from the aquarium to prevent other fishes from becoming infected.

Marine velvet disease

» **Causes:** The dinoflagellate *Amyloodinium ocellatum*

» **Symptoms:** The gills are usually the first site of infection, spreading to the skin, which becomes dull, patchy, and velvetlike; white spots are visible on sections of intact skin. As the disease progresses, the fish's behavior may include fasting, gasping, scratching against objects, and sluggishness. Lesions caused by the dinoflagellate can lead to secondary bacterial infection. This parasite is highly virulent and death can occur in as little as 12 hours. Tangs, clownfish, and angelfish are especially susceptible.

» **Treatment:** This organism has three stages to its life cycle, and only one of them is parasitic. No completely effective treatment is known, although copper-based products and some antibiotics, like chloroquine phosphate, malachite green, nitrofurazone, and acriflavin, are effective. A freshwater dip sometimes dislodges these parasites from the host but doesn't kill them. Treatments are often prolonged, and the entire tank must be treated to fully eradicate the infestation. If display tank treatment isn't possible, the best way to break the parasite's cycle is to remove all the fish and let the disease starve over an eight-week period.

Marine white spot, saltwater ich, marine ich

» **Causes:** The ciliate protozoan *Cryptocaryon irritans*

» **Symptoms:** Early signs include fasting, cloudy eyes, troubled breathing, excess skin mucus, and pale skin. White spots then appear on the skin, gills, and eyes, and death follows within a few days, most likely due to gill damage.

» **Treatment:** The white spot organism can be difficult to control. Like marine velvet, the encysted stage of this parasite is resistant to most treatments and remains in the gravel of the aquarium. More frequent water changes help, but they'll persist in the gravel. The freshwater dip may be effective in killing the parasites on the fish but does little to treat the aquarium. Therefore, you must maintain levels of treatment in the tank. Prolonged immersion in copper products is an effective treatment. Chloroquine phosphate is a drug also used to treat fish suffering from marine ich, but you need a prescription from a veterinarian.

Tang turbellarian disease, black spot, black ich

» **Causes:** *Paravortex* flatworms

» **Symptoms:** Although the name implies that only tangs are infected, this isn't the case. Many species of fish can be infected by this flatworm. In the parasitic phase, these organisms look like numerous dark spots distributed unevenly over the fins, gills, and body. Other signs include fasting, listlessness, paling or whitish skin, and scratching against objects. Secondary bacterial infections are also known to occur. These signs are common to other infestations by flatworms.

» **Treatment:** Flatworms are a type of worm in a phylum of their own, called *Platyhelminthes.* As with most parasitic infestations, crowding allows the disease to spread to other tank mates. Immersion in freshwater, trichlorfon, formalin, or praziquantel can be effective.

Trematode infestations

» **Causes:** Monogenetic trematode worms

» **Symptoms:** Many species of these worms are too small to see without a microscope. They normally infect the gills, eyes, skin, mouth, and anal opening. Infected fishes usually rub themselves against objects in the aquarium, trying to dislodge these parasites. This often causes damage that leads to secondary bacterial infections.

» **Treatment:** These infestations are difficult to eradicate because the life cycles of these animals are poorly understood. Immersion in freshwater, mebendazole, praziquantel, or trichlorfon has demonstrated effectiveness against trematodes.

Uronema disease

» **Causes:** The ciliate protozoan *Uronema marinum*

» **Symptoms:** External ulcers, muscle and skin bleeding, lethargic behavior, and sloughing of the skin are signs of this disease. Death may be rapid due to impaired circulation in the gills.

» **Treatment:** Little is known of this parasite, but it should be treated both externally with immersion in a formalin bath and internally with metronidazole.

Other health problems

Just when you thought there could be no more diseases, here are a couple more to motivate you to keep your aquarium in optimal shape.

Head and lateral line erosion

>> **Causes:** Poor water quality, nutrient deficiency, possibly a parasite

>> **Symptoms:** Like the freshwater disease called *hole-in-the-head,* holes develop and enlarge in the sensory pits of the head and down the lateral line on the body. The disease progresses slowly, and the fish doesn't seem to behave differently. Advanced stages can lead to secondary bacterial infection and death.

>> **Treatment:** There are no specific treatments for this disease, although some recommend the use of the freshwater antibiotic flagyl. Check your water quality and make necessary adjustments. You should also make sure that you're meeting the nutritional needs of your fishes. Diversify their diet and add vitamin supplements to their food.

Poisoning

>> **Causes:** Multiple causes, including buildup of nitrogenous compounds (ammonia, nitrite), household chemicals (smoke, cleaners, fumes), and tap water constituents (heavy metals, chloramine)

>> **Symptoms:** Low levels of toxins in the aquarium stress fish, thereby lowering their resistance to other diseases. Higher levels cause abnormal behavior, including darting movements, jumping, and gasping at the surface.

>> **Treatment:** Make sure that activated carbon is used to remove toxins and conduct a 20 to 40 percent water change. If pollutant levels are high, move the fish to a hospital tank until the main aquarium problems are corrected.

Do Invertebrates Get Sick?

The answer to this question is quite simple: Yes. But you probably noticed that all the diseases outlined in the preceding section are associated with fish. The fact of the matter is, invertebrates contract parasitic, fungal, bacterial, and viral diseases, but little is known about how to diagnose and treat them. Although fish and invertebrates share common pathogens, the extent to which the same remedies are effective isn't well known.

Until more research is conducted on invertebrate disease and home treatment, the most effective tool is prevention. High water quality, adequate aeration, optimal lighting, and good nutrition are keys to keeping your invertebrates healthy.

EUTHANIZING A FISH — A WORST-CASE SCENARIO

In some instances, your fish is so ill that you know it's going to die. At that point, you have a decision to make. You can either put the fish out of its misery and euthanize it or let nature take its course. This decision can be difficult because you generally have a lot of time and money invested in a fish, and you've probably become somewhat attached to your pet. I always make this decision by deciding what's best for each individual fish.

If you decide to dispatch the animal, the most humane way to do so is to use clove oil, which is a sedative that is deadly at high levels.

Don't discard a dead fish or invertebrate by flushing it down the toilet. Doing so may transmit disease pathogens to local fishes. Instead, place the dead animal in the trash or bury it in your backyard.

Chapter 19

Observing Your Fish

After you get your aquarium up and running, it's time to sit back and enjoy your pets. They'll interact with each other and with you, which is truly the most enjoyable part of aquarium keeping.

REMEMBER

You control every aspect of your aquarium. The health of your pets is in your hands, and you have to pay attention to them. Doing so requires patience, time, and a little start-up money. But as a result of that investment, maintaining your aquarium is fun. At times you'll throw your hands in the air in frustration, but those times will pass, and you'll likely realize that being an aquarist has rich rewards for you and your family. This chapter gives you some hints on how to get the most out of your new hobby.

Seeing Is Believing: Fish Can Be Fun

Keeping marine life happy and healthy in your home is great fun and very rewarding. In this section, I explain all the wonderful reasons to have a saltwater aquarium and give you a few ideas about how to enjoy your fish.

Fish watching

When you watch your aquarium and your pets, they're better off. Get to know all the subtleties of your fish and invertebrates and get a feel for their individual personalities. I, for example, like to name them after people I know. I have a cantankerous hermit crab that I named after my grandfather and a very pretty little damsel named after my niece, Anna.

TIP

Watch your fishy family members interact and have some fun with it. As you do this, you'll know immediately whether something is wrong because Maggie isn't fighting with Vickie or Evie is hiding all the time. This kind of game may sound goofy, but it's fun to play, especially with children.

REMEMBER

Each animal in your aquarium is your pet, and, as with any pet, watching it daily tells you when it acts normally and when something is wrong. You can diagnose problems as they arise and not after it's too late.

Relaxing

Keeping an aquarium does involve a little work. But after you have a good understanding of the basics, and if you keep up with the maintenance, you'll be able to relax with your aquarium.

Suppose it's the dead of winter, you're home from work, dinner is finished, and you want to relax. Well, look at your choices. Sit down and binge a bunch of mindless television shows, play video games, read a good book, or kick back in front of the aquarium and watch as the drama unfolds. Fish and invertebrates are entertaining creatures, and just sitting and watching them is relaxing. As far as I'm concerned, relaxation is one of the best reasons to have an aquarium.

REMEMBER

In fact, studies show that spending time in front of the aquarium reduces stress.

Having fun with your family

If you have children or nephews and nieces, include them in as many aspects of the aquarium as possible. Not only do they enjoy it, but they learn the responsibility of taking care of pets. You can even teach them how to properly feed the fish.

REMEMBER

Daily, weekly, and monthly maintenance duties become easier if they're shared by all. In addition, if everybody has a personal stake in the aquarium, the aquarium will be better off: Family pets often get more attention than those owned by a single person.

Showing off

Don't forget to show your fish and invertebrates off to all your friends. The beauty of a well-maintained aquarium is naturally impressive. Don't be surprised if your friends come over just to see your aquarium more than they come to see you. I guarantee you that anybody who enters the room where you have your tank will be drawn to it immediately.

TIP

Remind your friends and family members that they shouldn't tap on the glass, feed the animals, or add exotic drinks to the aquarium.

Experiencing marine biology in your home

I've been studying marine biology for more than 35 years, and that doesn't include my amateur years as a young aquarist. Believe me, those early aquarium years with my brother Burt and my friends Dave, Condo, and Carlo were extremely important in helping shape my future. If you, too, are an aspiring marine biologist, there's no better way to get started than to own an aquarium. Because many studies on fish biology have been conducted on fish kept in aquaria, an amateur biologist can discover a lot about fish in his or her own home.

Keeping a Log

A well-kept log helps you pinpoint when and how situations progressed in your aquarium. It also provides you with an interesting history of your aquarium that you and your friends and family will probably enjoy reading now and at some point down the road.

An aquarium log need not be complicated. Mine is just a simple notebook. I mark the date on the left side of the page and make all kinds of notes on the right. You can also subdivide your notebook into sections for each general category. For example, the fish section can have an individual page or two for each animal so that the history of that critter is all in one place.

You also can include the results of the water-quality tests, which I stress you keep track of in Part 3. This way, you're able to follow the water-maturation process.

TIP

Keep your notebook close to the aquarium and encourage all the fish watchers to make notations. This way, patterns of observations can be established even if you're not there all the time.

The following sections give you some idea of the types of notes to make in your log.

Comings and goings

Write down when you add fish and invertebrates to your aquarium and when you remove them. Doing so allows you to follow the progress of any new additions or the effects of taking a fish or invertebrate away. For example, if you suspect that one particular fish is bullying the others, but you haven't personally seen it, you may need to isolate that fish for a week. You can then follow the progress of your other fish to see whether conditions improve. To do this, you have to make note of when events happen.

Take notes about new arrivals — in particular, how they interact with others or with the aquarium. For example, "Just placed new lionfish in tank, and he immediately consumed the clownfish" or "New damselfish is shy and seems to hide a lot; need to keep an eye on it."

Fish interactions and behavior

Write down your observations on animal behavior and interactions. This doesn't only pertain to when you add or remove a tank inhabitant: Make notes whenever you see something worth noting.

Suppose you're relaxing and fish watching when suddenly your triggerfish nips your cardinalfish and the latter quickly swims away and hides. You should write this down for a couple of reasons. First, this agonistic behavior may be an isolated incident or a recurring situation. You won't know unless you make note of it. Second, if your cardinalfish starts to show signs of stress, you'll know why.

Most of the fish and invertebrate interactions you see are probably associated with aggressive or agonistic behavior (see Chapter 3 for a discussion of agonistic behavior). In many aggressive relationships, a pecking order is established, and the fish sort it out themselves. If not, one of the fish should be removed before the situation gets out of hand. If the aggressor is a general aquarium bully, it must go. However, if the fish being picked on is getting injured, it must be relocated to a more peaceful setting.

Feedings

Question: What is one of the first signs of stress? Answer: loss of appetite. If you notice that a fish or invertebrate isn't eating, write it down. If a fish or invertebrate is eating too much, write it down. If a fish is eating only one kind of food, write it down. If a particular food type isn't liked at all, write it down.

Face it, you can't remember everything. Writing down these observations helps determine whether there are any consistent patterns worth following. The older I get, the more I have to write things down . . . like my kids' names.

Because feeding is such an important aspect of keeping your fish and aquarium healthy, don't be afraid to keep detailed notes on feeding behavior, food types, feeding times, and food quantities.

New equipment

Any time you replace, maintain, or add equipment to your aquarium, note it in your log. This way, if anything changes dramatically after adding that equipment, you'll know why. Suppose, for example, your dealer recommends a different fluorescent light bulb for your aquarium to improve invertebrate health. You buy it, use it for several months, and find that your invertebrates are no better off. By checking your notes, you can pinpoint the amount of time you've been using the bulbs and evaluate their efficacy. Keeping track of equipment also helps with staying on top of routine maintenance.

It doesn't take long to write down, "Added new carbon to filter on May 1." Take the few seconds to do it, and you'll have an excellent maintenance record.

Problems

If something goes wrong, make note of it. This way, you can follow patterns if they develop. Filter failure, heater malfunction, and even air tube clogging are routine incidents that can stress your fish. If you know when they happened, you may be able to find the cause of any future problems.

Here's an example of a hypothetical but possible situation: You come home from a long weekend away and find your butterflyfish hiding in the corner of the tank and not interested in food. You haven't been there and don't know what might be wrong. Fortunately, your spouse took care of the fish, fed them, and made sure that aquarium conditions were stable. So, what happened? You pick up your log and notice that she found cooler water temperatures on Saturday and had trouble getting the heater to work. She also observed that the butterflyfish wasn't interested in food. Bingo, temperature stress and a possible heater problem. See what I mean?

General notes

You don't need to be feeding your fish, adding or removing an animal, having a problem, or adding equipment to make notes in your aquarium log. Any note that reminds you to do something is helpful. For example, my notes from last week say, "Need to stop watching fish and finish that book!"

This general note-taking will come in handy when you decide to write your own book about saltwater aquariums. Just remember me when you become a famous author.

Taking Pictures

Taking photos was one of my father's passions that he passed on to me and my brother Paul. There may come a time when you too want to photograph your aquarium and its inhabitants. Photography is truly my other favorite hobby, and I've spent literally thousands of hours and thousands of dollars underwater trying to get photos of fish and invertebrates in their natural environment. It's amazing how much time, effort, and money I could've saved had I just photographed the animals in my aquarium — and I wouldn't have had to get wet.

I can think of a number of great reasons to take photos of your pets: to show off, to follow the history of a particular animal, to preserve the memory of a critter, or to share and publish photos. Whatever your reason, I strongly encourage aquarium photography. Like maintaining the aquarium itself, photographing your fish can be frustrating because your subjects don't always cooperate. But the process is also a lot of fun.

Nowadays, many types of cameras are on the market. Years ago, I used to lug around a 35mm single lens reflex (SLR) film camera for all my photography. But film cameras are all but extinct and digital cameras are the way to go. They come sized for any pocketbook and produce incredible images that are easy to edit. In fact, the digital camera in your smartphone is far better than some of my ancient film cameras. And prices on digital SLRs keep coming down, though they are still more expensive.

Even though you can capture many of the fixed invertebrates (like corals) and slower tank inhabitants (like snails) without a *flash* or *strobe*, this piece of equipment is necessary for faster moving fishes. Also, the lights in your aquarium might not provide sufficient lighting for photography. Some lighting, like LED, usually results in strange colors, like green or orange, in your photos. Therefore, in these cases, you need to use a camera filter or add strong lighting from a flash unit or electronic strobe. Ideally, the flash should be separate from the camera and directed into the aquarium from above or the side.

This isn't a book on photography, so I don't cover any photography basics. However, the following are a few pointers to taking good aquarium photos:

>> **Mount the camera on a tripod or something sturdy.** Doing so ensures you avoid camera movement and blurred photos at slower shutter speeds.

>> **Set the camera perpendicular to the glass to avoid distortion of the subject.** The properties of glass can sometimes distort images, so doing so minimizes any distortion.

>> **Match the camera lens to the size of the subject and composition of the photograph.** A 50mm lens is good for larger fish, but a macro lens may be required for smaller subjects. A zoom lens gives you both options and allows you to vary your composition.

>> **Make every effort to direct the flash at a 45-degree angle to the glass of the aquarium.** If you don't, your photos will have a bright white spot from the reflection.

>> **Pay attention to focus and depth of field so that what you see is what you get.** The depth of field determines what's in focus and what isn't. For example, you may want the blenny on the coral in focus, but not the decorations behind it. You can manipulate your depth of field with your aperture setting.

>> **Compose your photo so that it has a subject.** I have lots and lots of photos of my aquarium that look busy because there is no center of interest. Now if I'm taking panoramic photos, I try to compose it with an element of central interest. This doesn't mean the center of interest needs to be in the center of the photo. In fact, most photographic experts feel that your subject should be positioned one third the way across the frame. In the case of close-ups, I try to fill the frame with the subject as much as possible.

>> **Be creative.** You may shoot something that you love, but everybody else looks at it and shrugs. So what? We all swim to a different current, or something like that, so go with what pleases you.

For more general information about photography, check out the latest edition of *Digital Photography For Dummies* by Julie Adair King (John Wiley & Sons, Inc.).

5

The Part of Tens

Meet and say good-bye to ten kinds of fish that you don't want to add to your new aquarium because they're difficult to maintain, too large, or dangerous to you or their tank mates.

Examine ten kinds of invertebrates to avoid because they aren't suitable for the average beginner aquarium.

Get to know how to convert from traditional U.S. units to metric for many of the measurements, like inches to centimeters, commonly used in the aquarium hobby.

See how the professionals keep marine animals happy and healthy by visiting one of these incredible public aquariums.

Chapter **20**

Ten Fish to Avoid

S ome families of fish tend to be a problem in captivity, particularly for the community aquarium or reef tank. Of course, each group may contain one or two exceptions. Chapter 3 lists the individual species that aren't well suited to the beginner's aquarium. This chapter builds on that list and points out fish that beginning aquarists probably should avoid.

Sharks

Having sharks in your aquarium probably is a natural desire, but you want to avoid them for a number of reasons. Most of the more than 500 species of sharks are simply too big for the average aquarist. Did you know that only a handful of shark species have been successfully kept in captivity, and that includes large, public aquaria? Besides, most sharks are predatory carnivores that will eat everything in your aquarium.

Skates and Rays

Skates and rays are flattened relatives of the sharks, and like their cousins, I don't recommend them for the average aquarium. Both groups grow to large sizes and prefer to eat invertebrates, so keep them out of your aquarium.

Stonefish

These fishes possess venom glands near the base of their needle-like dorsal fin spines. The neurotoxin of these fish is the most deadly of the fish venoms and can be fatal to humans. They typically camouflage themselves as rocks, which means they aren't very attractive, either. Leave stonefish care to the experts.

Moray Eels

Moray eels are cool-looking fish that belong to the family Muraenidae. Morays are generally nocturnal fish that feed on other fish and invertebrates (including yours) at night, spending most of their daytime hours in holes and crevices, so they're not much fun to observe. Also, in the wild, these fish grow very large and easily attain lengths in excess of 5 feet.

Lionfishes and Scorpionfishes

These predators hover or lie in wait for their prey, suddenly lunging at and engulfing them. Although their camouflaged coloration aids them in doing so, their venomous spines protect them from predators. For obvious reasons, these fish must be handled with great care. In captivity, they'll readily consume smaller tank mates. The novice is advised to avoid them — they don't belong in a reef tank.

Boxfishes and Trunkfishes

These box-shaped fishes of the family Ostraciidae release poisons into the water when threatened and are, therefore, poorly suited for the average aquarium. Some of the boxfishes are also intolerant of their own kind. Who needs this in an aquarium?

Groupers and Sea Basses

The family Serranidae comprises fast-growing, large, predatory fishes. Most species require a large aquarium that's populated with other large fish. Otherwise, groupers and sea basses will quickly outgrow your aquarium and will probably eat many of your smaller fishes in the process. Don't let their small size in the pet store surprise you: They grow up and grow up fast. In addition, many of the groupers are nocturnal, spending most of their day hiding or lying on the bottom. That's not fun to watch.

Parrotfishes

These fishes prefer to feed on algae, using their beaks to bite off pieces of dead coral to get at it. For this reason, parrotfishes aren't well suited to the reef aquarium. In general, these fish grow relatively large, which also makes them a poor choice for the average fish-only aquarium.

Snappers

Snappers are another group of fast-growing, highly active fishes that, as adults, aren't suitable for the average marine aquarium. They're predatory by nature, require a lot of space, and quickly dominate an aquarium.

Seahorses

Seahorses are delicate and exotic fishes that are difficult to feed and require very high water quality, so keeping them alive is challenging for the beginner. Because they don't compete well for food with other species, seahorses live best in a quiet aquarium by themselves.

Chapter **21**

Ten Invertebrates to Avoid

With so many kinds of invertebrates (see Chapter 4 where I discuss just a small number of them), I have a tough time singling out just ten that aren't for the average saltwater aquarium. In fact, thousands of them aren't suitable, but in this chapter, I list ten that you may encounter at your aquarium dealer.

Octopuses

These critters are incredible attractive cephalopods and every aquarist I know is intrigued by them. Unfortunately, most octopuses are large, crafty, and predatory in the tank. They're also quite delicate, rarely living very long in captivity. Why waste the money?

Crown of Thorns Starfish

This species of starfish isn't a friendly invertebrate. Instead, it's a predator on the reefs, eating corals left and right. If you plan to have a reef tank, avoid these funky-looking starfish.

Bristleworms

These polychaete worms are rarely purchased, but they usually end up in your aquarium hitchhiking on live rocks. They're named after the bristles that line their sides. These bristles are sharp and can easily irritate you if you handle them. Although small bristleworms are relatively harmless and can be helpful tank cleaners, larger ones can damage corals and must be removed.

Mantis Shrimp

Mantis shrimps are nasty, ill-tempered crustaceans capable of inflicting a serious injury with their powerful, spear-like arms. They're efficient predators of other invertebrates and fishes. This is one shrimp that doesn't act like one.

Jellyfish

Jellyfish aren't the most common aquarium invertebrates for a number of reasons. Although public aquaria do display jellyfish, they go through a lot of work to do so. Jellyfish require far too much work for the average aquarist in terms of water quality, aquarium conditions, and food. If someone offers you jellyfish, just say no.

Queen Conch

The shell of this large gastropod is probably the most popular curio in the tropics. The beauty of this animal and its shell often entices the new aquarists to add a small one to their aquarium. Don't do it! These snails get large. If you want a queen conch, collect a shell.

Lobsters

If you place a lobster in your aquarium in the evening, by morning you'll no longer recognize your aquarium. These feisty decapod crustaceans are disruptive and territorial, not to mention cannibalistic. Do yourself a favor; don't add a lobster to your peaceful community aquarium.

Bivalves

Clams, scallops, mussels, and oysters belong in this group. There are all different kinds of bivalves, and many of them are beautiful additions to the aquarium. I include them here because they're strictly filter feeders, which makes them difficult for a beginner to accommodate. Practice aquarium upkeep before you add these challenging species with special feeding requirements.

Sea Cucumbers

Although some species of sea cucumbers are okay for the aquarium, as a beginner, avoid these critters. When some sea cucumbers are stressed, they release toxins into the tank, and you don't want that.

Fire Coral

Although these cnidarians actually aren't coral, they're named after the feeling you get when you touch them. When these animals sting you, you feel as if you've been burned. For this reason alone, you don't need any species of fire coral in your aquarium.

Chapter **22**

Ten (Plus More) Simple Metric Conversions

T he units of measurement in this book are given in customary U.S. units (inches, feet, gallons, pounds). However, in the rest of the world and in the scientific community, the most common units of measurement are metric (meters, liters, kilograms). The 14 simple conversions in this chapter help you to translate your American aquarium into one that's recognized worldwide. *Tip:* Just look for the words "to convert" for a handy formula.

Temperature

To convert Fahrenheit to Celsius (which is the temperature scale used in most of the world), use the following formula:

$$°C = (°F - 32) \times 0.5556$$

To convert Celsius to Fahrenheit, use the following formula:

$$°F = (1.8 \times °C) + 32$$

Length Conversion

The metric system is based on units of 10, and the basic unit of length is the *meter*. Measurements are made in meters or increments of meters, which are named with different prefixes. The basic prefixes are *milli* (1/1000), *centi* (1/100), and *kilo* (1000), and each represents an increment of 10. Therefore:

» 1,000 millimeters (mm) = 1 meter (m)

» 100 centimeters (cm) = 1 m

» 1,000 m = 1 kilometer (km)

The U.S. uses inches and feet to measure length, whereas the metric system uses centimeters and meters:

To convert inches (in) to centimeters (cm), multiply by 2.54.

To convert feet (ft) to meters (m), multiply by 0.3048.

To convert centimeters to inches, multiply by 0.3937.

To convert meters to feet, multiply by 3.28.

Weight Conversion

Just as the meter is the basis for length, the *gram* is the basis for weight. The prefixes for length also apply for weight. Therefore,

» 1,000 milligrams (mg) = 1 gram (g)

» 1,000 g = 1 kilogram (kg)

The standard U.S. units of weight are pounds, whereas kilograms are standard metric units:

To convert pounds (lbs) to kilograms (kg), multiply by 0.4536.

To convert kilograms to pounds, multiply by 2.2.

REMEMBER

Always take into account the weight of your aquarium when it is full with water:

» One gallon of saltwater weighs 8.4 pounds.

» One liter of saltwater weighs 1.01 kilograms. See the "Volume Conversions" section for more on liters.

Area Conversion

The surface area of anything is simply the product of the length and the width or

$$\text{Area} = \text{length} \times \text{width}$$

Using the U.S. system, area is usually reported as square inches or square feet because the unit of measurement is squared (inches times inches = inches squared):

To convert square inches to square centimeters, multiply by 6.4516.

To convert square centimeters to square inches, multiply by 0.155.

Volume Conversions

Volume is equal to the product of length, width, and height or

$$\text{Volume} = \text{length} \times \text{width} \times \text{height}$$

The U.S. system usually reports this as cubic inches because multiplying inches times inches times inches results in the inches cubed. Americans also report volume in U.S. gallons. The metric system uses cubic centimeters and liters:

To convert cubic inches to cubic centimeters, multiply by 0.061.

To convert cubic centimeters to cubic inches, multiply by 16.39.

1,000 cubic centimeters = 1 liter (l) = 1 kilogram (kg).

To convert gallons to liters, multiply by 3.78.

To convert liters to gallons, multiply by 0.2642.

Chapter **23**

Ten Great Public Saltwater Aquariums

s there anybody who doesn't like going to a big public aquarium? I don't think so. You can see and discover so much at an aquarium, and there's usually not enough time to see it all in one day. For the home aquarist, the large public aquarium is also a great place to see just how a healthy aquarium should look. These places are loaded with information about fish, invertebrates, marine mammals, reptiles, and amphibians. Don't be afraid to steal an idea or two about aquarium decoration, species composition, and the re-creation of natural settings.

I've been to public aquariums all over the United States; here are a bunch that I really liked. This is in no way a comprehensive list of aquariums, just a smattering. No matter where you live, there's an aquarium not too far away. So, if you don't see one close to you listed here, poke around online and you'll find one.

New England Aquarium

Since I'm from the northeast and still live there, the New England Aquarium in Boston, Massachusetts, was one of the first large public aquariums that I ever visited. In fact, I dare say that the Giant Ocean Tank loaded with all kinds of fishes, including sharks, helped to inspire me to become a marine biologist and home aquarist. Check it out online as well at www.neaq.org.

Mystic Aquarium

Located in, you guessed it, Mystic, Connecticut, this aquarium not only houses all kind of fish and invertebrates, but it's well known for its incredible display of beluga whales. You can start your visit to Mystic Aquarium at www.mystic aquarium.org.

National Aquarium

The next time you're kicking around the beautiful waterfront in Baltimore, Maryland, you should make it a point to visit the National Aquarium (www.aqua.org). This aquarium is chock-full of all kinds of animals, including birds, amphibians, and reptiles; it also has an incredible dolphin amphitheater.

Georgia Aquarium

Touted as the largest aquarium in the world, the Georgia Aquarium in Atlanta (www.georgiaaquarium.org) is an incredible facility with more than eight million gallons of saltwater and freshwater and more than 120,000 animals representing 500 species. One of the highlights of the aquarium is the Ocean Voyager gallery, which allows you to view the largest fish species in the world, the whale shark, through a 100-foot underwater tunnel.

SeaWorld

The SeaWorld (www.seaworld.com) name is synonymous with ocean-oriented parks and combines animal attractions with rides, shows, dining, and shopping. With parks in Orlando, Florida, San Antonio, Texas, and San Diego, California, SeaWorld offers a little of everything for everyone, including that oddball family member who doesn't like fish.

Tennessee Aquarium

Now, granted, people usually don't think of Chattanooga, Tennessee when it comes to saltwater, but the Tennessee Aquarium (www.tnaqua.org) has a fantastic collection of marine animals. Also, this may a book for the saltwater enthusiast, but freshwater counterparts are people, too, and the Tennessee Aquarium is among the largest freshwater aquariums in the world.

Audubon Aquarium of the Americas

How do you combine great music, fantastic food, and marine life? You go to the Aquarium of the Americas in New Orleans, of course. Having conducted research in the bayous of Louisiana, I can tell you that these unique habitats house some of the toughest critters in the world, like bull sharks, alligator gars, and catfishes. But you don't have to brave the mosquitoes to see all these critters and more if you drop by this aquarium (www.auduboninstitute.org).

Monterey Bay Aquarium

Located in a quaint, historic Monterey, California, this aquarium offers a phenomenal and incredibly natural re-creation of Pacific marine habitats and their inhabitants. With exhibits ranging from kelp forests to the open ocean, this aquarium has all kinds of Pacific fishes and animals including sea otters and penguins. My personal favorite is the Open Sea exhibit, which houses giant bluefin tuna, ocean sunfish, and the scalloped hammerheads. See more of the aquarium at www.montereybayaquarium.org.

Shedd Aquarium

A trip to Chicago wouldn't be complete without a visit to the Shedd Aquarium. Touted as one of the largest indoor public aquariums, Shedd Aquarium has been around since 1930 and currently houses more than 30,000 animals. Don't let its location fool you; there are plenty of saltwater exhibits with an amazing assortment of marine animals from sharks to whales; check out `www.sheddaquarium.org/`.

The Seas with Nemo and Friends

Formerly called The Living Seas at Walt Disney World, The Seas with Nemo and Friends aquarium is a great way to cap off a family vacation at this amazing resort. Based on the popular fish-related movie, *Finding Nemo*, this aquarium combines entertainment with aquarium viewing. Visitors board Clamobiles and venture into the sea with popular characters of the film, then view all kinds of tropical fishes, dolphins, manatees, and sharks in the main pavilion. You can find out more at `https://disneyworld.disney.go.com/attractions/epcot/seas-with-nemo-and-friends/`.

6 The Appendixes

Appendix **A**

Additional Resources Every Saltwater Aquarist Needs

Home aquarists number in the millions throughout the world. As long as you have an aquarium, you will never be alone in this hobby. As you become more involved in aquarium keeping, you may be surprised at how many people share this avocation. I find myself going to my local pet dealer to see new fish arrivals, talk about aquarium problems, and exchange ideas with fellow aquarists. I've picked up some of the most valuable information on fishkeeping from amateurs who enjoy the thrills of this hobby. The resources for the home aquarist are almost limitless, ranging from books to the Internet.

Books

Though I'd like nothing better than to say that the book you're holding in your hand is the only one you're going to need, I can't. This book is really just the beginning, and literally thousands of books have been published on aquarium keeping. Some are good, some aren't. I happen to think the one you're reading is very good. Books have been written to address virtually every aspect of the hobby.

They cover broad topics, such as basic aquarium setup, and specialized topics, like the proper husbandry of a certain species. If you have any questions about aquarium keeping, it's covered in a book.

The following list of books includes some that I think are helpful, but this is a mere smattering of what's available for the new and experienced aquarist. Each one of the books listed below has its own bibliography, which can help you delve even further into the field.

- Burgess, W.E., *Dr. Burgess's Atlas of Marine Aquarium Fishes*, TFH Publications, 2000.

- Dakin, N., *The Macmillan Book of the Marine Aquarium*, Macmillan Publishing Co., 1992.

- Delbeek, C. J. and J. Sprung, *The Reef Aquarium: A Comprehensive Guide to the Identification and Care of Tropical Marine Invertebrates*, Vol. 2, Ricordea Publishing, 1997.

- Eschmeyer, W.M., *Catalogue of the Genera of Recent Fishes*, California Academy of Sciences, 1990.

- Gratzek, J.B., *Aquariology: The Science of Fish Health Management — Master Volume*, Tetra Press, 1994.

- Hargrove, M. and M. Hargrove, *Aquariums For Dummies, 2nd Edition.* John Wiley Publishing, New York, NY, 2006.

- Helfman, G.S., B.B. Collette, D.E. Facey, and B.W. Bowen, *The Diversity of Fishes: Biology, Evolution, and Ecology*, Wiley-Blackwell, 2009.

- Hunt, P., *The Marine Reef Aquarium*, B.E.S. Publishing, 2008.

- Michael, S.W., *PocketExpert Guide to Marine Fishees: 500+ Essential-to-Know Aquarium Species*, TFH Publications, 2003.

- Moe, M.A., *Marine Aquarium Handbook: Beginner to Breeder*, TFH Publications, 2009.

- Sandford, G., *An Illustrated Encyclopedia of Aquarium Fish*, Howell Book House, 1995.

- Shimek, R., *A PocketExpert Guide to Marine Invertebrates: 500+ Essential-to-Know Aquarium Species,* Microcosm Ltd., 2005.

- Skomal, G.B., *Clownfishes in the Aquarium*, TFH Publications, 2004.

- Skomal, G.B., *Setting Up a Saltwater Aquarium, An Owner's Guide to a Happy Healthy Pet.* Howell Book House, New York, NY, 1997.

- Skomal, G.B., *The Shark Handbook* Cider Mill Press, 2016.

>> Spotte, S., *Captive Seawater Fishes: Science and Technology*, John Wiley and Sons, 1992.

>> Sprung, J., *The Reef Aquarium, Vol. 3: Science, Art, and Technology*, Ricordea Publishing, 2005.

>> Stoskopf, M.K., *Fish Medicine*, ART Sciences LLC, 2010.

>> Tullock, J.H., *Your First Marine Aquarium*, Barrons Educational Series, Inc., 2008.

Clubs

In virtually every state in the United States and province in Canada, aquarium buffs have formed clubs and associations in which ideas and techniques are endlessly bantered about. The best way to find these organizations is to ask your local pet dealer or jump online and do a search — most clubs have websites. Also, most aquarium clubs belong to the Marine Aquarium Society of North America (MASNA), which is a nonprofit organization that promotes a sustainable future for marine environments and the marine aquarium hobby. The MASNA is an excellent organization composed of aquarium clubs, individual hobbyists, and industry partners. The organization's website (https://masna.org/) is a great place to find a local club.

REMEMBER

Not only are these kinds of organizations great for gathering information, but they also can help you acquire equipment and healthy, home-bred fish.

Magazines

Monthly or quarterly aquarium magazines provide you with some of the most up-to-date information on keeping an aquarium. Timely articles on breeding, feeding, disease, and species-specific husbandry both entertain and inform the new aquarist. In addition, product information and classified advertising are excellent features of any aquarium magazine. The photos are pretty cool, as well.

All of these magazines offer digital editions and some are also available in print. In some cases, the digital content comes at no charge:

>> *Advanced Aquarist Magazine* (digital), www.advancedaquarist.com/magazine

>> *Coral Magazine* (digital/print), www.coralmagazine.com/

>> *Reef Hobbyist Magazine* (digital/print), www.reefhobbyistmagazine.com/

>> *Reefs Magazine* (digital), www.reefs.com/magazine

>> *Tropical Fish Hobbyist* (digital/print), www.tfhmagazine.com

Internet

The amount of the aquarium information online is unbelievable. It's the place where people gather to exchange information about the hobby. This is by far the fastest way to obtain and exchange information on keeping a saltwater aquarium. On the Internet, you have unlimited access to a vast amount of information on this hobby. Internet resources include chat groups, equipment and fish retailers, photos, husbandry information, classified ads, events, and on and on and on.

Fish enthusiasts can join Internet networks, which provide you access to hobbyists, professional aquarists, researchers, breeders, and vendors of aquarium products. You can even get immediate advice from staff about sick fish.

With so much information on the Internet, you may be overwhelmed with all the options. Don't forget that many experts and vendors have home pages, as well. Any good search engine can help you access these resources, but here are a few that I like:

>> **Aquaria Central:** www.aquariacentral.com

>> **Aquarium Advice:** www.aquariumadvice.com

>> **The Aquarium Wiki:** www.theaquariumwiki.com/wiki/

>> **Fish Base:** www.fishbase.org

>> **Marine Aquarium Advice:** www.marineaquariumadvice.com

>> **Marine Aquarium Council:** www.marineaquariumcouncil.org

>> **Marine Aquarium Society of North America:** https://masna.org

>> **Reef 2 Reef:** www.reef2reef.com/

>> **Saltwater Aquarium Blog:** www.saltwateraquariumblog.com

>> **Saltwater Smarts:** www.saltwatersmarts.com

Appendix B

Glossary

acidic: Condition of the water in which the measured pH is less than 7. It is generally created by carbon dioxide buildup or decomposing organic matter.

actinic bulbs: Bulbs that produce light at the blue end of the spectrum, near ultraviolet.

activated carbon: Material used to mechanically and chemically filter aquarium water.

adipose fin: Small, fleshy fin between the dorsal and tail fin on some species of fish.

aeration: The introduction of air into the aquarium to create water movement and increase oxygen content.

aerobic bacteria: Bacteria that use oxygen for metabolism.

airstone: An air diffuser that produces tiny bubbles for aeration and water circulation.

algae: Simple, photosynthetic, aquatic organisms that range in size from one-celled microscopic types to large seaweeds.

alkaline: Condition of the water in which measured pH is greater than 7.

alkalinity: Carbonate hardness.

ammonia: The primary nitrogenous waste of fish that is highly toxic at elevated levels.

anaerobic bacteria: Bacteria that don't require oxygen for metabolism.

anal fin: An unpaired fin on the ventral side of the fish located between the anal opening and the tail fin.

aquarist: A person who owns and maintains an aquarium.

aquascape: To set up the inside of the aquarium.

barbel: Whisker-like growths on the mouth of some bottom-feeding fish, used for detecting food.

bioload: The volume of waste-producing animals, in terms of size and number.

biological filtration: The utilization of bacteria to convert toxic nitrogenous wastes to less-toxic compounds, thereby filtering the water.

brackish: Mixture of fresh and saltwater; pertains to fish habitats, like estuaries.

brine shrimp: Tiny saltwater crustaceans of the genus *Artemia*, which are excellent fish food, either live or frozen.

buffering: The ability of a solution to resist changes in pH.

calcareous: Containing calcium carbonate.

calcium carbonate: A crystalline mineral found in high concentrations in invertebrate skeletons and shells.

carbon dioxide: A common waste product of respiration in living things. It is used by plants during photosynthesis.

carnivore: Term describing fish that prefer to eat the flesh of other living creatures; meat-eaters.

caudal fin: The unpaired tail fin.

chloramine: Tap-water additive that kills harmful bacteria but may be toxic to aquarium fish.

community tank: An aquarium containing different species of compatible fish.

diatoms: Microscopic organisms with silica skeletons.

dinoflagellates: Single-celled algae with tails called flagella.

distilled water: Pure water that can be purchased at most pharmacies and food stores.

diurnal: Active during the day.

dorsal: Pertaining to the top of the fish.

dorsal fin: The unpaired fin(s) along the top of the fish.

family: The name for a group of related genera.

filter: A device that removes impurities from the aquarium.

filter feeders: Animals that filter plankton from the water for food.

foam fractionation: The separation of proteins from the water by a foaming action; the method used by a protein skimmer.

genus (genera): The name for a group of closely related species.

gills: The respiratory organs on fish that extract oxygen from the water.

habitat: The physical environment of a particular species.

hardness: The amount of dissolved minerals in water.

herbivore: Term that describes fish that prefer to eat vegetative matter; plant-eaters.

hydrometer: Instrument used to measure specific gravity in the aquarium.

ichthyology: The study of fish.

invertebrate: Animals that lack a spinal column.

kalkwasser: Lime water used to increase the buffering capacity of water.

lateral line: Sensory organ composed of receptors (lying along the surface of the fish's body in low pits or grooves) that detect water displacement and give the fish the sensation of touch.

length: Dimension of fish measured from the tip of the snout to the beginning of the caudal fin; used to calculate tank capacity for fish. Technically referred to as *standard length*.

live rock: Rock encrusted with live flora and fauna.

live sand: Sand containing live flora and fauna.

marine: Pertaining to the saltwater environment.

mechanical filtration: The physical removal of debris using filter media.

mineral: Naturally occurring inorganic substance in water.

mulm: An accumulation of decayed organic matter and detritus.

nauplii: Newly hatched brine shrimp.

nitrate: The end product of nitrification that is utilized by plants in aquariums; the least harmful of the nitrogenous compounds.

nitrification: Chemical conversion process carried out by bacteria in which toxic ammonia is converted to nitrite and nitrate.

nitrite: The intermediate compound of nitrification resulting from the conversion of ammonia by bacteria; can be toxic to fish in high concentrations.

nitrogen cycle: The conversion of toxic ammonia to nitrite and nitrate by bacteria.

nocturnal: Active during the night.

omnivore: Term that describes fish that have non-selective feeding habits and will eat a variety of foods.

operculum: Bony covering of the gill opening; also called *gill cover*.

osmoregulation: The biological control of salt balance in an organism.

osmosis: The movement of water through membranes.

ozone: Unstable molecule composed of three atoms of oxygen; sometimes used to disinfect aquariums.

parasite: A living creature that thrives on or in another living creature.

pectoral fins: Paired fins on each side of the body behind the gill opening.

pelagic: Term used to describe animals that live in the open ocean.

pelvic fins: Paired fins forward of the anal fin near the anal opening.

pH: A scale used to measure how acidic a solution is.

phosphate: Dissolved inorganic phosphorous that enters your aquarium through excretion by fishes, the breakdown of uneaten food, and tap water.

photosynthesis: The process by which plants produce compounds for energy-utilizing carbon dioxide and energy from the sun to produce oxygen.

plankton: Microscopic organisms living in the water column.

power filter: A filter driven by a motor.

powerhead: A water pump.

rays: The main supporting structures of fins.

reef tank: An aquarium that re-creates the natural coral reef ecosystem containing primarily invertebrates and peaceful species of fish.

refractometer: An instrument that measures the salinity of water.

refugium: A separate tank or container that shares water with your main display aquarium and provides biological and chemical filtration.

salinity: Measurement that refers to the amount of dissolved salts in water.

salt: A term commonly used to refer to sodium chloride, but also refers to various mineral compounds.

salt creep: The accumulation of salt deposits on the outside of the aquarium.

scales: Hard, bony structures that cover the skin and serve to protect the fish, reducing the chance of injuries and infection.

school: An organized group of fish swimming together in synchrony.

shoal: An unorganized group of fish.

spawning: The act of breeding.

specialty tank: An aquarium setup that re-creates a specific habitat with all its natural occupants of plants and fish.

species: The name applied to highly related living organisms capable of interbreeding; a subdivision of genus.

species tank: A tank containing only a single species of fish.

specific gravity: Ratio of density of seawater to that of pure water; used as an indicator of salinity.

substrate: Bottom material, such as gravel or sand.

sump: A separate tank with several chambers containing filtration and other equipment; water flows from your main aquarium to the sump where it's treated and returned to the aquarium.

swim bladder: Internal organ that regulates buoyancy in fish.

symbiosis: A mutually beneficial relationship between organisms.

taxonomy: The scientific classification of life.

temperate: Geographic areas that are seasonal.

thermometer: A device that measures temperature.

thermostat: A device within the aquarium heater that regulates the output of the unit.

tropical: Geographic areas that are warm throughout the year.

ultraviolet (UV): Short-wavelength light used to disinfect seawater.

ventral: Pertaining to the underside of the fish.

Index

bimetallic strip thermostats, 146

bioload, 207, 317

biological filtration, 117–118, 205, 317

biological stressors, 264

biowheels, 236

birdmouth wrasse (*Gomphosus caeruleus*), 63

bivalves, 301

black heniochus butterflyfish (*Heniochus acuminatus*), 51

black sea urchins, 91

black-cap gramma (*Gramma melacara*), 62

blanching vegetables, 253

blennies, 28, 49–50, 61

Blenniidae. *See* blennies

blood shrimp (*Lysmata debelius*), 87

blue damselfish (*Chrysiptera cyanea*), 57

blue devil (Pomacentrus caeruleus), 64

blue green chromis (*Chromis viridis*), 56

blue sea star (*Linckia laevigata*), 89

blue-face angelfish (*Pomacanthus xanthometopon*), 64

blue-green algae (*Cyanobacteria*), 225, 231

bluejaw fish, 38

body shape of fish, 18

books about aquariums, 313–315

boomerang triggerfish (white-lined triggerfish; *Sufflamen bursa*), 61

bottom-feeders, 22

boxfish, 28, 64, 296

brackish water aquariums
brackish, defined, 318
defined, 12
environment of, 186

equipment for, 186–188

fish for, 189–190

overview, 185

saltwater plants, 191–192

brain corals, 76

brine shrimp (*Artemia* species), 255–256, 318

bristleworms, 300

Brooklynella hostilis, 280

brown algae (*Phaeophyceae*), 228–229

brownout, 209

bubble corals, 76

bubble tip anemone (*Entacmaea quadricolor*), 72

buckets, 182

buffering, 215, 217, 318

bulb anemone (Entacmaea quadricolor), 72

butterflyfish, 9, 29, 50–51, 61–62

buying fish, 8–10

C

calcareous, defined, 318

calcareous calcium-based algae, 226

calcium (Ca), 219

calcium carbonate, 318

calcium hydroxide solution, 215

Callionymidae. *See* dragonets

camelback shrimps (*Lysmata debelius*), 88

canary wrasse (*Halichoeres chrysus*), 54

candy shrimp (camelback shrimp; *Lysmata debelius*), 88

canister filters, 195, 237

captive-bred fish, 8

carapace, 84

carbon dioxide (CO_2/c0), 204, 218–219, 318

carbonate hardness, 216

cardinalfish, 29–30, 48–49

carnivores, 44, 250, 261, 318

catfish, 30

caudal fins, 20, 37, 318

Caulerpa, 226

cauliflower disease (lymphocystis), 279

Centropyge, 55

Cephalopoda, 81–82

Chaetodontidae. *See* butterflyfish

Chaetomorpha, 226

changing water, 235–242

chemical filtration, 118

cherub angelfish (*C. argi*), 55

chevron butterflyfish (*Chaetodon trifascialis*), 62

chloramine, 318

Chondrichthyes. *See* sharks

choosing fish, 46–59
for beginners, 60–65
diurnal vs. nocturnal fish, 42
fish to avoid for beginners, 60–65, 295–297
habitats, creating, 45
interactions between fish, 43–45
night and day, 42
overview, 41
recommendations, 46–59
schools of, 43

Christmas tree worms, 82

chromatophores, 21

circulating oxygen, 135–139, 196

Cirrhitidae. *See* hawkfish

clams, 80–81

Clark's anemonefish (*Amphiprion clarkii*), 56

classes, 9

cleaner shrimp, 88

cleaning aquariums, 233
changing water, 238–242
cleaning filters, 235–238

cleaning tools, 182–184

conscientiousness and commitment, 234

vacuuming gravel, 234–236

clouded eyes, 272

clove oil, 284

clown coris (twin-spot wrasse; *Coris aygula*), 63

clown triggerfish (*Balistoides conspicillum*), 61

clownfish, 30

clownfish disease (*Brooklynella* disease), 280

clownfish host anemone (rose anemone; bulb anemone; bubble tip anemone; *Entacmaea quadricolor*), 72

clubs, 315

Cnidaria, 69–78

colt corals (*Alcyonium spp.*), 77

combination lighting, 157–158

common clownfish (*Amphiprion ocellaris*), 57

common porcupinefish (*Diodon hystrix*), 62

common sea urchins (short-spine sea urchins; black sea urchins), 91

community tanks, 318

complete water-management systems, 134

conditioning water, 241

condy anemone (*Condylactis gigantea*), 73

copepod crustaceans, 280

copper (Cu), 220, 276

copperband butterflyfish (*Chelmon rostratus*), 62

coral, 73–78, 169–171

coral beauty (*C. bispinosa*), 55

Coral Magazine, 315

coral trout (Cephalopholis miniata), 65

coralline red algae, 228

counter-current, 131–132

cowries, 80

crabs, 83–84

cross-hatch fish, 38

crown of thorns starfish, 300

crustacean infestations, 280

Cryptocaryon irritans, 281

cured live rock, 168–169

Cyanobacteria, 231

D

damselfish, 30–31, 56–57, 64

Dascyllus, 64

day fish, 42

dead heads, 169–170

dealers, 9–10, 95

decorating tanks

aquascaping, 160

background, 162–163

corals, 169–171

gravel, 163–165

natural look, 161

ornaments, 172

overview, 159–160

plants, 172

rocks, 165–169

denitrators, 133–134

denticles, 21

depth of gravel, 165

detritus, 231, 234–235

diatom filters, 133

diatoms, 209, 229, 318

diet, 44–45. *See also* feeding fish

Digital Photography For Dummies (King), 291

dinoflagellates, 230–231, 318

Diodontidae. *See* porcupinefish

dioramas, 163

dip method, 275

direct aquarium treatment, 274

discoloration, 271

diseases and treatments, 273

bacterial infections, 277–278

diagnosing, 272

euthanization, 284

fungal diseases, 279

head and lateral line erosion, 283

invertebrates, 283–284

medications, 276–277

parasites, 279–282

poisoning, 283

treatment methods, 274–276

viruses, 278–279

disinfecting water, 134

dissolved oxygen, 218

distended stomach, 272

distilled water, 242, 318

disturbances

light, 158, 269–270

minimizing, 184

stress from, 269–270

diurnal, 42, 318

dorsal fins, 20, 318

dottybacks, 32, 58, 65

dragonets, 32

drip method, 99

dry rock, 166–167

dwarf parrot wrasse (Cirrhilabrus rubriventralis), 63

E

Echinodermata, 87–92

electrical equipment, 113

electronic thermostats, 146

elegant sea star (*Fromia monilis*), 89

elkhorn corals, 76

emergency situations, 244–246

emperor snapper (*Lutjanus sebae*), 63

environment of brackish water, 186

epidermal (skin) tissue, 21

euthanization, 284

evaporation, salt levels and, 213

exophiala disease, 279

Exophiala fungus, 279

exoskeleton, 74

external power filters, 195

F

fairy basslets, 32, 62

false cleanerfish (*Aspidontus taeniatus*), 61

false gramma dottyback (*Pictichromis paccagnellae*), 64

families, 9, 318

fan worms, 82

featherduster worms (fan worms), 82

feeding fish, 249–262

  clipping food to side of tank, 257–258

  consistency, 257

  frequency, 257–259

  how much, 257–258

  keeping a log, 288–289

  nutrients and nutrition, 249, 251–252, 267–268

  observing fish during feeding, 259

  refusal to eat, 259, 270–271

  removing leftovers, 260

  strategies, 250–251

  types of food, 252–257

  varying diet, 251, 254, 260

  while traveling, 260

feeding invertebrates, 261–262

filefish, 32, 63

filling tanks (adding water), 197

filter feeders, 318

filters, 12–13

  adding, 194–195

  aerating and circulating oxygen, 135–139

  biowheels, 125–126

  for brackish water, 187

  breathing, 116

  canister filter, 126–127, 195

  choosing, 135

  cleaning, 235–238

  defined, 318

  disinfecting water with, 134

  external power filters, 125, 195

  fluidized bed filters, 195

  inside box filters, 120–121

  internal power filters, 126

  live rock and/or live sand, 129–130

  overview, 115, 119–120

  power filters, 125, 320

  protein skimmers, 195

  sponge filters, 121–122

  starting, 198

  sumps, 119

  trickle filters, 127–129, 195

  types of, 116–118

  undergravel filters, 122–124, 195

fin rot, 277

Finding Nemo (film), 310

finger corals (colt corals; *Alcyonium spp.*), 77

fins, 18–21

  adipose fins, 317

  anal fins, 20, 317

  caudal fins, 20, 37, 318

  dorsal fins, 20, 318

  fin rot, 277

  frayed fins, 272

  paired fins, 19

  pectoral fins, 20, 320

  pelvic fins, 20, 320

fire coral, 301

fire shrimp (blood shrimp; *Lysmata debelius*), 87

fish

  acclimating, 97–99

  anatomy of, 18–25

  avoiding certain species of, 14

  biological needs of, 11

  brackish water, 189–190

  buying, 8–10

  captive-bred, 8

  freshwater versus saltwater, 25–27

  healthy, choosing, 95–96

  keeping healthy, 13–14

  overview, 17–18, 93

  quarantining, 94, 99–100

  saltwater, 8–9

  senses of, 23–25

  taking home, 96–97

  temperature for, 141–143

  term usage of, 17

  tropical marine families, identifying, 27–39

  watching, 111–112

Fish Base, 316

fish tuberculosis (wasting disease), 278

fishnets, 180–181

flagella, 69

flame angelfish (*C. loricula*), 55

flame lobsters, 85

flamefish (flame cardinalfish; *Apogon maculatus*), 48

flash-back gramma (*Pictichromis diadema*), 58

fluidized bed filters, 130, 195

fluorescent lighting, 155–156

foam fractionation, 318

four-eye butterflyfish (*Chaetodon capistratus*), 62

fragging, 75

frayed fins, 272

invertebrates, 8–9, 283–284
  Annelida, 82–87
  Cnidaria, 69–78
  defined, 319
  description of, 67–68
  differences between fish and, 8–9
  Echinodermata, 87–92
  flatworms, 78
  invertebrates to avoid, 299–301
  Mollusca, 78–82
  overview, 67, 68
  phylum annelida, 82–87
  phylum cnidaria, 69–78
  phylum echinodermata, 87–92
  phylum mollusca, 78–82
  Platyhelminthes (flatworms), 78
  Porifera (sponges), 69
  sponges, 69
Iridophores scales, 21
iron stands, 110
isopod crustaceans, 280

J

jellyfish, 300

K

kalkwasser (limewater), 215, 217, 319
kelp, 228
King, Julie Adair, 291
king angelfish (*Holacanthus passer*), 64
kingdom Animalia, 9
Klein's butterflyfish (*C. kleinii*), 51
knobby black cucumber (*Stichopus chloronotus*), 91
koran angelfish (Pomacanthus semicirculatus), 64

L

Labridae. *See* wrasses
lagena, 24
large-polyped stony coral (LPS), 74
lateral line, 25, 283, 319
lava rock, 166
leaks, 197, 245
leather corals, 77
lemon goby (*Gobiodon citrinus*), 51–52
lemonpeel angelfish (*C. flavissima*), 55
length, 304, 319
light-emitting diodes (LEDs), 156–157
lighting, 199
  algae and, 222–223, 224
  for brackish water, 187
  combination, 157–158
  fixture options, 154
  fluorescent, 155–156
  importance of, 152–153
  LEDs, 156–157
  light-emitting diodes, 156–157
  mercury vapor, 157
  metal halide, 157–158
  natural lighting, 154
  on/off time switch, 158
  overview, 151–152, 154
  for photography, 290–291
  power compact fluorescent, 156
  tungsten lighting, 155
  wattage, 153
lined seahorse (*Hippocampus erectus*), 65
lionfish, 34, 65, 296
lipstick tang, 47
live coral, 171
live foods, 255–257

live sand and rocks, 164, 167–169
  adding, 199–200, 208
  brown algae on, 229
  cleaning, 237
  defined, 319
lobsters, 84–85, 301
locations for aquariums, 111–113
logarithmic pH scale, 214
logs and journals, 288–290
long tentacle anemone (*Macrodactyla doreensis*), 72
long-nose filefish (Oxymonacanthus longirostris), 63
long-spine porcupinefish (*Diodon holacanthus*), 62
long-spine sea urchins, 91
Lutjanidae. *See* snappers
Lymphocystis virus, 279
lyretail anthias (Pseudanthias squamipinnis), 58

M

macroalgae, 222
magazines about aquarium keeping, 315–316
maintenance schedule, 242–244
Malu anemones, 72
mantis shrimp, 300
marine, defined, 319
Marine Aquarium Advice, 316
Marine Aquarium Council, 161, 316
Marine Aquarium Society of North America (MASNA), 315, 316
marine biology, 287
marine families, 27–39
marine fish, 22
marine velvet disease, 281

white-lined triggerfish (*Sufflamen bursa*), 61

white-spotted puffer (*Arothron meleagris*), 65

whitetail damselfish (humbug damselfish; *Dascyllus aruanus*), 57

wimplefish (pennant coralfish; black heniochus butterflyfish; white heniochus butterflyfish; *Heniochus acuminatus*), 51

wood stands, 110–111

wormfish, 39

wrasses, 39, 53–55, 63

X

Xanthophores scales, 21

xanthophyll pigment, brown algae, 228

Y

yellow angelfish (*C. heraldi*), 55

yellow prawn goby (*Cryptocentrus cinctus*), 53

yellow seahorse (*Hippocampus kuda*), 65

yellow sweetlips (Plectorhinchus albovittatus), 58

yellow tang (*Zebrasoma flavescens*), 47–48

yellow wrasse (canary wrasse; *Halichoeres chrysus*), 54

yellowtail coris (*Coris gaimard*), 53

yellowtail damselfish (*Microspathodon chrysurus*), 57

Z

zooplankton, 229

zooxanthellae, 71, 74

About the Author

Gregory Skomal, PhD, is an accomplished marine biologist, underwater explorer, photographer, aquarist, and author. He has been a fisheries biologist with the Massachusetts Division of Marine Fisheries since 1987 and currently heads up the Massachusetts Shark Research Program. Greg holds a master's degree in marine biology from the University of Rhode Island and a Ph.D. from Boston University. His research, which centers on the ecology, natural history, and physiology of sharks, has spanned the globe from the frigid waters of the Arctic Circle to coral reefs in the tropical Central Pacific. He has written numerous scientific research articles and has appeared in a number of film and television documentaries, including programs for National Geographic, Discovery Channel, BBC, and PBS.

Although his research passion for the last 36 years has been sharks, he has been an avid aquarist for more than 40 years and has written 12 books on aquarium keeping. His home and laboratory are on the coast of Massachusetts.

Dedication

Like the first and second editions of this book, this third edition is dedicated to those people who helped me pursue this amazing hobby and my incredible career. It all started back in the 1970s with my parents, Bernard and Irene Skomal, who gave unwavering support to me and my six siblings for our passions and, often whimsical, pursuits. I only wish that they were alive today to see the fruits of their hard work manifested by the success of their children.

Since the second edition was published, I have had two children of my own, Wilson and Eve. I now share with them this incredible hobby and see the same beauty and wonder in their eyes that I had as a child. This has strengthened my passion for the ocean and instilled in me the urgency to protect the marine ecosystems of the world for future generations.

I dedicate this book to these incredible kids and my best friend and wife Kimberly, who provides me with limitless support and love despite my repeated efforts to test them.

Author's Acknowledgments

I want to thank the crew at Wiley for their continued faith in my work. Specifically, Acquisitions Editor Ashley Coffey for making this third edition come together, and Project Editor Chad Sievers for his patience, helpful comments, and editorial insight.

It has been many years since my first aquarium, and I have become much older and, in many ways, much wiser. One thing is for certain, my love and respect for the marine environment and its inhabitants have deepened, but human impacts on this planet have devastated coral reefs throughout the world. I can't impress upon the reader more our need to protect and conserve these valuable resources.

Publisher's Acknowledgments

Acquisition Editor: Ashley Coffey

Project Editor: Chad R. Sievers

Copy Editor: Chad R. Sievers

Technical Editor: Mark Valderrama

Production Editor: Magesh Elangovan

Cover Image: © Darya Bystritskaya/ EyeEm/Getty Images